TOWARD A GLOBAL CIVILIZATION OF
LOVE AND TOLERANCE

TOWARD A GLOBAL CIVILIZATION OF

LOVE & TOLERANCE

M. Fethullah Gülen

Foreword by Thomas Michel

The Light

New Jersey
2004

Published by The Light, Inc.
26 Worlds Fair Dr. Unit C
Somerset, New Jersey, 08873, USA
e-mail: contact@thelightinc.com
www.thelightpublishing.com

Library of Congress Cataloging-in-Publication Data is available

ISBN 1-932099-68-9

Printed by
Güzel Sanatlar Matbaası A.Ş., İstanbul, Turkey
June 2004

TABLE OF CONTENTS

Table of Contents

SUFISM AND METAPHYSICS

JIHAD – TERRORISM – HUMAN RIGHTS

EDUCATION

Table of Contents

GLOBAL PERSPECTIVES

FOREWORD

The need for dialogue among people of faith has been underscored by the events of the past few years. Interreligious dialogue is seen as an alternative to the much-discussed "clash of civilizations." Those who do not subscribe to the theory that a civilizational clash is inevitable are proposing instead a *dialogue of civilizations*, an exchange of views aimed at mutual enrichment, a sharing of insights that can lead all to a deeper understanding of the nature of God and God's will for humankind on this planet.

That is what this book is about. It presents the thoughts of one of the most influential Muslim scholars and spiritual leaders in the Islamic world today. The movement inspired and guided by Fethullah Gülen is offering Muslims a way to live out Islamic values amidst the complex demands of modern societies. From its origins in Turkey, the movement has spread rapidly, through its schools in many countries, through its cultural and media activities, and through the social projects and dialogue encounters of Turks in diaspora in Europe, North America, and Australia, to the point that the influence of the Gülen movement is being felt in virtually all regions where Muslims live as majorities or minorities.

This book has a double purpose. On the one hand, it is a call to Muslims to a greater awareness that Islam teaches the need for dialogue and that Muslims are called to be agents and witnesses to God's universal mercy. Mr. Gülen calls upon his broad knowledge of the Islamic tradition by bringing together the Qur'anic Scripture, the hadith (the Prophet's traditions) reports from Muhammad, and the insights of Muslims down through the ages, to build a convincing argument that tolerance, love, and compassion are genuinely Islamic values that Muslims have a duty to bring to the modern world.

On the other hand, the book is an invitation to non-Muslims to move beyond prejudice, suspicion, and half-truths in order to arrive at an understanding of what Islam is really about. Someone whose knowledge of Islam is limited to the headlines of the daily newspapers is likely to believe that the religion teaches terrorism, suicide attacks, oppression of women, and hatred for those outside its community. Who would ever want to be in dialogue with people who promote such actions? Who would ever want to live among people with such attitudes?

However, through the writings of Fethullah Gülen, the reader of this book will see that a proper interpretation of Islamic teaching leads rather to truly spiritual values like forgiveness, inner peace, social harmony, honesty, and trust in God. In expressing these Islamic values, which are shared by many religious believers of various faiths, the author is not only calling Muslims to engage in dialogue, but is engaging the non-Muslim in a discussion of commonly held ideals.

I can cite my own case as an example. I am a Catholic priest, an American living in Rome. I have known the members of the movement associated with Fethullah Gülen for more than a decade, and I can state that they are sincerely and impressively living the teachings of their spiritual guide. They respectfully call Mr. Gülen "Hoca Effendi," which simply means "Teacher." The lessons in this book, derived from the Qur'an and Islamic tradition, form and shape the attitudes by which these Muslims practice their Islamic commitment. In bringing together his writings which have appeared in a wide variety of journals and interviews, many of which have never previously appeared in English, Mr. Gülen has done a good service for those who wish to know the ideals that characterize this movement.

Last year I was delivering lectures in Urfa and Gaziantep in eastern Turkey. I was invited to address, on my way back to Rome, a group of young people in Istanbul at a gathering organized by the Gülen movement. On arriving, I discovered to my surprise an assembly of perhaps 4,000 youths. In speaking with them, I found that they represented a cross section of Istanbul youth, some university students in engineering, medicine, and computer science, others working men and women. Several of the women were employed as secretaries, travel agents, or school-teachers. I met young men who worked as bank clerks, drivers of delivery trucks, and in construction.

They were happy, enthusiastic young people who had come together to celebrate the birthday of their prophet Muhammad. It is significant that I, a Catholic priest, was invited to address them on the theme of "The Prophets, a Blessing for Humankind." My talk was followed by poetry readings in honor of Muhammad, and the evening concluded with a well-known Turkish folk singer singing hymns of praise to God accompanied by electric guitar. My feelings that evening, as on many other occasions, were that if Fethullah Gülen and his movement have been able to instill in so many young people the desire to praise and thank God and to live with love and respect for others, they must be engaged in a very valuable spiritual enterprise.

Non-Muslim believers will agree that these are people with whom we can live and cooperate for the benefit of all, but will undoubtedly ask about the views of Gülen and the movement toward others in the Muslim world who are prone to violence. In this book, the author also takes up these "hard" questions in the chapter on "Jihad-Terrorism-Human Rights," explaining the meaning of jihad and stating clearly that the true Muslim can never engage in terrorism.

I conclude this Foreword by citing a passage that sums up Gülen's approach as a spiritual teacher:

> If I had the ability to read people's minds, that is, if I had the ability to know everyone with his/her particular characteristics, I would direct each person to the hill of perfection that is the most appropriate for him/her. I would recommend continuous reflection, contemplation, reading; I would tell them to study the signs of God in the universe and in people themselves; I would advise people to busy themselves with the study of the Qur'an; I would advise others to recite a portion of the Qur'an and certain prayers on a regular basis; I would tell still others to continuously reflect on "natural" phenomena. That is, I would designate duties for people in the areas in which they have natural abilities.

Thomas Michel, S.J.
Rome, 25 May 2004

INTRODUCTION

The basic values that mark the twenty-first century are modernism, pluralism, individualism, and religion. Some claim that modernity embraces individual and social life as a whole, and that it has created new forms of religious, cultural, and political pluralism. Though described in various ways, modernism has yielded two sub-ideological phenomena: "advancement" and "globalism." Many theorists have depicted modernism from the perspective of the increased "sovereignty" of human beings over their surroundings, and their advanced "knowledge" of it. This direct relationship that was established between the "knowledge" and the "power and sovereignty" has presented opportunities and has given the authority to superpowers to set up new forms of domination over other lands and people. Imperialistic passions in the modern age have generated wider and broader consequences.

Because globalism has such an ideological aspect, some see it as being merely classical imperialism under another name. Ideological or not, globalism has caused fundamental changes in all areas, from economics to social sciences, from communication to politics, and from law, history and geography to state administration. In fact, globalism has popularized wealth, technology, democratic pluralism, production, and consumption. And then again, it has helped to spread all types of pollution; human, environmental, or political. Poverty, ecologic pollution, weapons of mass destruction, terrorism, and violence have all been globalized as well.

The globalization of knowledge, power, and technology has been followed up by theories of possible conflicts among cultures and civilizations. Consequently, all of these, be they the result of modernity or of globalism, have put a great many concepts on the agenda. A dozen concepts have been defined and re-defined within the context of modernity, democracy, and pluralism: the human being, the individual, freedom of thought and religion, political, social, and cultural tolerance, conflict versus concurrence, dialogue versus conflict . . .

There is no doubt that the world today is in need of dialogue between cultures and civilizations more than at any other time; this is of the utmost urgency. The knowledge and technology of weaponry—maybe not entirely, but to a significant degree—can worryingly be misused for ideological manipulation. This kind of ideological manipulation of knowledge, technology, and globalization threatens religious, cultural, social, and local differences. Mass reactions against globalization in all parts of the world is on the increase. These reactions cannot be read as reactions against modernism alone. Ideological dimensions of modernism are perceived, in a broader sense, as a threat to sovereign religious, national, historical, and social cultures and identities. And such a situation can cause new issues of conflict to arise.

On the other hand, for almost a quarter of a century, international relation platforms have witnessed a process of fierce discussions on theses of high risk and importance, such as the clash of civilizations. The political and ideological connotation that these theses have brought about worry hundreds, maybe even thousands of scientists, thinkers, and politicians who think and ponder upon the future of the humankind. Huntington's thesis of the clash of civilizations has been so much the focus of attention in international circles that it has now attained a place as the broadest and most fundamental issue of global discussion of the last decade. The echoes and effects of this theory on international relations still persist.

Then, can we not read into modernity and globalization a healthier meaning? Can modernity and globalization not be shaped more constructively; can they not be more concerned with humane and ethical values? Those who look for answers to these questions seem to try to reduce the problem to being no more than a problem of perception. Are modernity and globalization, in fact, so simple phenomena that they can be reduced to a problem of mere perception and understanding? Globalization and modernity in ideological terms are perceived by people coming from different cultures and civilizations as connoting past conflicts and unsettled scores. Thus, the theses of those, like Huntington and Fukuyama, who—to some extent—prophesize clashes, come into existence on this fragile platform.

On the other hand, along with the chronic problems of modern civilization, such as the spread of global terrorism, violence, and weapons of mass destruction—all of which go to support the theses of conflict—there have been other serious efforts which emphasize concordance among societies of different cultures and civilization through democracy, tolerance, love and dialogue; these too have marked the last quarter of the last century. These efforts do not involve, either directly or indirectly, any inner conflict with modernity or globalization. They produce more universal and fundamental humane and ethical values, as well as the dynamics to overcome the destructive aspects of globalization and modernity. Despite the fact that such initiatives of dialogue between civilizations and cultures have always been adopted by the majority, for some reason the "clash and destruction fans" have always been noisier. The international media, as if it is not bound by any humane or ethical virtues, has callously and recklessly popularized only terrorism, violence, and destructive values and issues, thus, unfortunately, magnifying the volume of these supporters. The fierce reaction against Huntington's theses, in fact, expresses the fervent need for concurrence and dialogue. However, the practical actions that can be taken toward laying the foundation for concurrence and dialogue are too few to mention. Or such efforts have not had global effect. The reasons for this general attitude of calm and indifference should be sought in modernity's transformative effect on humans and society.

It is a fact that modernity has injected egoism into human beings; making them so insignificant that they become almost invisible; stirring up the individual, material, and personal instinct of humans in opposition to society; distancing people from everything they hold sacred, humane, and ethical—from love, care, devotion, and self-sacrifice. In the end, an inferior human being has been the outcome, one who lives only for egoistic instincts. A person who lives only for egoistic instinct, indeed, is inferior. All monotheistic religions have tried to come to rescue of such people; but the fatal blow of modernity against the personality and cosmic coherence of human beings has made them captives of their individual instincts. It would, of course, be impossible to make a comprehensive investigation of modernity here. Nor is it the intention to pose an interrogation or any other type of questioning. What we see when we examine the rupture that contemporary human civilization has experienced—for whatever reason—is that everything comes down to the problem of humanity. When humans are destructive, detrimental, hostile, and aggressive, then they enslave the order of society and humanity, in which they are a part, to these instincts as well. Therefore, it is clear where the standard of humanity has been knocked down. The way to rescue contemporary civilization from imminent destruction is to re-educate human beings on the basis of love, tolerance, and dialogue, and to get organized.

Now, M. Fethullah Gülen's call finds its voice at the very spot where the standard of humanity has been knocked down. His call is neither passive, mere philosophical humanism, nor is it an elite discussion platform where only theoretical discussions take place. With hundreds of educational institutions spread all around the world, this project is applied to real life, where both the social foundations of dialogue and tolerance have been laid down, and where efforts are made to respond to the need of contemporary civilization—i.e., to act as a role model.

In fact, Gülen's model is—like the values of humanity, the individual, tolerance, and concurrence, values which mark the twenty-first century—the essence of the synthesis created by the coming together of Turkish culture with Islam. Muslim Turks have practiced tolerance and concurrence, which are the essence of the contemporary democracy, over a vast geography for centuries. Islam has been interpreted in this geography with the same tolerance for thousand years. This tolerance was initiated by Muslim Turkish Sufis, and was injected into the roots of the nation, follows a line that stretches from Yesevi to Rumi, then from Yunus to Hacı Bektaş-ı Veli it has a history that is long deep. Gülen, following this very basis, re-generates this tolerant interpretation and understanding of Muslim-Turkish Sufism within contemporary circumstances, albeit highlighting a broader, more active, and more socially oriented vision. Rumi, Yunus, and Hacı Bektaş-ı Veli called people to the dervish lodges to discover their inner worlds; while the etiquette of the lodges and their social surroundings emphasized tolerance and dialogue, Gülen opens up this framework and vision to all societies in the world, transforming and broadening it. In other words, his mission includes a transformative action; this is true to such a point that he unifies this mission and movement with the goal of existence of the humankind in this world. On one hand, through the movement of dialogue and concurrence he is able to organize meetings and discussion platforms based on good-will among different cultures of the world; on the other hand, he sets down a challenge to transform the human aspect—which has become self-centered with modernity—so that it can be of service to humankind and self-sacrifice. The modern humans are passive, unable to act due to individual burdens, sluggish, and selfish. One cannot find in such a person the strength to shoulder such a great and heavy responsibility as dialogue, tolerance, and concurrence among religions, cultures, and civilizations. The people who can take on such a burden must be devoted, sincere, self-sacrificing, and broad-hearted. Even those who have come to destroy, smash, and devastate must be revived, and be helped to find their fundamentals of humanity. Thus, humans, whom Gülen puts at the center of dialogue and tolerance, must always behave positively in terms of both thought and behavior. They should not act by instinct, or by reactions, or according to inner or outer considerations. They should be constructive, not destructive. Therefore, such people must volunteer to suffer. This is not something that can be accomplished by mere religiousness, or by existing only in one's own nook and letting oneself flow with social events. Gülen's model is an enduring one, open at both ends to infinity. There is neither an end to spiritual transcendence, nor a limit to material devotion, or to self-sacrifice; all of these are open to eternity. Nothing is enough when it is done for the sake of society, of humanity, of divine love.

Despite the broad vision Gülen has presented, there may be some circles which are unable to find themselves, or to identify their thoughts through his example. Different ideological concerns may produce different perspectives. However, when looked at from the standpoint of universal human values and concerns, his vision, has in fact the power to embrace all humane and social processes. This is because he has, leaving aside all ideological concerns, set up a model regarding humanity, which is the foundation stone of almost all ideologies. And the human in this model is the person who has been created by God and made the heir to the world, the person who is pure, self-sacrificing, and able to give up all individual requests and desires for the sake of divine love, and for the love of people and creation. Thus, you can place this person at the foundation of all kinds of relationships, societies, guidance, and leadership. You can create a myriad of social models based on such people. The spiritual, theoretical, and social characteristic of these people is such that they behave positively under all circumstances. The people who give their hearts to Gülen's call and thoughts behave in this way; they receive a warm reception from almost everybody throughout the world; from people from different ideological, political, religious, and socio-cultural situations. They accentuate the common values—humane, social and ethical values—with which everybody easily associates.

This book certainly does not include all the thoughts and approaches of Gülen. It most certainly touches on certain dynamics regarding the theoretical and cultural basis of the model he has developed based on dialogue, tolerance, and concurrence among different groups that come from different religions, cultures, and civilizations. This model focuses on human beings—those who surround all their world with thought and action, and who are directed toward love for God and for creation.

The articles in this book are a collection from various writings of Gülen and speeches he has given at different times and on different occasions. Nevertheless, all the articles give a general picture of the world of his thought. We hope that this book will make a plain, sincere, and great contribution to the wave of tolerance and dialogue that concerns the future of our people and our contemporary world.

M. Enes Ergene
Editor

AUTHOR'S BIOGRAPHY

Born in Erzurum, in eastern Turkey, in 1941, M. Fethullah Gülen is an Islamic scholar and thinker, and a prolific writer and poet. He was trained in the religious sciences by several celebrated Muslim scholars and spiritual masters. Gülen also studied the principles and theories of modern social and physical sciences. Based on his exceptional skills in learning and focused self-study, he soon surpassed his peers. In 1958, after attaining excellent examination results, he was awarded a state preacher's license, and was quickly promoted to a post in Izmir, Turkey's third largest province. It was here that Gülen started to crystallize his theme and expand his audience base. In his sermons and speeches he emphasized the pressing social issues of the times: his particular aim was to urge the younger generation to harmonize intellectual enlightenment with wise spirituality and a caring, humane activism.

Gülen did not restrict himself to teaching in the inner cities. He traveled around the provinces in Anatolia and lectured not only in mosques, but also at town meetings and corner coffee houses. This enabled him to reach a more representative cross-section of the population and to attract the attention of the academic community, especially the student body. The subject matter of his speeches, whether formal or informal, was not restricted explicitly to religious questions; he also talked about education, science, Darwinism, about the economy and social justice. It was the depth and quality of his speeches on such a wide range of topics that most impressed the academic community, and won their attention and respect.

Gülen retired from formal teaching duties in 1981, having inspired a whole generation of young students. His efforts, dating from the 1960s, especially in educational reform, have made him one of the best-known and respected figures in Turkey. From 1988 to 1991 he gave a series of sermons as preacher emeritus in some of the most famous mosques in major population centers, while continuing to deliver his message in the form of popular conferences, not only in Turkey, but also in Western Europe.

Main Ideas

In his speeches and writings Gülen envisions a twenty-first century in which we shall witness the birth of a spiritual dynamic that will revitalize long-dormant moral values; an age of tolerance, understanding, and international cooperation that will ultimately lead, through inter-cultural dialogue and a sharing of values, to a single, inclusive civilization. In the field of education, he has spearheaded the establishment of many charitable organizations to work for the welfare of the community, both within and without Turkey. He has inspired the use of mass media, notably television, to inform the public, of matters of pressing concern to them, individually and collectively.

Gülen believes the road to justice for all is dependent on the provision of an adequate and appropriate universal education. Only then will there be sufficient understanding and tolerance to secure respect for the rights of others. To this end, he has, over the years, encouraged the social elite and community leaders, powerful industrialists as well as small businessmen, to support quality education. With donations from these sources, educational trusts have been able to establish many schools, both in Turkey and abroad.

Gülen has stated that in the modern world the only way to get others to accept your ideas is by persuasion. He describes those who resort to force as being intellectually bankrupt; people will always demand freedom of choice in the way they run their affairs and in their expression of their spiritual and religious values. Democracy, Gülen argues, in spite of its many shortcomings, is now the only viable political system, and people should strive to modernize and consolidate democratic institutions in order to build a society where individual rights and freedoms are respected and protected, where equal opportunity for all is more than a dream.

Interfaith and Intercultural Activities

Since his retirement, Gülen has concentrated his efforts on establishing a dialogue among the factions representing different ideologies, cultures, religions and nations. In 1999, his paper "The Necessity of Interfaith Dialogue" was presented to the Parliament of World's Religions in Cape Town, December 1-8. He maintains that "dialogue is a must" and that people, regardless of nation or political borders, have far more in common than they realize.

Given all of this, Gülen considers it both worthwhile and necessary for a sincere dialogue to be established in order to increase mutual understanding. To this end, he has helped to establish the Journalists and Writers Foundation (1994), whose activities to promote dialogue and tolerance among all strata of the society have been warmly welcomed by people from almost all walks of life. Again to this end, Gülen visits and receives leading figures, not only from among the Turkish population, but from all over the world. Pope John Paul II at the Vatican, the late John O'Connor, Archbishop of New York, Leon Levy, former president of The Anti-Defamation League are among many leading representatives of world religions with whom Gülen has met to discuss dialogue and take initiatives in this respect. In Turkey, the Vatican's Ambassador to Turkey, the Patriarch of the Turkish Orthodox Church, the Patriarch of the Turkish Armenian community, the Chief Rabbi of the Turkish Jewish community and many other leading figures in Turkey have frequently met with him, portraying an example of how sincere dialogue can be established between people of faith.

In his meeting with Pope John Paul II at the Vatican (1998), Gülen presented a proposal to take firm steps to stop the conflict in the Middle East via collaborative work on this soil, a place where all three religions originated. In his proposal, he also underlined the fact that science and religion are in fact two different aspects that emanate from the same truth: "Humankind from time to time has denied religion in the name of science and denied science in the name of religion, arguing that the two present conflicting views. All knowledge belongs to God and religion is from God. How then can the two be in conflict? To this end, our joint efforts directed at inter-religious dialogue can do much to improve understanding and tolerance among people."

Gülen released a press declaration renouncing the September 11th terrorist attacks on the USA, which he regarded as a great blow to world peace that unfairly tarnished the credit of believers: ". . . terror can never be used in the name of Islam or for the sake of any Islamic ends. A terrorist cannot be a Muslim and a Muslim cannot be a terrorist. A Muslim can only be the representative and symbol of peace, welfare, and prosperity."

Gülen's efforts for worldwide peace have been echoed at conferences and symposiums. "The Peaceful Heroes Symposium" (April 11-13, 2003) at the University of Texas, Austin, produced a list of peacemakers over 5,000 years of human history. Gülen was mentioned among contemporary heroes of peace, in a list which includes names such as Jesus, Buddha, Mohandas Gandhi, Martin Luther King, Jr., and Mother Teresa.

Gülen contributes to a number of journals and magazines. He writes the editorial page for several magazines. He writes the lead article for *The Fountain, Yeni Ümit, Sızıntı*, and *Yağmur*, leading popular and spiritual thought magazines in Turkey. He has written more than forty books, hundreds of articles, and recorded thousands of audio and videocassettes. He has delivered innumerable speeches on many social and religious issues. Some of his books—many of which have been best-sellers in Turkey —have been made available in English translations, such as, *Prophet Muhammad: Aspects of His Life, Questions and Answers about Faith, Pearls of Wisdom, Prophet Muhammad as Commander, Essentials of the Islamic Faith, Towards the Lost Paradise, Key Concepts in the Practice of Sufism*. A number have also been translated into German, Russian, Albanian, Japanese, Indonesian, and Spanish.

The educational trusts inspired by Gülen have established countless non-profit voluntary organizations—foundations and associations—in Turkey and abroad which support many scholarships.

Though a well-known public figure, Gülen has always shied away from involvement in formal politics. Gülen's admirers include leading journalists, academics, TV personalities, politicians, and Turkish and foreign state authorities. They see in him a true innovator and unique social reformer who practices what he preaches. They see him as a peace activist, an intellectual, a religious scholar, a mentor, author and poet, a great thinker and spiritual guide who has devoted his life to seeking the solutions for society's ills and spiritual needs. They see the movement he helped to nurture as a movement dedicated to education, but an education of the heart and soul as well as of the mind, aimed at reviving and invigorating the whole being to achieve competence and providing goods and services useful to others.

LOVE AND MERCY

LOVE

Love is the most essential element of every being, and it is the most radiant light, and it is the greatest power; able to resist and overcome all else. Love elevates every soul that absorbs it, and prepares these souls for the journey to eternity. Souls that have been able to make contact with eternity through love exert themselves to inspire in all other souls what they have derived from eternity. They dedicate their lives to this sacred duty; a duty for the sake of which they endure every kind of hardship to the very end, and just as they pronounce "love" with their last breath, they will also breathe "love" while being raised on the Day of Judgment.

It is impossible for souls without love to be elevated to the horizon of human perfection. Even if they lived for hundreds of years, they could not advance on the path to perfection. Those who are deprived of love, as they are entangled in the nets of selfishness, are unable to love anybody else and die unaware of the love that is deeply instilled in the very being of existence.

A child is received with love when he is born, and grows up in a warm atmosphere composed of affectionate, loving souls. Even if children may not enjoy the same love to the same degree in later phases of their life, they always long for it and pursue it throughout their life.

There are impressions of love on the face of the sun; water evaporates, rising toward those impressions, and after it has been condensed in drops high above, the drops fall joyfully onto the earth on wings of love. Then, thousands of flowers burst through with love, offering smiles to their surroundings. Dew drops on leaves glitter with love and twinkle with amusement. Sheep and lambs bleat and skip about with love, and birds and chicks chirp with love and form choruses of love.

Each being takes part in the grand orchestra of love in the universe with its own particular symphony and tries to demonstrate, by free will or

This article was written in March 1987 and originally appeared in *Yitirilmiş Cennete Doğru*, Nil, Izmir, 1988, and in its English edtition *Towards the Lost Paradise*, Kaynak, Izmir, 1998, 2nd Edition, pp. 43-45.

through its disposition, an aspect of the deep love that is found in existence.

Love is ingrained in the soul of a human being so deeply that many people leave their home for its sake, many families are ruined, and, in every corner, a Majnun groans with love, longing for his Layla.[1] As for those who have not been able to uncover the love inherent in their being, they regard such manifestations of love as madness!

Altruism is an exalted human feeling, and its source is love. Whoever has the greatest share in this love is the greatest hero of humanity; these people have been able to uproot any feelings of hatred and rancor in themselves. Such heroes of love continue to live even after their death. These lofty souls who, by each day kindling a new torch of love in their inner world and by making their hearts a source of love and altruism, are welcomed and loved by people, have received the right to an eternal life from the Supreme Judge. Death, not even Doomsday, will be able to remove their traces.

A mother who can die for the sake of her child is a heroine of affection; individuals who dedicate their lives to the happiness of others are entitled "valiant devotees," but those who live and die for all of humanity are commemorated as monuments of immortality who deserve to be enthroned in the hearts of humanity. In the hands of these heroes, love becomes a magic elixir to overcome every obstacle and a key to open every door. Those who possess such an elixir and key will sooner or later open the gates to all parts of the world and spread the fragrance of peace everywhere, using the "censers" of love in their hands.

The most direct way of going to the hearts of people is the way of love, the way of the Prophets. Those who follow it are rarely rejected; even if they are rejected by a few, they are welcomed by thousands. Once they are welcomed through love, nothing can prevent them from attaining their ultimate goal, God's pleasure.

How happy and prosperous are those who follow the guidance of love. How unfortunate, on the other hand, are those who lead the life of "the deaf and dumb," unaware of the innate love deep in their souls!

O God, the Most Exalted! Today when hatred and rancor have enveloped everywhere like layers of darkness, we take refuge in Your infinite Love

---

[1] Layla and Majnun are legendary lovers in Eastern literature.

and entreat at Your door, begging You to fill the hearts of Your mischievous, pitiless slaves with love and humane emotions!

LOVE FOR HUMANKIND

Love is an elixir; a human lives with love, is made happy by love and makes those around him or her happy with love. In the vocabulary of humanity, love is life; we feel and sense each other with love. God Almighty has not created a stronger relation than love, this chain that binds humans one to another. In fact, the Earth is nothing but a ruin without love to keep it fresh and alive. Jinn and humans have sultans; bees, ants, and termites have their queens; for each of these there is a throne. Kings and queens come to power in different ways, and then they ascend their thrones. Love is the sultan that reigns on the throne of our hearts, with no power struggle being involved. The tongue and lips, the eyes and the ears only have a value as long as they carry the flag of love, yet love is only valuable in and of itself. The heart, the pavilion of love, is priceless because of the love it carries. Castles can be conquered without bloodshed merely by waving flags of love in front of them. Sultans become soldiers of affection when conquered by the soldiers of love.

We have been brought up in an atmosphere in which the victories of love are in our eyes and the sound of the drums of love resounds in our hearts. Our hearts beat with excitement when we see the flag of love waving. We have become so intertwined with love that our lives become purely dependent on love, and we dedicate our souls to it. When we live, we live with love, and when we die, we die with love. In every breath, we feel it with our whole existence; it is our warmth in the cold, and our oasis in the heat.

In this over-polluted world, where evil is everywhere, if there is something that has been left untouched and clean, that is love; among all the fading ornaments of this life, if there is a beauty that has preserved its magnificence and charm without fading, that is also love. There is nothing more real or more lasting than love in any nation or society in this world. Wherever the sound of love, softer and warmer than a lullaby, is heard, all other voices, all instruments, are muted, and they all join to-

This article originally appeared in *Işığın Göründüğü Ufuk* [The Horizon Where the Light Appeared], Nil, Istanbul, 2000, pp. 34-38.

gether in a contemplation of silence with their most melodic strains.

Creation is the result of lighting the wick of the candle of love, the wick of "being known and seen." If the Lord did not love creation, there would be neither moons, nor suns nor stars. The heavens are all poems of love, with the Earth being the rhyme. In nature, the heavy blow of love is felt, and in relationships between people, the flag of love can be seen to wave. In society, if there is a currency that maintains its value, it is love, and again the value of love is found in itself. Love weighs more if weighed against the purest gold. Both gold and silver can lose their value in different markets and places, but the doors of love are closed to any kind of pessimism and nothing can alter its inner stability and harmony. Up to this very moment, only those who are immersed in hatred, wrath and enmity plan to resist and struggle against love. Ironically, the only cure that will calm these brutal souls is love. Beyond the effect of worldly treasures there are other problems that only the mystical keys of love can solve. It is not possible that any value on this Earth can overcome or even compete with love. The cartels of gold, silver, coin, or any other object of value, are almost always conquered in this marathon by the devotees of affection and love. When the day comes, despite all the splendid, pompous life styles of the owners of material wealth, their coffers are empty, their fires have burned out; yet the candle of love always burns, giving light and diffusing this into our hearts and souls.

Those fortunate people who have kneeled in front of the altar of affection and who have devoted their lives to spreading love have not left even the smallest space in their vocabulary for words like hatred, wrath, conspiracy, or resentment, and even if it means putting their very lives at risk, they have never indulged in enmity. Their heads are humbly bowed, filled with love, they have never greeted anything other than love. When they rise, feelings of enmity try to find a haven in which to hide, feelings of hatred become jealous, recoiling from the blow delivered by love.

The only magic, the only spell that can destroy the tricks of Satan, is love. The messengers and prophets extinguished the fires of hatred and jealousy kindled by the pharaohs, the Nimrods, and other tyrannous kings; they used nothing but love. The saints have tried to gather together the undisciplined and rebellious souls, spread all over like loose pages; they have used love to try to introduce humane behavior to others. The power of love was great enough to break the spells of Harut and

Marut,[1] and effective enough to extinguish the fires of Hell. Hence, there is no doubt that a person who is armored with love needs no other weapon. Indeed, love is strong enough to stop a bullet or even a canon ball.

Our interest in our environment and our love for humankind—that is, our ability to embrace creation—depends on knowing and understanding our own essence, our ability to discover ourselves, and to feel a connection with our Creator. In parallel with the ability to discover and feel our inner depths and hidden potential within our essence, we will also be able to appreciate that others also possess the same potential. Moreover, because these inner values are directly related to the Creator, and because a respect for the riches that are hidden in every creature is nurtured, we will start to see every living thing from a different perspective and in a different manner. In reality, the level of our understanding and appreciation of one another depends on how well we recognize the qualities and riches that each person possesses. We can summarize this concept with a thought based on a saying of the Prophet, peace and blessings be upon him, "A believer is the mirror of another believer." We can enlarge on this saying as "a human is a mirror of another human." If we are able to succeed in doing this, as well as being able to understand and appreciate the riches hidden within every person, we will also understand how to relate these riches to their true Owner, and thus we will accept that anything in this universe that is beautiful, affectionate, or loving belongs to Him. A soul that can sense this depth says, as did Rumi[2] presenting us tales from the language of the heart: "Come, come and join us, as we are the people of love devoted to God! Come, come through the door of love and join us and sit with us. Come, let us speak one to another through our hearts. Let us speak secretly, without ears and eyes. Let us laugh together without lips or sound, let us laugh like the roses. Like thought, let us see each other without any words or sound. Since we are all the same, let us call each other from our hearts, we won't use our lips or tongue. As our hands are clasped together, let us talk about it."

---

[1] Two angels, whose story is told in the Qur'an (Al-Baqara 2:102), taught the fundamentals of magic to people and warned them against abusing it.

[2] Mawlana Jalal al-Din al Rumi (1207-73): A great Muslim saint. Mevlevi Sufi Order of whirling dervishes was founded by his followers.

In our present culture, it is not so easy to witness such a deep understanding of these humane feelings and values; we cannot find these easily in Greek or Latin thought or in Western philosophy. Islamic thought sees each one of us as a different manifestation of a unique ore, as different aspects of one reality. Indeed, the people who have gathered around common points, such as the Oneness of God, the Prophet, and the religion resemble the limbs of a body. The hand does not need to compete with the foot, the tongue does not criticize the lips, the eye does not see the mistakes of the ears, the heart does not struggle with the mind.

As we are all limbs of the same body, we should cease this duality that violates our very union. We should clear the way to unite people; this is one of the greatest ways in which God grants people success in this world, and how He transforms this world into a Paradise. It is in this way that the doors of Heaven will be opened wide in order to give us a warm welcome. Hence, we should remove all ideas and feelings that pull us apart, and run to embrace one another.

HUMANISM AND LOVE OF HUMANITY

L ove is not only one of the most frequently talked about issues today, it is also one of the most essential issues. Actually, love is the rose in our belief, a realm of the heart that never withers. Above all else, just as God wove the universe like lace on the loom of love, the most magical and charming music in the bosom of existence is always love. The strongest relationship among individuals that forms family, society, and nation is love. Universal love shows itself throughout the cosmos in the fact that each particle helps and supports every other particle.

This is true to such an extent that the most dominant factor in the spirit of existence is love. As an individual of the universal chorus, almost every creature acts and behaves in its own style, according to the magical tune it has received from God, in a melody of love. However, this exchange of love from existence to humanity and from one creature to another takes place beyond their will, because the Divine Will completely dominates them.

From this perspective, humankind "consciously" participates in this symphony of love that is being played in existence. By developing the love in their true nature, human beings investigate how they can demonstrate it in a human way. Therefore, without misusing the love in their spirit and for the sake of the love in their own nature, every person should offer real help and support to others. They should protect the general harmony that has been put in the spirit of existence, considering both the natural laws and the laws that have been made to govern human life.

Humanism is a doctrine of love and humanity which is articulated recklessly these days, and it has a potential to be easily manipulated through different interpretations. Some circles try to impose an abstract and unbalanced understanding of humanism by confusing people about jihad in Islam and awakening suspicion in their hearts. It should be difficult to reconcile with humanism the strange behavior of championing "pity and mercy" for those who are involved in anarchy and terror to demolish the unity of a country, for those who have heartlessly murdered innocent people as a part of centuries-long activities that are aimed at destroying the welfare of a nation, and even more horribly, for those who do this in the name of religious values, and those who recklessly accuse Islam of allowing terrorist attacks.

Every believer should follow God's Messenger, peace and blessings be upon him, in communicating the truth. They should never give up conveying to people the principles of happiness in both worlds. The Companions, who as a community were a vivid example of the truth embodied by the Prophet, became examples of moderation and balance in every matter.

Some remarkable people from the fortunate generation that immediately followed the Companions went to the Caliph to learn what their punishment would be if they accidentally stepped on a grasshopper. When we look at the outer walls of our mosques and minarets that radiate light, we see tiny holes made for birds to nest in; this is an expression of the depth of the love of our ancestors. History is intertwined with such tremendously humane acts; acts that protected animals as well as people.

In the framework of Islam's universal principles, the consideration and idea of love is very balanced. Oppressors and aggressors have denied this love, because just as love and mercy shown to oppressors makes them more aggressive, it also encourages them to violate the rights of others. For this reason, mercy should not be shown to people who threaten universal love. Mercy shown to an oppressor is the most merciless act toward the oppressed. However, we should show mercy for those who lapse unintentionally or feel remorse for their wrong. The Prophet said:

> Help your brothers whether they are oppressors or victims. You can help oppressors by making them stop their oppression (to others).[1]

---

[1] Bukhari, *Mazalim*, 4; Tirmidhi, *Fitan*, 68.

LOVE OF GOD

In these bleak and inauspicious days, when our hearts are overwhelmed with enmity, when our spirits are sickened, when hatred and antagonism are out of control, it is crystal clear that we need love and mercy as we need water or air. We seem to have forgotten love; what is more, compassion is a word rarely used. We have no mercy for each other, nor love for people. Our feeling of pity has diminished, our hearts are adamant and our horizon is pitch-black from hostility; it is for this reason that we see everything and everybody as being bleak. Throughout the world there are many tyrants that detest tolerance. The number of those who curse dialogue is not that small at all. What most of us do is to seek ways to fight, to blacken one another's name with various lies and we express ourselves with our fangs, our claws, our words that reek of blood.

There is a terrifying disunion among individuals as well as among the people. We begin our sentences with the words "We," "You," and "Others." Never does our hatred disintegrate and disperse. We conclude our nauseating rows, indicating that we will continue, still bearing feelings that will arise in future tension. We are distant from one another, and this distance or disunion is reflected in our every act. Like a burst rosary, we scatter here and there. We cause each other incomparably more suffering than unbelievers do.

As a matter of fact, we have forsaken God, and thus, He has disbanded us. Because we could not believe in and love Him to the degree required, He withdrew the feeling of love from our hearts. What we are now doing, deep in the abyss of our bosoms where we are condemned to suffer yearning for Him, is to utter the egotistic nonsense of "I," "you," and to label each other as "reactionary," "infidel fanatic," and to constantly produce scenarios to dethrone one another. It is as though we have been cursed, as if we have indeed been deprived of loving and being

This article originally appeared in *Örnekleri Kendinden Bir Hareket* [A Movement Originating Its Own Models], Nil, Istanbul, 2004, pp. 184-196.

loved, and we are craving mercy, compassion, and bliss. We did not love Him, so He took love away. No matter how long we wait, He will make us love one another if only we turn to Him and love Him. However, we are distant from the source of love. The roads we are on do not lead to Him, not at all. On the contrary, they are leading us away from Him. Our spirits, which used to receive streams of love, receive nothing now. Our hearts are like dry deserts; there are caves in our inner worlds, resembling the dens of wild animals. The love of God is the only remedy for all these negative things.

The love of God is the essence of everything and is the purest and cleanest source of all love. Compassion and love flow to our hearts from Him. Any kind of human relation will develop in accordance with our relation to Him. Love of God is our faith, our belief, and our spirits in the physical body. He made us live when we did. If we are to live today it is only through him. The essence of all existence is His love, and the end is an expansion of that divine love in the form of Paradise. Everything He created depends on love and He has bound His relationship with humankind to the holy pleasure of being loved.

The sphere of the manifestation of love is the soul. To whatever direction we may orient it, it always turns to God. The sufferings due to disorientation and getting lost in multiplicity, rather than in the Unity of God, are ours.[1] If we relate our love for everything to God, and thus, if we are able to take love in its real meaning, we will then be aloof from the various things that disperses love and we will avoid associating partners with God. Thus, we will remain like those who advance on the true path with our love and our relationship to all of existence.

Idolaters have considered idols as something to worship only because they were worshiped by their ancestors. God, on the other hand, is Beloved and worshiped because He is God. His Lordship and Greatness require us to be His servant. We always endeavor to worship Him, to express our love for Him, to thank Him for our attainments, and to voice our affection for Him, our relation with Him, and our connection to Him.

---

[1] The author touches upon "disorientation and getting lost in multiplicity" in association with failing to surrender to the Will of one single God, but instead, submitting to multiple worldly gods, like excessive wealth, abuse of power, indulging in illegitimate pleasures, etc. Idolatry is another manifestation of worshiping multiple gods.

In worldly love, aspects like beauty, perfection, form, harmony in appearance, greatness, reputation, power, position, status, prosperity, family and lineage, etc. have all been regarded as reasons for love. Occasionally, there have been people who fall into the error of associating partners with God; this is due to their excessive love and affection for these phenomena, which may explain why idolatry exists. Such people are usually fond of facial or physical beauty, or manners, they applaud perfection, prostrating themselves before magnificence and greatness, sacrificing their humanity and liberty for the sake of wealth and power, and flattering in their greed for position and status. In this way, by distributing their love and affection to many an impotent creature, not only do they waste their emotions, which are meant primarily to be used in relation to the True Opulent and Mighty One, they also experience death after death due to unreciprocated love, or to the indifference and unfaithfulness of their beloved ones.

As for believers, on the other hand, they love God in the very first place, and they feel affection to others through their love for Him. For the sake of the manifestation and blessings of the Just One, they keep in touch with every person and every thing, declaring their love and appreciating these things on His behalf.

Indeed, without taking God into consideration, any love for this or that object is futile, unpromising, indecisive, and fruitless. Above all else, a believer must love Him, and have a liking for all others only because they are colorful manifestations and reflections of His Divine Names and Attributes. Also, people must applaud these things with great admiration, and each time a person sees such a thing they must think, "This too, is by You," and experience a period of unification with the Lover. For this, however, we need pure and virtuous people that can read the verses of God in the faces of people. Verily, for those who can decipher, every creature is a shining mirror and a eulogy written in great verse; above all else is the human face, reflecting the secret of Mercy.

The All-Just made you a mirror of His Self,
A mirror of His Unique Self.

Hakani[2]

---

[2] Hakani Mehmed Bey (d. 1606): A divan poet whose *Hilya* (a literary genre which describes the physical features of the Prophet) was first of its kind.

How significant the above couplet is; not only does it remind us of our position, it also stresses reality. If a human being is a mysterious mirror of the concealed Beauty, which is, without a doubt, the case, then a person must turn to Him with the eyes of his or her heart, lying in wait to witness the manifestations, and expecting breezes that will take him or her to residences of deeper love. Also, in order to please Him, and thus, to become one favored by Him, a person must make use of each and every means available on the road leading to His intimacy. Like a key in the lock of the Hidden Treasure, his or her heart must keep turning all the time. As such, if love is Solomon and the heart is the throne of Solomon, it goes without saying that the sultan will ascend the throne, sooner or later.

Once Solomon ascends the throne, or in other words, when love meets the heart, people always think of Him, speak to Him in the inner world and taste His blessings, openly and explicitly, in the water they drink, in the food they taste and in the air they breathe. Moreover, they feel the warmth of His intimacy in all actions. The relationship of the tides of closeness and love deepens and their hearts begin to burn as if on fire. At times, they are destroyed by the fire of love, yet, never do any of them complain and thus, never do any of them tire others with their sighs. In contrast, such people consider these to be a gift bestowed by Him. They burn like a furnace without smoke or flames. Like chastity, they preserve their joy and love for God, never revealing any secrets to more tactless people.

This road is open to everybody. Nonetheless, it is essential that the traveler be sincere and determined. If believers find out that all of beauty, perfection, greatness, excellence, magnificence belong to God, then they turn to God with all the willingness, love, and affection that have been brought about by these means and they love God with a love that is fit for His Sublime Being. This love, if not passion, is for Him and it is the source of human love and desire in a unified manner. After all, in a heart that is confined to uniformity and that relies on Islamic principles, one can never observe any deviation, let alone any disorder of love. Believers love God because He is God, and their love for God is not connected to any earthly or unearthly considerations. They filter and test the gushing springs of love and the waterfalls of their desire for God with the Holy

Qur'an and the principles of the most exalted spirit.[3] Such people also use these as a barrier in the path that they follow with human fallibility. Even at times when they are completely consumed with the fire of love, they act righteously and justly. Never does presumption interfere in their love for God. Instead, regarding Him as the Real Owner and Protector of everything, Who is known with His Divine Names and Attributes, they love God wholeheartedly with a clean, sacred and reverent love.

Believers love God more than anything, prior to and in the aftermath of everything as the Real Beloved, the Real Desired, and the Real Worshiped. They desire God and through every possible action they cry out that they are the servants of God. For the sake of this devotion, they love in the first place Prophet Muhammad, the Pride of Humanity, who was the loyal attendant, the true interpreter of God's Essence, Names and Attributes, the end of the succession of prophets and the essence of messengership, peace and blessings be upon him. Following him, they love all the other prophets and people of sainthood who were the true vicegerents, the purest mirrors, and devout servants of Almighty God, who were in charge of representing divine purposes and supervising the building, design, and order of the world. Next they love youth, for it is conferred by God as an advance credit upon humankind so that they can better understand and evaluate this finite world. After that, they love this world, for it is an arable field of the other realms and also a manifestation of His Beautiful Names. Then they love their parents, for, being heroes of affection and mercy, they undertake the responsibility of looking after their children. Finally they love children, for they sincerely protect their parents and have an intimate closeness to them, as well. All these can be regarded as signs of cordial affection toward God and of love for the sake of God.

Unbelievers love people as if they were loving God, while believers love them because of God; these two are totally different. This sort of God-oriented love, which is experienced through faith and prayers, is unique to ideal believers. While the corporeal love based on waywardness and the evil-commanding self are the manifestations of sin and disobedience hidden in the nature of man, love of God and utterances of the lovers of God are like a sacred potion angels wish to drink. If this love grows to such an extent that the lovers forsake everything—material or spiri-

---

[3] Prophet Muhammad, peace and blessings be upon him.

tual—for the sake of the Beloved, leaving nothing for themselves, then there is merely the consideration of the Beloved in the heart. The heart girds itself with this consideration, beating accordingly, whereas eyes verbalize this love with tears. The heart reproaches the eye for releasing a secret, and the bosom for cooling down. Crying and bleeding inside, he tries not to let others discover his agony, and says:

You claim to be in love, then grieve not over the calamity of love,
Do not let others into your suffering from love.

(Anonymous)

Actually, love is a sultan, the heart is the throne, and the groans of hope and longing uttered on the prayer rugs in the remotest corners are the voice of that sultan.

Never should one let others into these groans of the remotest places, which indeed are the launching pads to reach God, and thereby help those ignorant ones make fun of them. If this spectacular love is for the Omniscient One, then it should be kept in the most private sphere, not letting it fly away from its nest.

Telling of their trivial love, these conventional lovers wander here and there, proclaiming their love to all, acting like mad men, making their love obvious to all. Lovers of God, on the other hand, are sincere and quiet. Leaning their heads on God's threshold, they express themselves merely to Him. From time to time they faint, but they never reveal their secrets. They are at His service with their hands and feet, their eyes and ears, their tongues and lips and they wander in the places of His Sublime Attributes. Immersed in His Light of Being they melt and disappear as a mortal in His love. As they feel and sense God, they burn and exclaim, "More!" Much do they feel at the peaks of their hearts and still they cry, "More!" They are never satisfied with love though they love and are loved. "More!" they keep repeating. And as they continue asking for more, the Glorious Beloved uncovers veils for them, presenting to their wisdom things never seen before, and also whispering to their spirits many a secret. After a certain point what they feel, what they love, what they think of becomes Him. In everything they see they find graceful manifestations of His Beauty. Leaving their strength entirely, at a certain time they connect their will power to His, melt in His demands, and evaluate this high rank with how much they love and are loved, and again with how much they know and are known. With obedience to Him and faithfulness, they express their love. They lock the door of their hearts with bolt after bolt in such a secure manner that no stranger can ever enter that pure house. With all their beings they are witnesses of God, and their praise and appreciation of God is far beyond their comprehension.

Their belief, on the other hand, in God's response to such loyalty is adamant. Their place in God's Presence is in direct proportion with His in their hearts, which is why they endeavor to stand upright before Him.

Never do they act like a creditor when they love Him deeply; on the contrary, they are as embarrassed as a debtor. As Rabi'a al-'Adawiya[4] put it, "I swear on Your Holy Being that I have not worshiped You demanding Your Paradise. Rather, I loved You and connected my slavery to my love." As such, they walk with gushing love toward His Realm, keeping His blessings and kindness in mind. With their hearts, they constantly endeavor to stay close to Him, and with their reason and intellect, they observe phenomena in the mirrors of the Divine Names. They hear voices of love in everything, are mesmerized by the fragrance of each and every flower, and consider every scene that is beautiful as a reflection of His Beauty. For Him, all they hear, feel, or think of is nothing other than love, as a result of which they watch the whole existence as an exhibition of love and, again, listen to it as a harmony of love.

Once love has put up its sumptuous tents in the valleys of the heart, all opposite events seem to be the same, such as peace-unrest, blessing-calamity, hot-sweet, comfort-discomfort, grief-pleasure, all giving the same sound and looking the same way. Indeed, for loving hearts, suffering is no different than pleasure. To them, suffering is the very cure, so they drink pain and agony as they drink from the rivers of Heaven. No matter how merciless the time and events get, they stay still with a profound feeling of loyalty. With their eyes fixed on the door to be opened, they lie in wait to welcome some manifestations and kindness in different dimensions. They crown His love by respecting and also obeying Him. Their hearts beat with submission and they shake due to the fear of disobeying the Beloved. So as not to fall, ironically, they take shelter again in the Unique Source of reliance and aid. This kind of quest for an agreement with and consent of God makes them in time very dearly sought by

---

[4] Rabi'a al-'Adawiya (c. 703-805): A female saint of exceptional piety.

everybody both on Earth and in the heavens. The only thing in their consideration is nothing but God. For them, expecting something in return is a kind of deception, yet they regard it as discourteous not to accept the blessings they have not asked for. They give these blessings high esteem but, cautiously, each of them moans; "I take refuge in You from their temptations."

An ardent longing is the highest rank for a lover, and to get lost in the lover's desires and wishes is the most unreachable attainment. Love is founded upon elementary principles, such as repentance, alertness, and patience, whereas once introduced, self-possession, familiarity, love, longing, and other principles are required in order to merit this position. The first lesson on the path of love is purification, to be deprived of personal desires, to relate all your thoughts and communication to Him, to be busy with things that hint of Him, to wait expectantly in case He manifests, and also to stay determinedly where you are for a lifetime in case He turns to you one day. In this path, love is to be madly in love; ardor is the gushing passion, enthusiasm and desire; when ardor becomes the true nature of humans then this is yearning; consent is meeting every act of the Lover with pleasure; self-possession is being cautious against becoming intoxicated with the blessings of hearing or feeling His Presence, or being under His direct guidance.

The more people develop in themselves one of the above features, the more changes there are that can be witnessed in their behavior. Sometimes they seek quiet bays where they can confide in Him. Sometimes under the influence of a variety of considerations, they talk to Him and state their grievance concerning separation. They are filled with joy expecting union and relax with tears of bliss. At times, they do not see what is going on around them, for they experience unity in multiplicity, and sometimes they get lost in the awe of peace and cannot even hear their own voices.

Love grows and develops in the bosom of wisdom. Wisdom is nourished by knowledge of the divine. Those who are not wise cannot love at all. And those whose perception is weak cannot reach wisdom, either. Occasionally, God himself implants love in hearts and activates the inner mechanism, an extra blessing which most people long for. Nevertheless, relying on some marvelous wonders and waiting impotently is one thing; an active waiting in endless contractions is totally different. The faithful servants at the Gate of the All-Just One put their expectations on action, take up a dynamic stance and, therefore, they generate with that seemingly still position enough energy to suffice the entire universe, materializing awesome activities.

These people are loyal lovers incarnating certain characteristics. They meet every act of the Beloved with pleasure and display faithfulness all the time, as if repeating Nesimi[5];

> *A desperate lover, I won't, O the Beloved, abandon You,*
> *I won't do so even if You rend my heart with a dagger.*

Despite the fact that they always seriously long for His Company, never ever do they whine. They remove all expectations that are not of Him from their minds, and think only of His Presence. Their conversations become those of the Beloved, and thus, their voices gain an angelic profundity.

For them, love is everything. They can survive without bodies; but without souls, they cannot. They believe that there is no room in their hearts for others, only for the love of the Beloved. As such, even if they are the poorest and weakest of the world, they hold a status envied by kings as well. They are big in their smallness, mighty in their impotence, wealthy enough in their neediness to command the entire universe. Though they look like a puny candle, they are like an energy source rich enough to light up suns. Even if everyone were to run toward the loyal lovers, it is still clear to where and to Whom the lovers are running. With the wealth of their essential characters they transcend the entire universe. But when they turn toward Him, they become a spark, even less—they become nothing by forgetting all that pertains to their existence.

A life without Him counts little for them. A life without Him is not a life at all. Leading a life without loving is a wasted life, and the delights and pleasures not related to Him are nothing but a placebo. They ceaselessly talk about love and longing and regard those who are not familiar with these as being somehow different.

---

[5] Nesimi (d. 1404). A famous Sufi poet from Baghdad, Nesimi is considered to be one of the first masters of divan literature. He has two *divans* (book of poems) in Turkish and Persian.

APPEAL TO MERCY

It is patently obvious that those who do not share the same values inherited from the past, or who do not rely on the same sources as us are not likely to appreciate our affliction; nor can they help but be puzzled by our general attitudes. In fact, for those who view the present and the future from only a materialistic point of view and who deal with life merely in accord with its corporal aspects, it is not possible to feel or taste anything but the transient and shallow pleasures of the body. And, again, according to the same corrupt view, things not related to corporeality or to the body are not worth mentioning. Neither the past nor the future holds any meaning. The past and the future are merely refuges in which those who have lost the present can take shelter. What such people consider essential is the present; they see the rest as being a waste of time. Truly, these people, imprisoned within such a narrow perspective, are not likely to understand such statements as, "Were you to know what I know, you would seldom laugh, and often weep."[1] Nonetheless, the Sultan of the Words, the Prophet who uttered this hadith, knew well over what he was crying, just as those mature spirits, satisfied only with faith, divine knowledge and love, and prepared with their armament for eternity, also know why they are weeping and of what they are in pursuit. There are many reasons for such people to cry.

As well as belief and finding peace—a problem in which everybody is interested—or the danger of being drowned in disbelief, there is a multitude of problems that need to be solved—social, economic, political, and cultural. There are cases of injustice that are considered to be the root of unease in society. There are rights that need to be reconsidered and redistributed in accordance with human values and along the principles of fairness and conscience. There are our hopes and ideals that are concerned with eternity, and, opposing these, there are antidemocratic obstacles that

This article originally appeared in *Işığın Göründüğü Ufuk*, [The Horizon Where the Light Has Appeared], Nil, Istanbul, 2000, pp. 189-195.

[1] Bukhari, *Kusuf*, 2; Muslim, *Kusuf*, 1; Tirmidhi, *Zuhd*, 9; Ibn Maja, *Zuhd*, 19.

cannot be contemplated, as well as the propaganda of power. In many areas, emotions still dominate reason, and orders are given in accordance with the recklessness of power. In many parts of the world, human mistakes and acts that are considered to be wrong are still swept away with blood and tears. People, from time to time, are forcefully taken off in the direction of Paradise, or roughly pushed toward Hell, their will power and opinions disregarded. New camps are being formed every day, each team fighting for their perspective or their commandments; every ideology is depicting a life style befitting their principles. Furthermore, people are forced to fit into this narrow portrait and to live accordingly. Throughout the world, in hundreds of places, individual consciences are still being crushed, the will of the community is still being ignored and the eyes of the conscience are still being blinded.

In fact, the shortest way to relieve their pains and to rid them of personal and social repression is to cease interfering with their consciences and to show them how to exist with their own awareness and will. Indeed, only when the mechanism of the conscience is kept alive, and will power and awareness are respected in society, can the people stay human and be directed toward human values. Individuals can only be regarded as true citizens when they exist with their own conscience and will power, thus growing mature enough to help others spiritually. Otherwise, society is inescapably inflicted with various social, political, administrative, and economic problems. A community that is made up of inadequate, inconsistent or patched together pieces cannot be called a nation. Likewise, a mass that appears to be a nation, yet which has deteriorated beyond recovery cannot promise a bright future. If we want salvation as a whole society, it is essential that each and every individual be alert and motivated. The star of the good fortune of our society will appear in a surprisingly comforting manner if we plead for the salvation of others, shoulder to shoulder, with our palms opened to the sky.

The essence of the fundamentals that help us reach the desired maturity is composed of our being aware of the faith with all its peculiar depths, of undergoing pain and effort in our worship, of being moral in all our acts, of being spiritually, consciously and sensuously revitalized, and of weighing everything against the righteousness of the heart. Enlightened with these, we will transcend the limits of individuality, make demands in accordance with these principles, and be aware of the things that we demand as well. Going one step further, we will be able to connect everything with eternity, and evaluate everything with the supreme criteria. Thus, sharing in all the advantages of humanity, we will be able to voice once again our eligibility to be "in the most perfect form and nature"[2] as the humans we are. I believe that those blessed ones who understand this pivotal point will not only attempt to lead others to the straight path, but will also guarantee their own future.

I feel obliged to restate again that individual projects of enlightenment that are not planned to aid the community are doomed to fruitlessness. Moreover, it is not possible to revive values that have been destroyed in the hearts of the individual in society, nor in the conscience or the will power. Just as plans and projects for individual salvation that are independent of the salvation of others are nothing more than an illusion, so, too, the thought of achieving success as a whole by paralyzing the individual awakening is a fantasy.

In this light, we believe that, having clarified in our individual wills and consciences the fact that everybody has hands of their own, but by joining hands we can solve all the problems with a collective conscience and will power. With this kind of attitude, we hope to retain, and even to increase, the fruitfulness of our individual lives while presenting to others the elixir of life, and, therefore steadily augmenting our material and spiritual value. To us, the more altruistic a plan or an attempt is, and the more often it is directed for the good of others, the more consistent and promising it is. This is true because what keeps a person alive is the goal of lifting others up. The converse of this is that it is personal interest that kills or paralyzes human beings. Those who waste their lives in pursuit of personal interest are sooner or later corrupted, although they are not necessarily involved in dirty politics. Those who stay alive by inspiring the awakening of others, on the other hand, walk safely providing the elixir of life, in places where all others are being blown around like leaves. And such are the people who have been nominated to "contentment" in this marathon that takes place in both this world and the next.

The camaraderie of the politician who seems to have accepted the existence and right to life of others just because they serve his or her personal interests can never be trusted, nor can anyone be safe when such politicians are antagonized. What such people think of all the time is their

---

[2] "We have indeed created man in the most perfect form and nature." (at-Tin 95:4)

own personal interests. This is why they flatter and even submit themselves to the whims of other people. Such people crush, if need be, those they can afford to, and those whom they need are ceaselessly plotted against. When in power, these tyrants are ruthless; yet, when weak, they begin to cringe and fawn. Because they are consistently insincere, they are mostly beaten by their own tricks, preparing their own evil and wicked end. They make themselves believe that they are tricking and deceiving everybody, and that they are doing the right thing. These poor politicians, however, have placed themselves in a strange position, destroying their reputations for the sake of their careers. Such a deceptive intelligence, witnessed in some people, is a very serious disorder and is an incurable psychological illness. People of this kind always seek their own personal interest, despite the fact that these people are good for nothing. Nevertheless, this does not win them a reputation or credit in their career, and they end up cringing, licking boots.

On the other hand, what lies at the roots of the behavior of people of service is a long period of preparation and severe suffering followed by an appeal to mercy aimed at a search for human rights. This appeal almost always lies beyond individual responsibility, transcending the limits of the awareness of social responsibility with a depth of sincerity, and is a task fitting to a person of heart. People of heart are the leaders in each and every charitable act, reflecting their own style in their works, and they are open and honest in all their deeds. No matter how relentless and merciless the circumstances may be, such people are determined not to be diverted from their routes and, relying on their own foundations, they do, not become disturbed. With their inner and outer feelings, they are programmed to see and hear God in a certain way, to know and to be with God. They are people of this world and the next, people whose contact with others, from the aforementioned point of view, can be considered as contact with God. Apparently, it is possible to observe the zenith of the Hereafter from this sort of worldliness. Moreover, the life that such people lead, with all its variants, is clear and boundless enough for them to enjoy a glimpse of the quiet of a harbor in the next world. Indeed, these purest of pure hearts have already achieved the blissful result that others can only dream of reaching after millions and millions of years of toil. They are considered to have reached the company of God and to have sat down with the dwellers of the highest rank, knee to knee, shoulder to shoulder, proving that such people are the eternal winners. Always sincere and profound, these people of heart constantly seek grand projects and summits. They think of mercy, speak of mercy, and seek ways to express themselves through mercy. They endeavor so heartily in the name of conducting everyone, without discrimination, to the infinite bliss that they sacrifice the pleasures of the future world and spiritual power, not to mention materialistic interests and desire for position. They display in their spiritual position and in their relationships with others a spiritual attitude that reflects the fact that they are in the presence of the Supreme Power. And where others die, they realize successive revitalizations.

Over and above the maxim "Desire not for others what you do not desire for yourself," such people ceaselessly try harder for others so that others will benefit from what these people of heart have already found useful. With the boundlessness of the horizon of such people, they are able to revive the feeling of mercy in the hearts of tyrants. At the same time, they believe that being with the oppressed is the same as being with God, and thus support them.

Living for others is the most important factor that determines the behavior of such heroes. Their greatest worry is their quest for eligibility for such missions, whereas their most prevalent characteristic is that their utmost ambition is their search for God's consent. When striving to enlighten others, they feel no pain nor do they undergo any shock caused by the delight of enlightening others. The achievements that such people accomplish are regarded as revelations of His holy aid, and such people bow in modesty, nullifying themselves again and again, every day. In addition to all this, they tremble at the idea that their emotions are bound to interfere with the works that they have caused to come into existence, and groan; "You are all I need."

For ages we have waited impatiently for such blessed hands to transform what can be depicted as "the devastated lands, ruined homes, and remote deserts" into a new realm. And we are determined to wait for many more years with faith, desire, and resoluteness. May the expectation of these pure, compassionate hearts for this Infinite Mercy, not go unanswered.

FORGIVENESS, TOLERANCE, AND

DIALOGUE

FORGIVENESS

Humans are creatures with both exceptional qualities and faults. Until the first human appeared, no living creature carried such opposites within its nature. At the same time as humans beat their wings in the firmaments of heaven, they can, with sudden deviation, become monsters that descend to the pits of Hell. It is futile to look for any relationship between these frightening descents and ascents; these are extremes because their cause and effect take place on very different planes.

At times humans are like a field of wheat bending in the wind; at other times, although they appear as dignified as a plane tree, they can topple over, not to rise again. Just as the times that the angels envy them are not few, neither are the times when even the devils are shocked by their behavior.

For humans, whose natures contain so many highs and lows, even if committing evil is not essential to their nature, it is inevitable. Even if becoming sullied is accidental, it is likely. For a creature which is going to spoil his good name, forgiveness is paramount.

However valuable it is to ask for and expect forgiveness and to bemoan the things that have escaped us, forgiving is that much greater an attribute and virtue. It is wrong to think of forgiveness as being separate from virtue or of virtue as being separate from forgiveness. As the well-known adage says, "To err is human, to forgive divine," and how well this has been said! Being forgiven means being repaired; it consists of a return to our essence and finding ourselves again. For this reason, the most pleasing action in the eyes of Infinite Mercy is any activity pursued amidst the palpitations of this return and search.

All of creation, animate and inanimate, was introduced to forgiveness through humanity. Just as God showed His attribute of forgiveness through humanity, He also put the beauty of forgiveness into the human heart. While the first man dealt a blow to his essence through his fall,

This article was written in 1980 and originally appeared in *Çağ ve Nesil* [The Age and New Generations], Kaynak, Izmir, 2003 (first edition 1982), pp. 57-60.

something which was almost a requirement of his human nature, forgiveness came from the heavens because of the remorse he felt in his conscience and because of his sincere pleas.

Humans have preserved gifts, such as hope and consolation, which they have obtained from their ancestors over the centuries. Whenever people err, by boarding the magical transport of seeking forgiveness and by surmounting the shame caused by their sins and the despair caused by their actions, they are able to attain infinite mercy and are shown the generosity that is involved in veiling their eyes to the sins of others.

Thanks to their hope for forgiveness, humans can rise above the dark clouds that threaten their horizon and seize the opportunity to see light in their world. Those fortunate ones who are aware of the uplifting wings of forgiveness live their lives amidst melodies that please their spirits.

It is impossible for people who have given their heart to seeking forgiveness not to think of forgiving others. Just as they desire to be forgiven, they also desire to forgive. Is it possible for someone not to forgive if they know that salvation from the fires of suffering caused by his/her mistakes in the inner world is possible by drinking deeply from the river of forgiveness? Is it possible for people not to forgive if they know that the road to being forgiven passes through the act of forgiving?

Those who forgive are honored with forgiveness. One who does not know how to pardon cannot hope to be pardoned. Those who close the road to tolerance for humanity are monsters that have lost their humanity. These brutes that have never once been inclined to take themselves to task for their sins will never experience the high solace of forgiveness.

Jesus Christ said to a crowd that was waiting rocks in hand to stone a sinner: "If anyone of you is without sin let him be the first to throw a stone."[1] Can anyone with a sin on their conscience still be inclined to stone another if they truly understand this idea? If only those unfortunate ones of today who spend their lives putting the lives of others to the litmus test could understand this! In fact, if the reason for stoning a person is our malice and hatred, if this is the reason why we have passed judgment on them, then it is not possible to pass this sentence on them. The truth is, unless we destroy the idols in our ego as courageously as Abraham destroyed the idols, we will never be able to make a correct decision in the name of our selves or in the name of others.

---

[1] Gospel of John, Chapter 8, Verse 7.

Forgiveness emerged with and reached perfection through humanity. In this respect, we can witness the greatest forgiveness and the most impeccable tolerance in the greatest exemplars of humanity.

Malice and hatred are the seeds of Hell that have been scattered among humans by evil spirits. Unlike those who encourage malice and hatred and turn the Earth into a pit of Hell, we should take this forgiveness, and run to the rescue of our people who are confronted by countless troubles and who are being continually pushed toward the abyss. The past few centuries have been turned into the most unpleasant and foul years by the excesses of those who do not know forgiveness or recognize tolerance. It is impossible not to be chilled by the thought that these unfortunate ones could rule the future.

For this reason, the greatest gift that the generation of today can give their children and grandchildren is to teach them how to forgive—to forgive even when confronted by the worst behavior and the most disturbing events. However, thinking of forgiving monstrous, evil people who enjoy making others suffer would be disrespectful to the idea of forgiveness. We have no right to forgive them; forgiving them would be disrespectful to humanity. I do not believe that there is any probability that anyone could see an act that is disrespectful to forgiveness as being acceptable.

A generation which was raised in a particular past under constant hostile pressure saw continuous horror and brutality in the dark world into which they had been pushed. They saw blood and pus, not just in the dark of night, but also at the break of day. What could be learned from a society whose voice, breath, thought, and smile were tainted with blood? The things that were presented to this generation were the complete opposite and totally contrary to what they needed and what they desired. This generation took on a second nature, caused by years of neglect and misleading suggestions; the disorder and sedition caused by these became a flood. If only by now we could have understood them. Alas! Where is such insight?

We believe that forgiveness and tolerance will heal most of our wounds, if only this celestial instrument will be in the hands of those who understand its language. Otherwise, the incorrect methods of behavior, those used up until now, will cause many complications and will only confuse us from now on.

Diagnose the illness, then set out to treat it:
Do you think any ointment will be a cure for every wound?

Ziya Pasha[2]

---

[2] Ziya Pasha (d. 1880): An influential literary figure in the nineteenth century who was a member and advocate of the Young Turks, a secret nationalist organization formed in Istanbul in June 1865.

TOLERANCE AND LIBERALITY

Be as vast as the oceans and take every soul to your bosom! Let faith keep you alert, cherish a never-ending affection for humanity, and leave no broken heart forgotten or ignored! Applaud the good for their goodness, appreciate those who have believing hearts, and be kind to them. Approach unbelievers so gently that their envy and hatred melt away. Like a Messiah, revive people with your breath.

Remember that you travel the best road and follow the Prophet, an exalted guide. Be mindful that you have his guidance through the most perfect and expressive revelation. Be fair-minded and balanced in your judgment, for many people do not enjoy these blessings.

Fend off evil with goodness and ignore rudeness! The attitude of a person reveals their character. Favor tolerance and be magnanimous toward those who do not know better.

The most distinctive feature of a soul overflowing with faith is to love all love that is expressed in deeds and to feel enmity for all deeds in which enmity is expressed. To hate everything is a sign of insanity or of infatuation with Satan.

Accept how God treats you. Make it the measure by which you treat others, so that you may represent the truth among them and be free of the fear of loneliness in either world.

Only those who do not use their reason or who have succumbed to plain stupidity and desires of the flesh are convinced that believers might harm them. Apply to a spiritual master to stir up your heart, and fill your eyes with tears.

Judge your worth in the Creator's sight by how much space He occupies in your heart and your worth in people's eyes by how you treat them. Do not neglect the Truth even for a moment. And yet still "be a human among other humans."

This collection of aphorisms was written in 1984 and recently appeared in one volume *Ölçü veya Yoldaki Işıklar*, Kaynak, Izmir, 2000; English edition *Pearls of Wisdom*, The Fountain, New Jersey, 2000, pp. 61.

Take note of and be attentive to any behavior that causes you to love others. Then remind yourself that behaving in the same way will cause them to love you. Always behave decently and be alert.

Do not allow your carnal self to be a referee in any contest, for it will rule that everyone but you is sinful and unfortunate. Such a judgment, according to the word of the Prophet, the most truthful, signifies your destruction. Be strict and implacable with your carnal self, and be relenting and lenient toward others.

To preserve your credit, honor, and love, love for the sake of the Truth, hate for the sake of the Truth, and be open-hearted toward the Truth.

TOLERANCE

As a nation we are experiencing an intense fervor of recovery and revival. If a wind of opposition does not hinder us, the coming years will be our "years of becoming." However, there are differences in methods of recovery and revival. There has been a difficulty in arriving at a mutual agreement as to which methods we should accept and which we should reject regarding the renewals in our intellectual and cultural life over the last few centuries. Also there has been a difference in style and method used in blowing a new spirit into society. The nuances that appear in building a bridge between the past and future fill us with hope, yet at the same time it seems that troubled days await us.

Thus, while walking toward the future as a whole nation, tolerance is our safest refuge and our fortress against the handicaps that arise from schism, factions, and the difficulties inherent in reaching mutual agreement; troubles that lie waiting at every corner.

We should have such tolerance that we are able to close our eyes to the faults of others, to have respect for different ideas, and to forgive everything that is forgivable. In fact, even when faced with violations of our inalienable rights, we should remain respectful to human values and try to establish justice. Even before the coarsest thoughts and the crudest ideas, ideas that we find impossible to share, with the caution of a Prophet and without losing our temper, we should respond with mildness. This mildness is presented in the Qur'an as "gentle words"; it will touch the hearts of others. This mildness is the result of a tender heart, a gentle approach, and mild behavior. We should have so much tolerance that we can benefit from opposing ideas in that they force us to keep our heart, spirit, and conscience active and aware, even if these ideas do not directly or indirectly teach us anything.

Tolerance, a term which we sometimes use in place of the words respect, mercy, generosity, or forbearance, is the most essential element of moral systems; it is a very important source of spiritual discipline and a

This article was written in 1996 and originally appeared in *Yeşeren Düşünceler* [The Thoughts Growing to Yield Fruit], Kaynak, Izmir, 1996, pp. 19-22.

celestial virtue of perfected people.

Under the lens of tolerance the merits of believers attain new depths and extend to infinity; mistakes and faults become insignificant and whither away until they are so small that they can be placed into a thimble. In fact, the treatment of He Who is beyond time and space always passes through the prism of tolerance, and we wait for it to embrace us and all of creation. Because of the broadness of this embrace, when a corrupt woman who had given water to a thirsty dog touched the knocker of the "Door of Mercy," she found herself in a corridor extending to chastity and Heaven. Similarly, due to the deep love he felt for God and His Messenger, a drunk suddenly shook himself free and attained companionship of the Prophet. In another example, with the smallest of Divine favors, a bloody murderer was saved from his monstrous psychosis and headed toward the highest rank; a rank that far surpassed his natural ability and, one that in the end he actually reached.

We all want everyone to see us through this lens and we expect the breezes of forgiveness and pardon to constantly blow in our surroundings. All of us want to refer our past and present to the climate of tolerance and forbearance that melts, transforms, cleans, and purifies and then to walk toward the future securely, without feeling any anxiety. We do not want our past to be criticized or our future to be darkened because of our present. All of us expect love and respect for a whole lifetime, hope for tolerance and forgiveness, and want to be embraced with feelings of liberality and affection. We expect tolerance and forgiveness from our parents in response to mischievousness at home, from our teachers in response to our misbehavior at school, from those innocent victims toward whom we have acted unjustly and oppressed, from the judge and prosecutor in court, from our army commanders, from police officers and from the Judge of Judges in the Highest Tribunal.

However, deserving what we expect is very important. Anyone who does not forgive has no right to expect forgiveness. Everyone will receive disrespect to the degree that he has been disrespectful. Anyone who does not love is not worthy of being loved. Those who do not embrace all of humankind with tolerance and forgiveness have lost their worthiness to receive forgiveness and pardon. An unfortunate one who curses others does not have the right to expect respect from others. Those who curse will be cursed and those who beat will be beaten. If true Muslims observed such Qur'anic principles as the following and were to go on their way and tolerate curses deep in their breasts, then others would appear in order to implement the justice of Destiny on those who cursed us.

> When they meet hollow words or unseemly behavior, they pass them by with dignity. (Al-Furqan 25:72)

> If you behave tolerantly, overlook, and forgive (their faults) . . . (At-Taghabun 64:14)

In countries rife with corruption, intolerance, and mercilessness, such things as freedom of thought, polite criticism, and the exchange of ideas according to norms of equity and fair-minded debate are absent; it would be meaningless to talk of the results of logic and inspiration. In my opinion, this must be the real reason that for years no progress has been made, in spite of plenty of empty boasting.

For years, there have been numerous examples of immorality—my values do not allow me to speak about them openly—although their perpetrators have received their share of tolerance. Despite this, attempts continue to be made to label innocent people as "backward fanatics who support theocratic regimes." "Fundamentalism" is another fashionable term with which to smear them. Moreover, Islam has been accused of not keeping up with the times. We frequently observe with sorrow today that those who did nothing more than express their religious feelings have been branded as reactionaries, fanatics, and fundamentalists. Unfortunately some people do not distinguish between being truly religious and blind fanaticism.

It is not possible to talk about common ideas or a collective consciousness in communities where individuals do not look upon one another with tolerance or in countries where the spirit of forbearance has not become fully entrenched. In such countries, ideas will devour one another in the web of conflict. The work of thinkers will be futile, and in such countries it will not be possible to establish sound thought or freedom of belief or thought. These things will not be allowed to flourish. In fact, it cannot be said that in such a country the state has been based on a true system of justice; even if this appears to be the case, it is nothing more than a sham. Actually, in a place where there is no tolerance, it is not possible to talk about a healthy media, scholarly thought, or pertinent cultural activities either. What we see when we look at the things that carry such names are only some fruitless, one-sided efforts made according to certain thoughts and a certain philosophy; expecting something fresh, beneficial and promising for the future from these is futile.

TOLERANCE IN THE LIFE OF THE INDIVIDUAL AND SOCIETY

First of all, I would like to indicate that tolerance is not something that was invented by us. Tolerance was first introduced on this Earth by the prophets whose teacher was God. Even if it would not be correct to attribute tolerance to God, He has attributes that are rooted in tolerance, like forgiveness, the forgiveness of sins, compassion and mercy for all creatures, and the veiling of the shame and faults of others. The All-Forgiving, the All-Merciful, and the All-Veiling of Faults are among the most frequently mentioned names of God in the Qur'an.

The golden era when tolerance was represented at its apex was the Age of Happiness, and I would like to give some true examples from that historical time, events that extend in a line from that "period of roses" until today.

An Example of Forgiveness

As is known, in the historical "Event of Slander" the hypocrites made slanderous accusations against 'A'isha, the chaste wife of the Prophet and the spiritual mother of all believers. 'A'isha has a special place among the pure wives of the Prophet because the Prophet was the first man she saw when she awakened to womanhood. In a period when she became fully conscious of her womanhood, 'A'isha became a member of the Prophet's pure household and there she breathed only an atmosphere of chastity and honor. 'A'isha, an exemplar of chastity, became subjected to a planned slander campaign during this period. Both herself, her family and the Prophet, peace and blessings be upon him, suffered much because of this slander. However, the verse revealed approximately one month later declared 'A'isha's unadulterated purity and innocence. However, her father Abu Bakr, who had been giving financial support to one of those who was involved in the slander, took an oath not to give any more support to this person. But, the verse that was revealed warned that

The author occasionally delivers impromptu speeches to visiting groups and answers questions on various issues. This section is one of those speeches, which was recorded on January 13, 1996.

the most faithful friend of the Prophet, Sultan of Tolerance, should be more lenient.[1] The verse reads:

> Let not those among you who are endowed with grace and amplitude of means resolve by oath against helping their kinsmen, those in want, and those who have left their homes in God's cause: let them forgive and overlook. Do you not wish that God should forgive you? For God is the All-Forgiving, the All-Merciful. (An-Nur 24:22)

I want to draw you attention in particular to the expression at the end of this verse: *Do you not wish that God should forgive you? For God is the All-Forgiving, the All-Merciful*. In reality, the All-Merciful God Whose mercy is unequalled and compared to which all the mercy in the world is but a drop in the ocean, continually secrets Himself and, in spite of everything, forgives us, forgives everything, from the unbecoming words that enter our ears and darken our spirits to the filth that flows into us from the universe and back to the society that we have polluted. His question, *Do you not wish that God should forgive you?* directed at people like us who are always in need of purification, is very fine and sincere and worthy of being coveted. By means of this verse, God indicates that just as He forgives us, so too should we forgive one another for the mistakes we make, and this is illustrated to us as a Qur'anic virtue in the character of Abu Bakr.

Forgiveness and tolerance are given great importance in the messages of the Prophets, which are from divine and celestial sources. A prophet has the duty of educating and training others. In order for the truths that he is conveying to influence the hearts of others, his own heart must beat with forgiveness and tolerance. When some faults that are the result of a person's nature collide with the tolerant atmosphere of a person of truth, they melt and disperse like a meteor. Instead of splitting open someone's head, the legions of light, which resemble the lamps lit on nights of celebration, will soothe the eyes and give joy to the heart. As I mentioned before, there is in actual fact such a divine virtue recommended in our Prophet's hadith, "Take on the virtue of God."[2] Does not God Himself always forgive those who deny Him? On the cosmic plane this crime is unforgivable murder and rebellion. But look at the vastness

---

[1] Bukhari, *Shahadah*, 15:30; Muslim, *Tawbah*, 56.
[2] Mansur Ali Nasif, *al-Tac*, 1:13.

of God's forgiveness and pardon. In spite of the ungratefulness of His servants, He says:

Without doubt My Mercy precedes My Wrath.[3]

and

My Mercy extends to all things. (Al-Araf 7:156)

With His attribute of Mercy, without showing any bias, He nurtures and protects all human beings and, indeed all animate creatures, and He continues to give sustenance even to those who deny Him.

Here it is possible to view all the prophets from the same perspective and present some examples from all of them, but let it suffice to give a few from Prophet Muhammad, the essence of existence, peace and blessings be upon him.

Hamza was one of the Companions whom the Prophet loved most. He was not just an ordinary Companion, he was also the Prophet's uncle and they had both been nursed by the same wet-nurse. Suppressing his honor and pride, this lion-hearted giant of a man entered the spiritual atmosphere of the Pride of Humanity, peace and blessings be upon him. Supporting his nephew and saying "I am with you" at a critical time when the Muslims were weak in numbers raised his value manifold. Thus, by demonstrating the qualities of his closeness on the spiritual plane as well as on the physical plane, he was able to reach what seemed to be an unattainable height of greatness. Of course, the loyalty of this great hero was rewarded by the Prophet. He was martyred one day while fighting at Uhud; his bloody murderers had sworn to raid Madina and to run every man and woman through. At the hands of his murderers, their hands, eyes and thoughts bloody, Hamza was chopped into pieces. His sacred eyes were gorged out, his ears and lips cut off, his chest was split open and his liver was torn out and bitten into. The Messenger of God, peace and blessings be upon him, whose bosom was full of compassion and mercy, looked at this horrifying scene and his eyes filled with tears like clouds of rain. There were seventy martyrs at the battle of Uhud—

---

[3] Bukhari, *Tawhid* 15, 22, 28, 55, *Badi'ul'-Halk* 1; Muslim, *Tawba* 14, (2751); Tirmidhi, *Daawat* 109, (3537).

twice as many again had been wounded—women were widowed and children were orphaned. When he looked at this scene with the compassion of a prophet, it was almost unbearable. The children of Hamza and the children of other martyrs appeared before the Prophet, shivering like newly hatched chicks. As related in his biographical works, no sooner than the thought "In retribution for what they have done . . ." had crossed his mind was the following verse revealed:

> And if you have to respond to any wrong, respond to the extent of the wrong done to you; but if you endure patiently, this is indeed better for he who endures. (An-Nahl 16:126)

In this verse he was being directed to a horizon of understanding according to his level, and in other words he was told, "You should not think like that." That sun of leniency and tolerance, peace and blessings be upon him, buried all the pain in his chest and chose the road of patience.

Actually, the Prophet interwove the whole of his life, not only that moment, with tolerance. The polytheists did not spare him any torture or trouble. They drove him out of his homeland, formed armies, and attacked him. But even after the conquest of Makka, when the pagans were anxiously waiting to see how they would be treated, as a sign of his vast compassion and mercy the Prophet said:

> I speak as Joseph spoke to his brothers: There is no reproach for you today (because of your previous acts). God will forgive you also. He is the Most Merciful of the Merciful. Go; you are free.[4]

The Qur'an is the source of leniency and tolerance, and because these concepts have flowed to us like an exuberant stream from the Conveyor of the Qur'an, peace and blessings be upon him, we cannot think any differently on this matter. Any contrary idea would mean that we do not know the Qur'an and God's Messenger. From this perspective, because tolerance derives from the Qur'an and the Sunna, it is a Muslim's natural virtue and, because of the sources it is derived from, it is permanent. The covenant that the Messenger of God presented to the Chris-

---

[4] Ibn al-Athir, *Usd al-Ghabah*, 1:528-532.

tians and Jews is truly worthy of attention (the original text of the cove-nant is preserved today in England). Compared to the principles that our Prophet put forth, humanity today has not attained his level, neither with the declarations of human rights put forth in The Hague or Stras-bourg nor that in Helsinki. That Man of Great Forbearance lived to-gether closely with the People of the Book in Madina. In fact, he was even able to find points of agreement with the dark souls who, even though they said, "We are Muslims," continuously caused friction eve-rywhere and tried to play those with clear consciences one against an-other. He embraced them by means of forbearance. Upon the death of Abdullah ibn Ubayy, who had been a lifelong enemy, the Prophet even gave his shirt as a burial shroud. Saying, "As long as there is no revela-tion forbidding me, I will attend his funeral," and he showed his respect to the deceased.[5] There is no message similar or equal to the message given to humankind by Prophet Muhammad. Thus, it is not possible for those who try and follow "the Most Beautiful Example" to think differ-ently from what he thought.

In this respect, it is not possible to think of tolerance as something that is separate from us; it is a different color and tone of our feelings and thoughts. From this time on platforms for tolerance should be de-veloped in our society. Tolerance should be rewarded, it should be given precedence at every opportunity, and those who behave with forgiveness to others should have a chance to express themselves.

Tolerance Awards

Gathering around these ideas and feelings, the Journalists and Writers Foundation formed a committee and recently gave awards for tolerance to people who had been seen as having made a significant contribution to social reconciliation. This action was approved of by almost every segment of society—from politicians to people involved in the arts, from academics to journalists, writers, and the people in the street. Of course, a marginal group that was not synchronized with the general public, due to their different worldview, expressed their displeasure at an activity that everyone else had embraced; they made the mistake of reproaching the individuals and institutions that said yes to this consensus.

---

[5] Bukhari, *Janaiz*, 85; *Tafsir al-Baraa*, 12; Muslim, *Fadail al-Sahaba*, 25.

But let them say what they will. At a time when the world has become like a large village and at a point when our society is on the verge of great change and transformation, if we are talking about dialogue with other nations, then it will not be possible to explain away our disagreements with one another. In this respect, tolerance is a matter that needs to be rewarded and for this reason, tolerance must permeate all of society. So much so that universities should breathe tolerance, politicians should talk about tolerance, people in the music world should write lyrics about tolerance, and the media should give support to positive developments concerning tolerance.

Tolerance does not mean being influenced by others or joining them; it means accepting others as they are and knowing how to get along with them. No one has the right to say anything about this kind of tolerance; everyone in this country has his or her own point of view. People with different ideas and thoughts are either going to seek ways of getting along by means of reconciliation or they will constantly fight with one another. There have always been people who thought differently to one another and there always will be. It is my humble opinion that those people who are the mouthpiece for certain marginal groups that neither affirm the divine scriptures God sent nor the realities of today and who start fights at the drop of a hat should review their position one more time. Are they making their claims for the sake of human values or for the sake of destroying human values?

Today, more than anything else, our society is in need of tolerance. In fact, our nation should have this dynamic today and should give it priority; it should represent tolerance to the world because our glorious ancestors captured the hearts of people by means of tolerance and became the protectors of the general peace. The longest period of peace in the Balkans and the Middle East, which have always been volatile areas, was realized with the enduring tolerance of our ancestors. From the moment that tolerance and those great representatives left history, this region became void of peace and contentment. Thanks to the grace of God, after several centuries of life in limbo, this great nation has begun walking toward resurrection. This great "plane tree," the leaves of which are beginning to bud in the bosom of Anatolia, with the grace and bounty of God, should once more breathe tolerance itself and teach others to breathe tolerance.

At the same time, our citizens in European countries can only live in harmony in those countries by means of a vast atmosphere of tolerance.

Here, I would like to underscore one point. Being tolerant does not mean foregoing the traditions that come from our religion, or our nation, or our history; tolerance is something that has always existed. The Ottomans were faithful both to their religion and to other values and, at the same time, they were a great nation that could get along with other world states. If the people of today, who are civilized, enlightened, and open to the world, are going to fall short of those who lived in that period, then this means they have not understood this age. In this respect, as individuals, as families and as a society, we have to speed up this process that has already begun. I personally believe that even the people who do not share our feelings and thoughts will soften when we go to see them. Thus, in the name of dialogue we can unite on common ground and shake hands with all. This is because the things that God gives most value to are human beings, love, and compassion.

The Value the Messenger of God Gave to Humanity

More than anything else, with the training he received from his Lord, the Pride of Humankind gave value to every human being, regardless of whether that person was a Muslim, Christian, or Jew. Before leaving this subject, it would be beneficial to see what kind of a visionary man he was. He was the Pride of Humanity—his spirit was the beginning of the book of existence, and his message was the end. This is self-evident to those who know the Prophet's mission. We know him as one by whose light the universe can be observed and read like a book. However much humankind, the Prophet's followers in particular, take pride in their connection with the Prophet of Mercy, it is not too much. As one who loved him said, how fortunate we are to be connected with him. In fact, regarding the great blessing he received, the Messenger of God said:

> The first thing God created—the first seed that was sown in the bosom of non-existence—was my light.[6]

This is true because he is the seed, the essence, and the summary of existence. If we express this same sentiment in Sufi terms, the existence of

---

[6] Ajluni, *Kashf al-Khafa'*, 1:266.

Muhammad was both the reason for creation and its final goal. Existence was created for him to be able to come into it as the embodiment of all human values and as a theatre in which all the manifestations of God's Names would be apparent.

As I have mentioned at other times in different contexts, the Pride of Humanity, the reason for creation and the Prince of Prophets, one day stood up as a Jewish funeral was passing by. One of the Companions at his side said, "O Messenger of God, that's a Jew." Without any change in attitude or alteration of the lines on his face, the Prince of Prophets gave this answer: "But he is a human being!"[7] May the ears ring of those followers who do not know him in these dimensions and those human rights advocates who are ignorant of the universal message he brought in the name of humankind! There is nothing I can add to these words, but if we are disciples of the glorious Prophet who spoke these words, it is not possible for us to think any differently. Thus, it would be beneficial for those who oppose the recent activities made in the name of dialogue and tolerance to review their situations in respect to their heedlessness or their obstinacy that has permeated their personalities and spirits.

Tolerance and Democracy

Democracy is a system that gives everyone who is under its wing the opportunity to live and express their own feelings and thoughts. Tolerance comprises an important dimension of this. In fact, it can be said that democracy is out of the question in a place where tolerance does not exist. But come and see some of those who, on the one hand, talk about democracy, but who at the same time want the source that nurtures it to dry up. In a democratic country everyone should be able to take advantage of democratic rights and responsibilities. If one segment of society becomes upset by the existence of another segment, then it is obvious that those who are upset are not sincere, to say the least, in their claim that "we are democrats and supporters of democracy." As I mentioned above, it is not possible for democracy to take root in a place where there is no tolerance. In fact, advocates of democracy should be able to accept even those who do not share their views, and they should open their hearts to others.

---

[7] Bukhari, *Janaiz*, 50; Muslim, *Janaiz*, 81; Nasai, *Janaiz*, 46.

Here it is beneficial to stress this point. Accepting all people as they are, regardless of who they are, does not mean putting believers and unbelievers on the same side of the scales. According to our way of thinking, the position of believers and unbelievers has its own specific value. The Pride of Humanity has a special position and his place in our hearts is separate from and above all others. In relation to this point, I would like to inform you of my feelings. After returning from a visit to the resting-place of our Prophet, I was very sad that I had not died there. I thought that if I really loved him then I should have clung to the iron railing and died on the spot. Until that day, I had thought that my attachment to the Prophet was that great. Of course, he has a very high place in our hearts and we would not want anyone to harm him in any way, but even though I have such strong feelings and thoughts about him this does not prevent me from entering into dialogue with someone who does not think or believe the same.

Tolerance and the Future

Even if we have different feelings and thoughts, we are all people of this society. Even though we may not have common grounds on some matters, we all live in this world and we are passengers on the same ship. In this respect, there are many common points that can be discussed and shared with people from every segment of society.

In all probability, time will clarify everything and prove that those who started the trend of tolerance were right. Again, time will discard feelings and thoughts of grudge and vengeance. Only feelings fed with love, forgiveness, tolerance, and dialogue will continue. People of tolerance will build a world based on tolerance. Those whose lot is not tolerance will drown in their malice, hatred, and anger in the well of intolerance. It is my wish that people such as these will wake up and not drown in the swamp into which they have fallen. Or else we will have to cry for them as well. I can already feel this pain and I am greatly grieved by it!

MAKING THE ATMOSPHERE OF TOLERANCE PERMANENT

In addition to our "lost paradise," we have also lost some of our exalted characteristics. Knowledge, research, work, work method, organization of the work place, helping one another, and reading the book of the universe are some of the things we have lost. Among the many things we have lost, perhaps the first and most important is tolerance. From this word we understand embracing people regardless of differences of opinion, world-view, ideology, ethnicity, or belief. It also means putting up with matters we do not like by finding strength in a deep conscience, faith, and a generous heart or by the strength of our emotions. From another approach, it means, in the words of the famous Turkish poet Yunus,[1] loving the created simply because of the Creator.

Loving the Created Simply Because of the Creator

Love is the reason for existence and its essence, and it is the strongest tie that binds creatures together. Everything in the universe is the handiwork of God. Thus, if you do not approach humanity, a creation of God, with love, then you will have hurt those who love God and those whom God loves. For example, being an opponent of the paintings of an artist like Picasso will hurt both Picasso and those who admire him. Another example would be to remain indifferent to the grace of the Alhambra Palace, the lines of grace that express the ways from the finite to the infinite; this would be to show disrespect to that masterpiece and its artists. In the same way, every aspect of the universe's mind-boggling beauty, grandeur, and splendor is an example of God's artistry. In this respect, humans, animals, other animate creatures, and, in fact, all the inanimate objects as well, were created with a nature that is worthy of being embraced by us with love. Showing indifference or being condescending to them means

---

[1] Yunus Emre (c.1238-c.1320): A poet and Sufi who had a powerful influence on Turkish literature. He was well versed in Sufi philosophy, especially that of Rumi, and, like Rumi, became a leading representative of Sufism in Anatolia (but on a more popular level).

showing indifference and acting with condescension to the Maker. On the contrary, our approach to creation and other human beings should be based on loving them for the sake of their Creator. If Muslims talk about weapons, armories, killing and the butchering of others and if by doing so they put vast distances between people, then this means that in fact we have been far removed from our essence.

But we should be thankful that at a time when there are signs of the paradise we have lost, we have also found tolerance again; this is one of the characteristics that we had lost. We are rediscovering tolerance, something that is inherent in the spirit of Islam and something that was explained to us in the Qur'an and by Prophet Muhammad, peace and blessings be upon him. In the matter of tolerance, our people have welcomed the activities involved with tolerance and have warmly embraced this spirit; this is of vital importance. Along with the institutions that have been established, the voluntary services provided by people have aroused a great deal of interest. The Qur'an states:

> On those who believe and work deeds of righteousness will the All-Merciful bestow love. (Maryam 19:96)

In other words, both inhabitants of the sky and inhabitants of the Earth will love them. As expressed in a hadith, God tells those in the sky which people He loves and orders them, too, to love these beloved ones. When the angels in the sky love them, the people on Earth love them, too.

The seed that has been sown by tolerance is growing. It will blossom when the time is right. Of course, this depends, to a certain extent on the newspapers, TV, magazines, and foundations giving the appropriate support.

There Is No Turning Back from the Road of Tolerance

Acceptance in the heavens always brings about an affirmative response on Earth. The signs of this are obvious. The most obvious signs are that doors everywhere are opened wide in the name of acceptance to heroes of love and tolerance. It can be said that tolerance is on its way to growing and flourishing. This is true to such an extent that after the season of tolerance began conflicts were staged to disrupt these developments. But sides that for years had been seen and shown as being separate reacted with great farsightedness, and a calamity was averted.

I think it is probable that from now on many other intrigues will take place and attempts will be made to disturb the general peace. However, we, who have begun this process, must be determined to carry it through to the end. We have to be determined and act in accordance with the way indicated in the Qur'an:

> Those who witness no falsehood, and when they meet hollow words or unseemly behavior, they pass them by with dignity. (Al-Furqan 25:72)

Everyone reflects their own character with their actions. It is the duty of perfected people to act leniently. If one ridicules the Qur'an, and makes light of prayer, fasting, and chastity, this behavior should be considered as an indication of the style and character of that person. But as believers, we must not be aggressive or ridicule people, even toward those who act in a disagreeable manner. We should not return aggressiveness and ridicule in kind. Another verse says:

> Tell those who believe to forgive those who do not look forward to the Days of God. (Al-Jathiya 45:14)

This is actually the voice of our conscience. When you see a blind man, do you kick and beat him or do you take his hand and show him the way?

From this point of view, the duty that befalls the makers of ideas for tomorrow is to bring harmony to the incongruities in society, to protect the balance that is under attack and to view unpleasant incidents with far-sightedness. Just as is said in the Turkish saying, "Take what is pleasant, and leave what causes grief," we should remain indifferent to unpleasant things and not cause any conflicts or disturbances.

If we can continue like this, then in a short time it will be possible to go much further than where we are now. Of course, there will be many attempts made, domestically and abroad, to destroy this balance. But for the sake of the continuation of tolerance, we will die many times and be born again in the efforts to prevent this. There will be floods of love everywhere, and love will flow from the eyes and hearts of people. Everyone will embrace one another with love and, God willing, the twenty-first century will be called the age of tolerance. I am so eager for this to come about that one or two years of tolerance is not enough for me. We are determined that there will be one or two centuries of tolerance, in fact, we want tolerance to last until the end of time, we want to experience eras of tolerance, and we have no intention of turning back from this road.

THE TWO ROSES OF THE EMERALD HILLS: TOLERANCE AND DIALOGUE

Dialogue means the coming together of two or more people to discuss certain issues, and thus the forming of a bond between these people. In that respect, we can call dialogue an activity that has human beings at its axis. Undoubtedly, everyone is rewarded according to their sincerity and intention. If people direct their actions with sincerity and with good intentions, then they may be winners even if others should consider them losers. The Prophet of God said: "Deeds are judged by intentions,"[1] and he emphasized that the intention of the believer is more important than the act itself. If the deed is founded upon good intentions, it will turn out well. So, whatever one may do, one must first be sincere in one's intentions and seek the approval of God. Thus one should not ill-judge or slander the ties that are being established between various groups in the name of love, dialogue and tolerance.

Society cannot endure more tremors after having suffered so many wounds and after having been shaken so many times. If anti-democratic concentrations of power become the unshakeable burden of this nation and logic and judgment are supplanted through the power and means available to these concentrations, then this noble nation might not be able to recover again. As a result of such a calamity, this heaven-like land may be pushed 15 or 20 years back. It is possible that we might lose some things, that we might long for these lost things, even if they were to be among those things that we criticize today. In that respect, if we start our efforts for dialogue with the belief that "peace is better" (Al-Nisa 4:128), then we must demonstrate that we are on the side of peace at home and abroad. Indeed, peace is of the utmost importance to Islam; fighting and war are only secondary occurrences which are bound to specific reasons and conditions. In that respect, we can say that if an environment of peace where all can live in peace and security cannot be achieved in this

---

[1] Bukhari, *Bad'ul-Vahy* 1, *Itk* 6; Muslim, *Imarat*, 155; Abu Dawud, *Talak*, 11.

land, then it would be impossible for us to do any good service for society or for humanity.

Misconceptions about Islam

If we approach the issue from a different perspective, Muslims have from time to time been misunderstood and as a result they have been subjected to pressure and insults. We have even witnessed Muslims being deprived of their most natural and basic rights, for example their right to work. This oppression that believing people has been subjected to is executed in the name of virtues, like humanism, human rights, generosity, love, and tolerance; these are in fact characteristics of Islam. Yet, it is these very characteristics and virtues that are being used against people who believe and these concepts are being exploited. Always there has been this basic attitude, an attitude that is subtle and deceitful, on the part of those who do not want to give room to Islam and Muslims to exist, either here or abroad. Things that have been claimed are not true; a Muslim can never be a bigot. Even if some people with such characteristics may have appeared within the Islamic community, it is unthinkable to conceive of all Muslims as being distanced from understanding and tolerance. Indeed, to this day what harm have the Muslims done and what evil have they committed and against whom? Despite their good intentions, some people have always been falsely stereotyped and have been weighed up on faulty scales; they have become the scapegoats for various accusations in the name of love, tolerance, freedom, and democracy. Despite being at the receiving end of all these false accusations, real Muslims never injure anyone and satisfy themselves merely by stating the fact that they are not the way they have been imputed to be. Still, a certain group has never ceased to attack them. Indeed, beauty has always sprung from the pure and blameless souls of the Muslims and the holy and exalted sources that are in their hands. It cannot be any other way; in the Qur'an, the Sunna, and in the pure and learned interpretations of the Great Scholars there is no trace of a decree or an attitude that is contrary to love, tolerance or dialogue in the sense of meeting with all, and declaring and expressing our emotions or thoughts. We cannot conceive of a religion that wills the good of all and who calls all—with no exception—to salvation, as being otherwise. The following verses in the Glorious Qur'an express this truth perfectly:

And if you behave tolerantly, overlook, and forgive, then verily God is Forgiving and Merciful. (at-Taghabun 64:14)

God does not forbid you, regarding those who did not fight you on account of religion and did not drive you out of your homes, to show kindness and deal with them justly. (Al-Mumtahana 60:8)

Tell those who believe to forgive those who do not look forward to the Days of God; in order that He may recompense each people according to what they have earned. (Al-Jathiya 45:14)

Indeed, when we look at the Qur'an we see that it is molded in love. In that respect, believing hearts must reclaim these beauties which are already ours, changing the negative image of Muslims. This negative image has been fed to the world and now we must once more communicate the essential facet of Islam to those who are presumed to be civilized, using the principle of "gentle persuasion."

Let there be endless thanks to the Excellent Just One who feeds us with His bounty for the devotees of truth and heroes of love who have been carrying messages of love, tolerance and dialogue all over the world and who are trying to build the "new image of the Muslim" with hearts full of love.

Seeking the Approval of God

I would like to stress the fact that Muslims will lose nothing by employing dialogue, love, and tolerance. Muslims continuously seek the approval of God; this is the greatest gain of all. In that respect, things that may appear as losses to some people are seen as gains by Muslims, while certain other events may actually be detrimental even when they appear to be lucrative. Moreover, we have no doubts concerning Islam, its holy book the Qur'an or its most glorious representative, the Pride of Humanity, peace and blessings be upon him. We know that Islam will certainly continue on the path that leads to the future despite all obstacles; every subject of the Qur'an is proven by reason; it is a book that is strong enough to solve all the problems of the future. The Prince of the Prophets, a man about whom Bernard Shaw said, "He solves all problems the ease of drinking coffee," was sent to humanity in order to present the solutions for all of its problems until Judgment Day. As in previous centuries, the problems of our age and the coming ages, which seem to be far removed from a sound solution, will be solved by the architects of hearts and mind who base their solutions on these holy sources.

Indeed, we do not need to have any worries as we believe that the illuminating expressions and statements of the Holy Qur'an and our Prophet offer lasting solutions to a myriad of problems. In my opinion, those who are equipped with these torches will suffer no loss, with the help and bounty of God, wherever they may go in the world and with whomever they may enter into dialogue. Thus, there is no cause for concern. The important fact here is that we should understand the sources that we possess, and we should employ them as necessary. Moreover, we should not abuse them by associating them with our own faults, our bodily or earthly desires. With their assistance and guidance we should seek only the approval of God and the afterlife.

Indeed, just as we have not even the slightest doubt concerning the Qur'an and the Prophet of God and just as we have no doubts concerning their justice, there is no reason why anyone should have doubts about us. But, if there still are some people who are frightened due to groundless fears, they will only be those people who are worried about the reliability of the dynamics and sources on which they rely.

WITHOUT HANDS AGAINST THOSE WHO STRIKE YOU, WITHOUT SPEECH AGAINST THOSE WHO CURSE YOU

From the day the Journalists and Writers Foundation was established until now—even if things have not always been as we would have wished—we can say that the Foundation has always organized important activities. But somehow I have never fully been able to participate in any of them. For this reason, I cannot claim a share in their success.

For instance, it brought world-famous soccer players here to raise aid for Bosnia. Every year it has brought together special groups, like the one here tonight, to talk on various platforms, providing at the very least an exchange of ideas. The Foundation has suggested the ideas to be discussed, regardless of our personal ideas or opinions. As a result, we have seen with our own eyes that there is no reason to fear one another, and that everyone can meet with whomever they want. If we have not been able to come together before today, it only means that we have been obstructed by our mistaken conjectures, and as a result, neglected this important responsibility toward each other.

The Foundation is known in Turkey mainly as a representative of tolerance. In fact, it has identified itself with tolerance. Whenever it is mentioned, tolerance is immediately mentioned afterwards. In fact, the Foundation's image has created much jealousy, causing several alternative organizations to appear. Now, fortunately, everyone is singing the same tune. For this reason, I believe that tolerance will spread faster to the grassroots, diffuse throughout the country and, as an artist friend said, we will be able to walk head to head, heart to heart, and hand in hand toward "a happy tomorrow," God willing.

When the Prophet was dying and about to pass over to the next world, he said:

The author delivered this speech at a Ramadan dinner gathering organized by the Journalists and Writers Foundation, February 11, 1995, Istanbul.

I place in your trust the People of the Book, the Christians and Jews.[1]

When 'Umar had been stabbed and was in the throes of death, he warned:

I place the People of the Book among us in your trust. Fear God regarding them and treat them justly.[2]

After defeating the enemy at Malazgirt,[3] the Turkish commander Sultan Alparslan[4] hosted the military chiefs and the ruler of the rival state in his tent. He then had them conveyed safely to their capital, Constantinople (now Istanbul), escorted by some of his officers. In Jerusalem, the commander and ruler, Sultan Salahaddin Ayyubi, went at night to the tent of Richard, the commander of the Crusader's army, to treat his wounds—despite the fact that Richard's forces had killed thousands of Muslims.

We are the children of a culture that gave birth to such people. We are the heirs of the culture that has the world's broadest, most comprehensive and most universal tolerance. This concept is spreading today like the waves of the sea, reaching across the entire world. I fully believe that the coming years will be years of tolerance and love. In this framework, we will give the world much and we will receive much. Not only will we not be fighting our own people, we will not even be fighting other cultures, civilizations, or the people of other beliefs and worldviews. Issues that lead to argument and conflict will be completely resolved, and once again by understanding the power of love, we will be able to open our hearts to all with love and compassion. With the help of God, we will be able to concentrate on the important matters of dialogue and tolerance; matters which today's world needs very much.

---

[1] Abu Dawud, *Imarat*, 33; Muttaqi al-Hindi, *Kanz al-Ummal*, 4.362.
[2] Yahya ibn Adam, *Kitab al-Haraj*, 54.
[3] Battle of Malazgirt (or Manzikert): This battle, fought in 1071, pitted the Byzantine Emperor Romanus IV Diogenes against the Seljuk Turk Sultan, Alparslan. The Emperor's defeat resulted in the Seljuk conquest of most of Anatolia.
[4] Sultan Alparslan (1032-1072). The greatest and most famous of the Seljuk sultans. He defeated the Byzantine army in Malazgirt in 1071, and opened the doors to Anatolia for the Seljuks.

When I saw Mr. İzzettin Doğan,[5] I remembered an important event in Muslim history. Mentioning the Kharijites[6] who rebelled against the lawful government and gathered in Nahrawan to attack him, Caliph 'Ali said, "It would have been unjust for us to attack them before they attacked us."

We are a society nurtured by the culture of such leaders. At a time when we are in great need of tolerance, with the grace of God, every sector of society will stand up for tolerance and dialogue, and the good things that come from this will spread faster than ever hoped for in all directions.

Maybe I am taking up too much of your time, but I cannot proceed without mentioning the anxiety I feel. Turkish society, which has been wrung by internal conflict at this time, has been awaiting tolerance. Upon finding it, when one step toward it was to have been made, the society responded by leaping forward three steps. But it also is obvious that certain weak and insignificant persons, by ranting and raving, have demonstrated their own weaknesses and have tried to show themselves as being strong by being destructive, lying in ambush to attack tolerance and attempting to blow up the bridges that lead to dialogue. We will face great tests now. Our nation, which has already passed through many trials, will face these future tests with solidarity among individuals, and will overcome every obstacle on the path to social harmony.

What we are seeking is very valuable. The goal of the tolerance and dialogue that we want to reach will be very expensive. Just as it is not easy to obtain precious and exclusive things, it is also difficult to protect them once they have been achieved. Attaining social harmony through dialogue and tolerance is a matter of achieving two valuable things in order to realize a third. God is going to test us in different ways so that we realize how great the values of these are and, accordingly, to force us to stand up for them. We will endure all these trials and say as Yunus did:

If harshness comes from the Majesty of God
Or generosity from His Grace,
Both are delights to the soul.
Both His blessings and His wrath are pleasing.

---

[5] Dr. İzzettin Doğan (b. 1940): Professor of law and current president of Cem Vakfı, a foundation of Turkish Alevi citizens.
[6] A minority group who withdrew from the community and assassinated Caliph 'Ali.

We must be as if "without hands against those who strike us and without speech against those who curse us." If they try and fracture us into pieces even fifty times, we still will remain unbroken and embrace everyone with love and compassion. And, with love toward one another, we will walk toward tomorrow.

I wish for this happy evening to be an occasion for mercy and forgiveness. I greet you all with my deepest respect.

ISLAM—A RELIGION OF TOLERANCE

Islam is a word derived from the root words *silm* and *salamah*. It means surrendering, guiding to peace and contentment, and establishing security and accord.

Islam is a religion of security, safety, and peace. These principles permeate the lives of Muslims. When Muslims stand to pray, they cut their connection with this world, turning to their Lord in faith and obedience, and standing at attention in His presence. Completing the prayer, as if they were returning back to life, they greet those on their right and left by wishing peace: "Remain safe and in peace." With a wish for safety and security, peace and contentment, they return to the ordinary world once again.

Greeting and wishing safety and security for others is considered one of the most beneficial acts in Islam. When asked which act in Islam is the most beneficial, the Prophet replied, "Feeding others and greeting those you know and those you do not know."[1]

Accusing Islam of Terrorism

How unfortunate it is that Islam, which is based on this understanding and spirit, is shown by some circles to be synonymous with terrorism. This is a great historical mistake; wrapping a system based on safety and trust in a veil of terrorism just shows that the spirit of Islam remains unknown. If one were to seek the true face of Islam in its own sources, history, and true representatives, then one would discover that it contains no harshness, cruelty, or fanaticism. It is a religion of forgiveness, pardon, and tolerance, as such saints and princes of love and tolerance as Rumi, Yunus Emre, Ahmed Yesevi,[2] Bediüzzaman,[3] and many others have so

---

[1] Abu Dawud, *Adab*, 142.
[2] Ahmed Yesevi (d. 1166): Sufi poet and early Turkish spiritual leader who had a powerful influence on the development of mystical orders throughout the Turkish-speaking world.
[3] Bediüzzaman Said Nursi (1877-1960): An Islamic scholar of the highest standing with deep spirituality, a wide knowledge of modern science and the contemporary world. He

beautifully expressed. They spent their lives preaching tolerance, and each became a legend in his own time as an embodiment of love and tolerance.

Jihad can be a matter of self-defense or of removing obstacles between God and human free choice. Our history is full of examples that show how this principle has been implemented in life.

Of course there are and should be occasions where war is unavoidable. However, the Qur'anic verses on jihad that were revealed for particular conditions have been generalized by some short-sighted individuals. Whereas in actual fact war is a matter of secondary importance, it has been given priority as an essential issue by these people. Such people do not understand the true meaning and spirit of Islam. Their failure to establish a proper balance between what is primary and what is secondary leads others to conclude that Islam advocates malice and hatred in the soul, whereas true Muslims are full of love and affection for all creation. Regarding this, how apt is the following couplet:

> *Muhammad was born out of love,*
> *What can be born out of love without Muhammad?*

Love Is the Essence of Creation

The Pride of Humanity was a man of love and affection. One of his names was *Habibullah* (the Beloved of God). In addition to meaning one who loves, *habib* means one who is loved, one who loves God, and one who is loved by God. Sufi masters like Imam Rabbani,[4] Mawlana Khalid,[5] and Shah Waliyyullah[6] state that love is the ultimate station of the spiritual journey.

---

believed that humanity could be saved from its crises and could achieve true progress and happiness only by knowing its true nature, and by recognizing and submitting to God. His *Risale-i Nur* (The Epistles of Light) deals with the Islamic essentials of faith, thought, worship, and morality and Qur'anic descriptions of Divine activity in the universe. Containing rational and logical proofs and explanations of all Qur'anic truths, it is his reply to those who deny them in the name of science. In his work, he reveals their many discrepancies and illogical statements.

[4] Imam Rabbani (Shaykh Ahmad al-Sirhindi) (1564?-1624): Indian Sufi and theologian who reasserted and revived the principles of Islamic faith and Sufi tradition in India against the syncretistic religious tendencies prevalent under the Mogul emperor Akbar. He was given the posthumous title: *Mujaddid-i Alf-i Thani* (Renovator of the Second [Islamic] Millennium).

[5] Mawlana Khalid al-Baghdadi (1778-1827): Naqshbandi master considered the *mujaddid* (reviver) of the thirteenth Islamic century. The Khalidi order, a new Naqshbandi branch,

God created the universe as a manifestation of His love for His creatures, in particular humanity, and Islam became the fabric woven out of this love. In the words of Bediüzzaman, love is the essence of creation. Just as a mother's love and compassion compels her to allow a surgeon to operate on her sick child to save his or her life, jihad allows war, if needed, to preserve such fundamental human rights as the right to life and religious freedom. Jihad does not exclusively mean war.

Once a friend said to me: "Without exception and regardless of differences in faith, you meet with everyone, and this breaks the tension of Muslims toward probable opponents. But it is an Islamic principle to love those things or people who must be loved on the way of God and dislike those things or people who must be disliked on the way of God." Actually this principle is often misunderstood, for in Islam all of creation is to be loved according to the rule of loving on God's way.

"Disliking on the way of God" applies only to feelings, thoughts, and attributes. Thus, we should dislike such things as immorality, unbelief, and polytheism, not the people who engage in such activities. God created humanity as noble beings, and everyone, to a certain degree, has a share in this nobility. His Messenger once stood up out of respect for humanity as the funeral procession of a Jew passed by. When reminded that the deceased was a Jew, the Prophet replied: "But he is a human," thereby showing the value Islam gives to human.

This action demonstrates how highly our Prophet respected every person. Given this, the involvement of some self-proclaimed Muslim individuals or institutions in terrorist activities can in no way be approved of by Islam. The reasons for this terrorism should be sought for in the actions themselves, in false interpretations of the faith, and in other factors and motives. Islam does not support terror, so how could a Muslim who truly understands Islam be a terrorist?

If we can spread the Islamic understanding of such heroes of love as Niyazi-i Misri,[7] Yunus Emre, and Rumi globally, if we can extend their messages of love, dialogue, and tolerance to those who thirst for this mes-

---

arose under his leadership and had acquired a large following by the end of the nineteenth century.

[6] Shah Waliyyullah Muhaddith of Delhi (1702-1762): A great scholar of the twelfth Islamic century. Some writers call him *Khatam al-Muhadditheen* (the last of the hadith scholars).

[7] Niyazi-i Misri (1618-1694). A Sufi poet and member of the Khalwati order.

sage, then everyone will run toward the embrace of love, peace, and tolerance that we represent.

The definition of tolerance in Islam is such that the Prophet even
prohibited verbal abuse of unbelievers. For example, Abu Jahl died before
embracing Islam, despite all the Prophet's efforts. His unbelief and enmity toward the Prophet was such that he deserved the title Abu Jahl:
Father of ignorance and impudence. His untiring opposition to Islam was
a thorn in the side of the Muslims.

Despite such hostility, when in an assembly of Companions where
Abu Jahl's son Ikrimah was present, the Prophet one day admonished a
Companion who had been heard insulting Abu Jahl: "Do not hurt others
by criticizing their fathers."[8] Another time, he said: "Cursing your
mother and father is a great sin." The Companions asked: "O Messenger
of God, would anyone curse their parents?" The Prince of Prophets replied: "When someone curses another's father and the other curses his
father in return, or when someone curses another's mother and the other
does the same in return, they will have cursed their parents."[9]

While the Prophet of Mercy was inordinately sensitive when it came
to respecting others, some Muslims today justify unpleasant behavior on
the basis of religion. This shows that they do not understand Islam, a
religion in which there is no place for malice and hatred.

The Qur'an strongly urges forgiveness and tolerance. In one verse, it
says of pious people:

> They swallow their anger and forgive people. God loves those who do
> good. (Al-Imran 3:134)

In other words, Muslims should not retaliate when verbally abused
or attacked. If possible, as Yunus says, they should act as if they had no
hand or tongue with which to respond and no heart with which to resent.
They must swallow their anger and close their eyes to the faults of others.
The words selected in the verse are very meaningful. *Kazm*, translated as
swallowing, literally means swallowing something like a thorn, an object
that actually cannot be swallowed; thus it denotes swallowing one's

---

[8] Hakim, *al-Mustadrak*, 3:241; Muttaqi al-Hindi, *Kanz al-'Ummal*, 13:540.
[9] Muslim, *Iman*, 145; Tirmidhi, *Birr*, 4.

wrath, no matter how difficult. Another verse, while mentioning the characteristics of believers, says:

> When they meet hollow words or unseemly behavior, they pass them by with dignity. (Al-Furqan 25:72)

When we look at the exalted life of God's Messenger, peace and blessings be upon him, we see that he always practiced the precepts presented in the Qur'an. For example, a Companion once repented of a sin and admitted: "I am guilty of fornication. Whatever my punishment is, give it and cleanse me." The Prince of Prophets said: "Go back and repent, for God forgives all sins."[10] This event was repeated three times. Another time, a Companion complained to the Prophet that someone had stolen his belongings. But as the punishment was about to be carried out the Companion said: "I have changed my mind and do not want to pursue my case. I forgive this individual." The Prophet asked: "Why did you bring this matter to court? Why didn't you forgive him from the outset?"[11]

When such examples are studied from their original sources, it is clear that the method of those who act with enmity and hatred, who view everyone else with anger, and who blacken others as infidels is non-Islamic, for Islam is a religion of love and tolerance. A Muslim is a person of love and affection who avoids every kind of terrorist activity and who has no malice or hatred for anyone or anything.

---

[10] Muslim, *Hudud*, 17, 23; Bukhari, *Hudud*, 28.
[11] Abu Dawud, *Hudud*, 14(4394); Nasai, *Sarik*, 4 (8, 68); Muwatta, *Hudud*, 28, (2, 834).

ISLAM AS A RELIGION OF UNIVERSAL MERCY

Life is the foremost and most manifest blessing of God Almighty, and the true and everlasting life is that of the Hereafter. Since we can deserve this life only by pleasing God, He sent Prophets and revealed Scriptures out of His Compassion for humanity. While mentioning His blessings upon humanity, He begins:

> All-Merciful. He taught the Qur'an, created humanity, and taught it speech. (Al-Rahman 55:1-4)

All aspects of this life are a rehearsal for the afterlife, and every creature is engaged toward this end. Order is evident in every effort, and compassion resides in every achievement. Some "natural" events or social convulsions may seem disagreeable at first, but we should not regard them as being incompatible with compassion. They are like dark clouds or lightning and thunder that, although frightening, nevertheless bring us the good tidings of rain. Thus the whole universe praises the All-Compassionate.

Prophet Muhammad, peace and blessings be upon him, is like a spring of pure water in the heart of a desert, a source of light in an all-enveloping darkness. Those who appeal to this spring can take as much water as is needed to quench their thirst, to become purified of their sins, and to become illuminated with the light of faith. Mercy was like a magical key in the Prophet's hands, for with it he opened hearts that were so hardened and rusty that no one thought they could be opened. But he did even more: he lit a torch of belief in them.

The compassion of God's Messenger encompassed every creature. He desired that everyone be guided. In fact, this was his greatest concern:

> Yet it may be, if they believe not in this Message, you will consume (exhaust) yourself, following after them, with grief. (Al-Kahf 18:6)

But how did he deal with those who persisted in oppression and per-secutions; those who did not allow him and his followers to worship the One God; those who took up arms against him to destroy him? He had to fight such people, yet his universal compassion encompassed every creature. This is why when he was wounded severely at the Battle of Uhud, he raised his hands and prayed:

O God, forgive my people, for they do not know.[1]

The Makkans, his own people, inflicted so much suffering on him that he finally emigrated to Madina. Even after that, the next 5 years were far from peaceful. However, when he conquered Makka without blood-shed in the twenty-first year of his Prophethood, he asked the Makkan unbelievers: "How do you expect me to treat you?" They responded unanimously: "You are a noble one, the son of a noble one." He then told them his decision: "You may leave, for no reproach this day shall be on you. May God forgive you. He is the Most Compassionate."[2] 825 years later Sultan Mehmed II[3] said the same thing to the defeated Byzan-tines after conquering Constantinople. Such is the universal compassion of Islam.

The Messenger displayed the highest degree of compassion toward believers:

There has come to you a Messenger from among yourselves; grievous to him is your suffering; anxious is he over you, full of concern for you, for the believers full of pity, compassionate. (At-Tawbah 9:128)

He lowered unto believers his wing of tenderness through mercy . . . (Al-Hijr 15:88)

. . . was the guardian of believers and nearer to them than their selves. (Al-Ahzab 33:6)

When one of his Companions died, he asked those at the funeral if the deceased had left any debts. On learning that he had, the Prophet

[1] Qadi 'Iyad, Shifa', 1:78-9; Hindi, Kanz al-'Ummal, 4:93.
[2] Ibn Hisham, Sirat al-Nabawiyah, 4:55; Ibn Kathir, Al-Bidayah wa al-Nihayah, 4:344.
[3] Sultan Mehmed II (the Conqueror) (1431-1481). The 7th Ottoman Sultan who conquered Istanbul in 1453.

mentioned the above verse and announced that the creditors should come to him for repayment.

His compassion even encompassed the hypocrites and unbelievers. He knew who the hypocrites were, but never identified them, for this would have deprived them of the rights of full citizenship that they had gained by their outward declaration of faith and practice. Since they lived among the Muslims, their denial may have been reduced or changed to doubt, thus diminishing their fear of death and the pain caused by the assertion of eternal non-existence after death.

God no longer destroys unbelievers collectively, although He had eradicated many such people in the past:

> But God would never chastise them while you were among them; God would never chastise them as they begged forgiveness. (Al-Anfal 8:33)

This verse refers to unbelievers regardless of time and place. God will not destroy whole peoples as long as there are some who follow the Messenger. Moreover, He has left the door of repentance open until the Last Day. Anyone can accept Islam or ask God's forgiveness, regardless of how sinful they consider themselves to be.

For this reason, a Muslim's enmity toward unbelievers is a form of pity. When 'Umar saw an 80-year-old man, he sat down and wept. When asked why, he replied: "God assigned him so long a lifespan, but he has not been able to find the true path." 'Umar was a disciple of God's Messenger, the prophet who said:

> I was not sent to call down curses on people, but as a mercy.[4]

> I am Muhammad, and Ahmad (the praised one), and *Muqaffi* (the Last Prophet); I am *Hashir* (the last Prophet in whose presence the people will gather); the Prophet of Repentance (the Prophet for whose sake the door of repentance will always remain open), and the Prophet of mercy.[5]

Archangel Gabriel also benefited from the mercy of the Qur'an. Once the Prophet asked Gabriel whether he had any share in the mercy con-

---

[4] Muslim, *Birr*, 87.
[5] Hanbal, *Musnad*, 4:395; Muslim, *Fada'il*, 126.

tained in the Qur'an, Gabriel replied that he did, and explained: "I was not certain about my end. However, when the verse: *(One) obeyed, and moreover, trustworthy and secured* (At-Takwir 81:21) was revealed, I felt secure."[6]

The Messenger of God was particularly compassionate toward children. Whenever he saw a child crying, he sat beside him or her and shared his or her feelings. He felt the pain of a mother for her child more than the mother herself. Once he said:

> I stand in prayer and wish to prolong it. However, I hear a child cry and shorten the prayer to lessen the mother's anxiety."[7]

He took children in his arms and hugged them. Once when he hugged and kissed his grandson Hasan, Aqrah ibn Habis told him: "I have 10 children, none of whom I have ever kissed." God's Messenger responded: "One without pity for others is not pitied."[8] According to another version, he added: "What can I do for you if God has removed compassion from you?"[9]

He said: "Pity those on the Earth so that those in the heavens will pity you."[10] Once when Sa'd ibn 'Ubadah became ill, God's Messenger visited him at home. Seeing his faithful Companion in a pitiful state, he began to cry and said: "God does not punish because of tears or grief, but He punishes because of this," and he pointed to his tongue.[11] When 'Uthman ibn Mad'un died, he wept profusely. During the funeral, a woman remarked: "'Uthman flew like a bird to Paradise." Even in that mournful state, the Prophet did not lose his balance and corrected the woman: "How do you know this? Even I do not know this, and I am a Prophet."[12]

A member of the Banu Muqarrin clan once beat his female slave. She informed the Messenger of God, who then sent a message to the master.

---

[6] Qadi 'Iyad, *as-Shifa' al-Sharif*, 1:17.
[7] Bukhari, *Adhan*, 65; Muslim, *Salat*, 192.
[8] Bukhari, *Adab*, 18.
[9] *Ibid.*, *Adab*, 18; Muslim, *Fada'il*, 64.
[10] Tirmidhi, *Birr*, 16.
[11] Bukhari, *Jana'iz*, 45.
[12] *Ibid*, *Jana'iz*, 3.

He said: "You have beaten her without any justifiable right. Free her."[13] Setting a slave free was far better for the master than being punished in the Hereafter because of a wrong act. The Messenger of God always protected and supported widows, orphans, the poor, and the disabled, even before his Prophethood. When he returned home in excitement from Mount Hira after the first Revelation, his wife Khadijah told him:

> I hope you will be the Prophet of this community, for you always tell the truth, fulfill your trust, support your relatives, help the poor and weak, and feed guests.[14]

His compassion even encompassed animals. We hear from him:

> A prostitute was guided to truth by God and ultimately went to Paradise because she gave water to a poor dog dying of thirst inside a well. Another woman was sent to Hell because she made a cat die of hunger.[15]

Once while returning from a military campaign, a few Companions removed some young birds from their nest to caress them. The mother bird came back and, not being able to find its babies, began to fly around, calling out for them. When told of this, God's Messenger became angry and ordered the birds to be put back in the nest.[16]

While in Mina, some of his Companions attacked a snake in order to kill it. However, it managed to escape. Watching this from afar, he remarked: "It was saved from your evil, as you were from its evil."[17] Ibn Abbas reported that God's Messenger, upon observing a man sharpening his knife directly before the sheep to be slaughtered, asked him: "Do you want to kill it more than once?"[18]

His love and compassion for creatures differed from that of today's self-proclaimed humanists. He was sincere and measured in his love and compassion. He was a Prophet raised by God, the Creator and Sustainer of all beings, for the guidance and happiness of conscious beings—

---

[13] Muslim, *Ayman*, 31, 33; Ibn Hanbal, *Musnad*, 3:447.
[14] Ibn Sa'd, *al-Tabaqat al-Kubra'*, 1:195.
[15] Bukhari, *Anbiya*, 54; Muslim, *Salam*, 153.
[16] Abu Dawud, *Adab*, 164; Ibn Hanbal, *Musnad*, 1:404.
[17] Sunan al-Nasa'i, *Hajj*, 114; Ibn Hanbal, *Musnad*, 1:385.
[18] Hakim, *Mustadrak*, 4:231.

humanity and jinn—and the harmony of existence. As such, he lived not for himself but for others. He is a mercy for all the worlds, a manifestation of Compassion.

He eradicated all differences of race and color. Once Abu Dharr got so angry with Bilal that he insulted him: "You son of a black woman!" Bilal came to the Messenger and reported the incident in tears. The Messenger reproached Abu Dharr: "Do you still have a sign of *jahiliyah* (ignorance)?" Full of repentance, Abu Dharr lay on the ground and said: "I will not raise my head (meaning that he would not get up) unless Bilal puts his foot on it." Bilal forgave him, and they were reconciled.[19] Such was the bond of kinship and humanity that Islam created among a once-savage people.

---

[19] Bukhari, *Iman*, 22.

TOLERANCE AND DIALOGUE IN THE QUR'AN AND THE SUNNA

The Qur'an always accepts forgiveness and tolerance as basic principles, so much so that "the servants of the All-Merciful" are introduced in the following manner:

> And the servants of (God) the All-Merciful are those who move on the Earth in humility, and when the ignorant address them, they say: "Peace." (Al-Furqan 25:63)

> When they meet hollow words or unseemly behavior, they pass them by with dignity. (Al-Furqan 25:72)

> And when they hear vain talk, they turn away therefrom and say: "To us our deeds, and to you yours." (Al-Qasas 28:55)

The general gist of these verses is that when those who have been favored with true servanthood to God encounter meaningless and ugly words or behavior they say nothing unbecoming, but rather pass by in a dignified manner. In short: "Everyone acts according to his own disposition," (Al-Isra 17:84) and thus displays his or her own character. The character of heroes of tolerance is gentleness, consideration, and tolerance. When God sent Moses and Aaron to a man who claimed to possess divinity, as the Pharaoh had done, He commanded them to behave tolerantly and to speak softly (Ta Ha 20:44).

The life of the Pride of Humanity, peace and blessings be upon him, was led in an orbit of forgiveness and forbearance. He even behaved in such a manner toward Abu Sufyan, who persecuted him throughout his lifetime. During the conquest of Makka, even though Abu Sufyan said he still was not sure about Islam, the Messenger said: "Those who take refuge in Abu Sufyan's house are safe, just as those who take refuge in the Ka'ba are safe." Thus, in respect of providing refuge and safety, Abu Sufyan's house was mentioned alongside the Ka'ba. In my humble opinion, such tolerance was more valuable than if tons of gold had been given to

Abu Sufyan, a man in his seventies, in whom egoism and chieftainship had become ingrained.

In addition to being commanded to take tolerance and to use dialogue as his basis while performing his duties, the Prophet was directed to those aspects in which he had things in common with the People of the Book (Jews and Christians):

> Say: "O People of the Book! Come to common terms as between us and you: that we worship none but God; that we speculate no partners with Him; that we take not some from among ourselves for Lords other than God." (Al-Imran 3:64)

In another verse, those whose hearts are exuberant with belief and love are commanded to behave with forgiveness and tolerance, even to those who do not believe in the afterlife:

> Tell those who believe to forgive those who do not look forward to the Days of God: It is for Him to recompense each people according to what they have earned. (Al-Jathiya 45:14)

Those who consider themselves addressed by these verses, all devotees of love who dream of becoming true servants of God merely because they are human beings, those who have declared their faith and thereby become Muslims and performed the mandated religious duties, must behave with tolerance and forbearance and expect nothing from other people. They must take the approach of Yunus Emre: not to strike those who hit them, not to respond harshly to those who curse them, and not to hold any secret grudge against those who abuse them.

DIALOGUE IN THE MUHAMMADAN SPIRIT
AND MEANING

I do not like to make claims and I have a poor memory, but in spite of this I can recite tens of verses, one after the other, that are concerned with forgiveness, dialogue and opening one's heart to all. This demonstrates the all-embracing nature or universality of Islam.

For example, the Qur'an states, "peace is good" (An-Nisa 4:128). The verse does not necessitate its being particular to a certain event, meaning or framework. The rule is general. Moreover, does not the root of the noun "Islam" express soundness, surrender, peace, safety, and trust? Then it is not possible for us to be true Muslims without fully representing and establishing these characteristics. In addition to this, underlying the meaning of this sacred name is an essence that incorporates embracing all and approaching everything with love. But if we do not approach the subject in this spirit, then we cannot be considered as having understood Islam or having made its call or having represented it.

In addition to rules that guarantee peace and security, there are also verses in the Qur'an related to attitudes that should be taken against criminals and people who cause anarchy and terror; for such people there are legal sanctions, punishments, and retaliations. However, whether regarding verses and hadiths on these subjects or their implementations, if we do not take into consideration the conditions, if we do not separate the essence from the detail and the goal from the means, if we do not evaluate the verses in the context of the situation both before and after they were revealed, then we will always arrive at false conclusions.

I can and do say that peace, love, forgiveness, and tolerance are fundamental to Islam; other things are accidental. Yet, it is necessary to give priority to basic Muslim issues according to their degree of importance. For example, if God gives importance to love, if he has informed us that He loves those who love Him, and if he has given to the person He loved most the name "Habibullah," i.e. one who loves God and is loved by Him, then we have to take this as a fundamental principle. Rules like jihad against hypocrites and unbelievers are secondary matters that are necessitated by circumstances. Rules are tied to various reasons and conditions. If there are no such reasons, then the rules will not be enforced.

Rules regarding things like execution, exile and war have been tied to various reasons. What is essential here is explaining and conveying the principles of Islam with kind words and gentle behavior. Also, peace, justice and stability are essential in Islam, war being a by-product of circumstances and dependent on certain conditions. Unfortunately, those who ignore the essence and do so without taking into consideration the reasons for the secondary rules and regulations, those who (by reading the Qur'an in the manner of a crude kind of Zahiris[1]) emphasize violence—these people have not understood the rules, the reasons for them nor their source, nor have they understood Islam.

When the relevant reasons appear, of course the rules necessitated by the reasons become operative. For example, when foreign enemy armies attack our country, we will, of course, not be expected to sit passively in a corner and say to the attackers, "How nice of you to come."

Look at the world in which we find ourselves! According to some news recently reported in one of the newspapers, "bloody wars" are continuing in 56 places in the world. There are still floods of tears and blood flowing in many parts of the world. In many of these wars, some of the countries that defend democracy and human rights are on both sides. In that case, opposing war means opposing a human reality. For this reason, the moment someone touches our democratic rights and freedoms, we are, of course, going to defend ourselves and fight when necessary. But as I mentioned at the beginning, these are secondary things. The basis of Islam is peace and embracing humankind with love.

A Call to the Common Word

Another aspect of establishing and maintaining dialogue is the necessity of increasing the interests we have in common with other people. In fact, even if the people we talk with are Jews and Christians, this approach still should be adopted and issues that can separate us should be avoided altogether. For example, when the Qur'an calls the People of the Book, it says, "O People of the Book! Come to a word (that is) common between

---

[1] Zahiris approach the Qur'an and the Sunna only from the perspective of their outward meaning, devoid of insight and proper perception. They are very few in number.

us and you." What is that word? "Let us not worship anything but God." Because real freedom is realized only by being saved from being someone else's slave. When someone becomes a servant of God they are rescued from being anyone else's slave. So come and let us unite on this matter. The Qur'an continues, "Let us not take some of us for Lords." (Al-Imran 3:64) What is meant here is that our primary common point is belief in God; mentioning the Messengership of Muhammad has not even been mentioned yet. In another verse: "Say to those who believe: Let them forgive those who have no hope for the afterlife." What is being said here is let those who do not believe in the afterlife and resurrection after death be forgiven, because "God only rewards or punishes a people with what they have earned," (Al-Jathiya 45:14) i.e., if someone is going to be punished, then God will punish them and this matter does not concern anyone else.

Another clear example of this issue is related in particular to our Prophet who received a mild warning from God regarding the time he prayed against some guilty pagans. According to a report, a Bedouin Arab tribe requested that the Messenger send them teachers of the Qur'an. The Messenger sent them some, but they were ambushed and cruelly martyred at Bi'r Al-Maunah (the well of Al-Mauna). After this event, God's Messenger prayed to God for their punishment. However, God revealed the following verse:

> Not for you, (but for God), is the judgment concerning My servants: whether He turns in mercy to them, or punishes them because they are indeed wrongdoers. (Al-Imran 3:127-128)

Today there is an interest in religion all over the world. In my opinion, representing faith with its true values has gained an even greater importance than before. Today there is a need for people who are virtuous, self-possessed, cautious, sincere and pure of heart, people who do not steal or think too highly of themselves, and who prefer the well-being of others to their own, and who have no worldly expectations. If society can educate people with these characteristics, then it means that a much better future is imminent.

DIALOGUE WITH THE PEOPLE OF THE BOOK

The attitude of believers is determined according to the degree of their faith. I believe that if the message is put across properly, then an environment conducive to dialogue will be able to emerge in our country and throughout the world. Thus, as in every subject, we should approach this issue as indicated in the Qur'an and by the Prophet, peace and blessings be upon him. God says in the Qur'an:

> This is the Book; in it is sure guidance, without doubt, to those who are God-conscious, pious. (Al-Baqara 2:2)

Later on, these pious ones are identified as follows:

> Who believe in the Unseen, are steadfast in prayer, and spend out of what We have provided for them; and who believe in the Revelation sent to you and sent before your time, and (in their hearts) have the re-assurance of the Hereafter. (Al-Baqara 2:3-4)

Using a very gentle and slightly oblique style, the Qur'an calls people to accept the former Prophets and their books. The fact that such a condition has been placed at the very beginning of the Qur'an seems to be very significant to me when it comes to talking about the establishment of a dialogue with Jews and Christians. In another verse God commands:

> And argue not with the People of the Book unless it be in (a way) that is better. (Al-Ankabut 29:46)

In this verse, the Qur'an describes the method and approach we should use and the behavior we should display. Bediüzzaman said some extremely significant words in order to clarify this: "Those who are happy about their opponent's defeat in debate have no mercy." He explains the reason for this: "You gain nothing by defeating someone. If you are defeated and the other person is victorious, then you would have corrected one of your mistakes."

Debate should not be for the sake of ego, but rather to enable the truth to appear. When we look at political debates in which the only thought is to vanquish the other person, there can be no positive result. For the truth to emerge in a debate of ideas, such principles as mutual understanding, respect, and dedication to justice cannot be ignored. As a Qur'anic rule, debate can only take place in an environment that is conducive to dialogue.

Reading the above verse (29:64) further, we notice that the condition "unless it be with those who disbelieve and inflict wrong (and injury)" is placed. Wrong is also mentioned in another verse:

> It is those who believe and confuse not their beliefs with wrong—that are (truly) in security, for they are on (right) guidance. (Al-Anam 6:82)

According to the interpretation of this above verse by the Prophet, associating partners with God is equal to unbelief in the sense that one has contempt for the universe. The greatest tyranny is to silence all the voices in one's conscience that express God. Tyranny also means committing an injustice against others, oppressing them, and imposing one's ideas onto others. In that respect, as tyranny includes both polytheism and unbelief, it is the greater sin. Every polytheist or unbeliever may not be a wrongdoer in the sense outlined above. However, those who oppress others, who arm themselves in the name of committing evil, and who violate the rights of other people and the justice of God must be confronted within the framework of the law.

When dealing with People of the Book who are not oppressors, we have no right to behave violently against them or to think about how to destroy them. Such behavior is non-Islamic, contrary to Islamic rules and principles, and it can even be said that it is anti-Islamic. Elsewhere in the Qur'an it is stated:

> God does not forbid you, regarding those who did not fight you on account of religion and did not drive you out of your homes, to show kindness and deal with them justly. (Al-Mumtahana 60:8)

This verse was revealed when an emigrant lady called Asma asked the Prophet if she should meet with her polytheistic mother, who wanted to come from Makka to Madina to see her daughter. The verse suggests that such a meeting was perfectly acceptable, and that Asma could also be kind to her mother. I leave it to your discretion as to what approach should be used toward those who believe in God, the Judgment Day, and the prophets.

Hundreds of Qur'anic verses deal with social dialogue and tolerance. But care must be taken to establish balance in one's tolerance. Being merciful to a cobra means being unjust to the people the cobra has bitten. Claiming that "humanism" is more merciful than Divine Mercy is disrespectful to mercy and violates the rights of others. In truth, except in certain special cases, the Qur'an and the Sunna always advocate tolerance. The shielding canopy of this tolerance extends not only to the People of the Book, but, in a sense, to all people.

SPORTS AND THE PROCESS OF DIALOGUE

It is a fact that the concepts of democracy, peace, dialogue, and tolerance have spread and are now being taken seriously with the expansion of communication networks throughout the world. In order for these concepts to become more widespread and for everyone to benefit from them, a number of responsibilities fall on all people, both as individuals and as societies.

In connection with this matter, one important source of power and means of communication that can influence society is without a doubt sports. All manner of sports programs, indeed, anything that pertains to sports, are instantly transmitted from one side of the globe to the other. Of course, there are other, more conventional ways to spread ideas, but by employing this means we can help the ideas of dialogue and tolerance spread; ideas that we believe to be so essential that they must be made known to everyone can be publicized by this means for the sake of the well-being of both our own people and all of humanity.

For example, the 90 minutes spent on the field during a football match could be well utilized. The game itself will give pleasure to the spectators in the stands and, at the same time, without any objections, a number of human virtues could be easily displayed. It is important to utilize this 90 minutes in this way. For example, as was formerly done in sports matches, the victors and the defeated would come together, embrace, shake hands and radiate sportsmanship to all around them. Such behavior would in time be reflected by the behavior of the people in the stands. This would be an important lesson to the people who occasionally feel inclined to burn their seats, curse one another, or even attack one another with weapons; for them it would be highly beneficial to see and show the sports profession in a light that radiates good feelings and thoughts. Even if the spectators of today do not respect the fact that the players are shaking hands before leaving the stadium, in time the behavior of the players will break the cycle of hate and vengefulness, or at least, neutralize it. At this time, this is what the world desperately needs.

Both internally and externally certain people have a desire for conflict and have been brought up in an environment of conflict, and therefore they do not desire dialogue or the improvement of human relationships. It is for this reason that we must act very cautiously. In every task undertaken, there should be a certain meaning, sincerity should be sought, and reason and good judgment should be the priority. In addition, every profession should be given its due and it should behave accordingly. An imam uses his voice in the mosque, but a film star, an actor, or an author does not act in the same way. The actor gives precedence to body language or acting ability and the author to writing style and the writing of ideas in a literary way. This is how it should be; otherwise, the impact of the message and its effect is diminished and the message is of no benefit. The same thing is true for sports. An athlete should demonstrate his or her abilities through success, good behavior, and an exemplary lifestyle.

Unfortunately, today the importance of some values has not been perceived. People have a greater need for religion than they do for bread and water, for the peace and security provided by religion, and for the guarantee of an afterlife; I believe that when these facts have been properly explained, then there will be no doubting this matter. There are many people throughout the world who want to do something in the name of Islam. But when this important subject is approached in a crude manner, hate is evoked in the place of love, and unbridgeable abysses appear between people. Yet, what is expected and needed is for Islam to be a bridge and a road between people, as well as a factor that breaches the abysses.

If we do not respond to those who are extending their hands in order to express their love and respect, we will become unlovable. In fact, we will cause some undesirable negative developments to occur. In short, we can say that as an important factor in realizing social dialogue and tolerance, sports can also be utilized, if done so in a well-thought out manner.

THE IDEAL HUMAN

THE NEW MAN AND WOMAN

History has carried us to the threshold of a new age that is open to the manifestations of Divine favor. Despite, or in parallel with, advances in science and technology, the last two or three centuries have witnessed a global break with traditional values and, in the name of renewal, an attachment to different values and speculative fantasies. It is our hope, strengthened by promising developments, that the next century will be the age of belief and moral values, an age that will witness a renaissance and revival for the believers.

Among wavering crowds that lack sound thinking or reasoning, a new type of people will appear. They will rely equally on reason and experience, but give as much importance to conscience and inspiration as they do to the former. They will pursue the perfect in everything, establish the balance between this world and the next, and wed the heart to the intellect.

The coming-to-be of such people will not be easy. All births are painful, but these blessed births will take place and provide the world with a new, brilliant generation. Just as rain pours out of slowly gathering clouds and water wells up from underground, so too will the "flowers" of this new generation one day appear among us.

These new people will be individuals of integrity who, free from external influences, can manage independently of others. No worldly force will be able to bind them, and no fashionable -ism will cause them to deviate from their path. Truly independent of any worldly power, they will think and act freely, for their freedom will be in proportion to their servanthood to God. Rather than imitating others, they will rely on their original dynamics rooted in the depths of history and try to equip their faculties of judgment with authentic values that are their own.

They will think, investigate, believe, and overflow with spiritual pleasure. While making the fullest use of modern facilities, they will not neglect their traditional and spiritual values in building their own world.

This article originally appeared in *Zamanın Altın Dilimi* [The Golden Slice of Time], Kaynak, Izmir, 1998, pp. 157-160.

If changes and reforms are linked to and dependent on eternal universal values, they may be welcomed eagerly. Otherwise, there will be a plethora of speculative fantasies that are appealing because of their novelty and modernity. Standing on the firm ground of those eternal values, the new man and woman will always look to the future to illuminate the darkness enveloping the world.

They will be completely truth-loving and trustworthy and, in support of truth everywhere, always ready to leave their families and homes when necessary. Having no attachment to worldly things, comforts, or luxuries, they will use their God-given talents to benefit humanity and plant the seeds of a happy future. Then, constantly seeking help and success from God, they will do their best to protect those seeds from harm, just as a hen protects its eggs. Their entire lives will be dedicated to this way of truth.

To stay in touch and communicate with people's minds, hearts, and feelings, these new men and women will use the mass media and try to establish a new power balance of justice, love, respect, and equality among people. They will make might subservient to right, and never discriminate on grounds of color or race.

These new people will unite profound spirituality, diverse knowledge, sound thinking, a scientific temperament, and wise activism. Never content with what they know, they will continuously increase in knowledge: knowledge of self, of nature, and of God.

Equipped with the good morals and virtues that make them truly human, these new men and women will be altruists who embrace humanity with love and are ready to sacrifice themselves for the good of others when necessary. As they shape themselves in the mold of universal virtue, they will simultaneously strive to illuminate the way of others. They will defend and support what is good and recommend it to others, while seeking to challenge, combat, and eradicate all evils.

These new people will believe that All-Mighty gave them life here so that they could know and worship Him. Without discriminating between the Book of the Universe (where the Divine Names are manifested and which is therefore full of signs of Him and acts as a "stairway" leading to Him) and the Divine Scripture (the translation of the Book of the Universe), they will see science and religion as two manifestations of the same truth.

They will never be reactionary. They will not pursue events, for they will be the dynamism of history that initiates and shapes events. With due perception of their age and surrounding conditions, and in devotion to their essential values and with utmost reliance on God, they will be in a state of continuous self-renewal.

These new people will conqueror their selves, thoughts, and hearts, and those of others, and they will discover the unknown. They will regard any time spent in not taking a new step into the depths of the self and the universe as being wasted. As they remove, through faith and knowledge, the veils covering the face of reality, they will become even more eager to advance further. With the messages and answers received from the Heavens, the Earth, and the seas, they will continue to journey until they return to their Creator.

THE PORTRAIT OF PEOPLE OF HEART

With their vision, faith, and deeds, people of heart are integrated heroes of both spiritualism and meaning. Their profundity relies not on their knowledge or acquisitions, but on the richness of their hearts, the pureness of their souls and their closeness to God. They believe that the principles presented to humanity in the name of knowledge are valuable only if they lead humanity to the truth. Similarly, they regard information, and especially abstract knowledge that has no practical uses, as being insignificant, as they do not assist human beings to understand the reality of the creatures, the matter and human beings themselves.

People of heart are monuments of humility and modesty who are devoted to a spiritual life, determined to stay away from all the material and spiritual dirt, always vigilant to corporeal desires of the body, and ready to struggle with such evils as hatred, resentment, greed, jealousy, selfishness and lust. They always endeavor to give what is right the highest esteem, to convey to others what they feel about this world, as well as the next, and they are always patient and cautious. People of faith and action who, rather than talking and making noise, live as they believe, present an exemplary personality for others. Such people move on, never pausing, teaching those who are walking toward God how to do so. Inside, they have a pyre that can never be extinguished. Yet, in order not to disclose this painful burning inside, such people never complain to others. As such, they are constantly emitting heat to the spirits of those who seek shelter in them.

A longing for the transcendent realms is evident in the eyes of people of heart. Dedicated to the consent of God, they are such people of progress and of struggle with distances that they run like a purebred Arabian steed until they reach their Beloved One, without expecting, in the meantime, anything in return.

People of heart are such sincere adherents of the truth that all they think of is to stabilize the justice on Earth and they are willing, when it comes to His consent, to give up their own desires and wishes. They open their hearts to everyone, welcoming them affectionately, and appearing as an angel of preservation in society. Regarding their deeds and attitudes, they try to be compatible with everybody, they try to avoid vicious competition with others, and they avoid resentment. Even though such people make choices from time to time in favor of their convictions, beliefs, methods and ways, they do not compete with others. On the contrary, they love all who serve in the name of their religion; they love their country and their ideals. Furthermore, they give generously to other people in pursuit of positive activities and they try to show as much respect as possible to the philosophy and ideas that other people adopt.

Along with such endeavors and activities, people of heart who are seeking ways to incur His help also give utmost importance to God's aid and assistance. They pay particular attention to union and solidarity, which are considered a means of God's aid. They are ready, wholeheartedly, to cooperate with anybody who is on the straight path. Moreover, for such an understanding of union, they, in spite of themselves, follow a path. Believing that union incurs mercy, and dissension and disunion lead nowhere, such people do their best to gain the help and good will of all, ever receptive to showers of Divine aid.

People of heart are lovers of God, and devoted seekers of God's consent. They connect their deeds to His pleasure, regardless of the circumstances. They display great ambition to please Him, and are willing for the sake of this purpose to use or abandon all that they possess—of this world or not. There is never any room in the realm of their thoughts for unpleasant expressions like "I did it," "I succeeded," or "I managed it." Such people take pleasure in the fulfillment of the tasks of others, as if they had carried such actions out themselves, they take the same amount of pleasure in such achievements as if it were their own and they follow humbly after these people, leaving also the honor and the title of leading to them. What is more, as they consider others to be more eligible and successful in serving religion and humanity, they provide other people with more comfortable facilities, and, taking a step back, continue in their service as an "ordinary person."

People of heart are too busy fighting their selves and their misdemeanors to be interested in the misdeeds of others. In contrast, they set an example to others of what a good person should be, leading others to attain higher horizons. They turn a blind eye to what other people may do wrong. Responding with a smile to those who have displayed negative attitudes, such people nullify bad behavior with kindness, not thinking to hurt anybody, even when they have been hurt over and over again.

For the man of heart, a soldier of the reality that has been devoted to gaining God's good pleasure with feelings, ideas and deeds, the first priority is to lead a life based on perfect faith and equipped with sincerity. Thus, it is unlikely that such a person will be dissuaded from reaching their goal, even if they were offered the heavens in addition to the world.

People of heart never compete with those who bear the same ideals and who walk on the same path, nor do they envy them. In contrast, they complete what has been left incomplete by others, and, when interacting with other people, they treat them as if they were as closely connected as organs of the same body. With a complete understanding of renunciation, pushing their counterparts into the limelight, in every earthly as well as unearthly matter, they withdraw to the background. They act as spokespersons for the accomplishments of others, applauding them and welcoming their achievements with the same joy that they feel on a festival.

Relying to a great extent on method and manner, people of heart conduct all of their acts in accordance with their nature. They try, however, to remain respectful to the acts and thoughts of others. They are able to live harmoniously and to share, developing common projects. They struggle to replace the word "I" with the word "we." Over and above all this, they sacrifice their happiness for that of others. In so doing, they never expect any appreciation or respect from anyone. They even think that such expectations are a form of moral corruption and, thus, they avoid appearing in the limelight, they avoid fame and fortune, much as they would a snake or a scorpion, hoping only to be soon forgotten.

People of heart do not violate the rights of any other people, nor do they seek revenge. Even in the most critical circumstances, they tend to behave calmly, and do whatever a person of heart should do to the utmost. They always reply to evil acts with kindness, and, considering badness to be a characteristic of evil, treating those who have harmed them as monuments of virtue.

People of heart lead a life illuminated by the light of the Qur'an and the Sunna, and also within the framework of the consciousness of *taqwa* (piety), blessing, and sainthood. They are on constant guard against feelings of egoism, pride, fame, etc., feelings which kill the heart. The glories performed by such people are attributed to the Real Owner, saying, "All is from Him." With those things that depend on will power, they avoid uttering "I," instead taking refuge in "We."

People of heart are afraid of no one. No single event can send them into a panic. "Relying on God, he works hard, expecting the rest from His aid," sums up their character, and they never break their promise.

People of heart never lose their temper with anybody, nor are they offended by those whose hearts are attached to God. When they see any of their brothers or sisters-in-religion doing wrong, they do not abandon them. In order to avoid embarrassment they do not make any wrong-doing publicly or personally known, either. On the contrary, they blame and question themselves for witnessing any immoral act.

People of heart avoid commenting on the attitudes of believers that are apt to be interpreted differently. They think positively of what they see and hear and never perceive such actions as being negative.

In every act and deed, people of heart keep in mind that here, this world, is not a place of reward, but rather one of service. Accordingly, they perform the duties that they are responsible for in strict discipline, regarding it as being discourteous to God to be concerned about the consequences. They consider it a priority to perform actions in the name of God and with God's consent in order to serve the religion, belief, and humankind, and however great their achievements may be, they attribute all to God, without thinking about taking a personal share for themselves.

The destruction of order cannot leave people of heart in despair, nor does the opposition of other people disturb them. "This world is not a place for conflicts or rows, but one for endurance," they say, and patiently clench their teeth. They seek ways out of any situation that they may find themselves in, not losing hope even at the most critical of times, and they are constantly producing with adamant perseverance multifarious strategies. Today, when we find that human values are despised, when there are cracks appearing in religious thinking, when every place resounds with the disturbance caused by the carefree ones, we need people of heart as much as we need air to breathe and water to drink.

THE IDEAL BELIEVER, THE IDEAL MUSLIM

The Muslims are those from whose tongues and hands other Muslims are safe and sound. The emigrants are those who leave behind and abandon those things God has prohibited.[1]

Let us briefly analyze the above hadith. Notice the presence of the definite article (*al* in Arabic) before *Muslim*. What can be extrapolated from this is that there are ideal believers who enter an atmosphere of safety and security, having so immersed themselves in that atmosphere that they harm no one with their hands or tongues. This refers only to the true and ideal Muslims who leave their mark on all minds, not those who appear or claim to be so, or to those whose identity cards or passports have "Muslim" written on them. We understand this from the article used in the Arabic, which indicates something specific, definite. This is derived from the grammatical rule of the Arabic language: "When something is described by a definite article, the item's highest and most perfect condition is indicated." So, when one hears "the believer," the first thing that comes to mind is the most perfect meaning of "believer," and that is what is meant in this hadith.

Moreover, one cannot learn such a fine grammatical point by oneself, for it is a topic that belongs to formal education. Hence, such an educational experience was not possible for the Messenger of God; he was illiterate. Thus, he was not speaking his own thoughts, but rather he was relaying what the Eternal Teacher taught him to say. For this reason, there are many subtle grammatical points found in the Prophet's expressions and declarations, and there are no errors in usage.

Let us return to the above hadith: Real Muslims are people in whom one can feel confidence and trust, so much so that other Muslims can turn their backs on them without a second thought. One can entrust a family member to such people without fear; this person will suffer no injury from the hand or tongue of the Muslim. If one were to attend a gathering

---

[1] Bukhari, *Iman*, 4.

with a true Muslim, one could leave in full confidence that no one will gossip about one, nor would one have to listen to gossip about others. Such Muslims are as sensitive to the dignity and honor of other people as they are to their own. They do not eat; they feed others. They do not live for themselves; they live to enable others to live. They will even sacrifice their spiritual pleasure for others. I derive all these meanings from the fact that the definite article in Arabic also means *hasr*; a restraining, a devotion to a specific purpose.

Security and Muslims

Etymologically speaking, the word *Muslim* and the verb *sa-li-ma* both come from the root *silm*. This means that for Muslims, every matter takes place in line with *silm* (security), *salamah* (safety), and Muslim-ness. Muslims are seized by such a divine attraction that all of their actions take place around this powerful center.

They greet everyone with *salaam*, thereby placing love for themselves in everyone's heart.[2] They end their prayers with *salaam*. All people, jinn, angels, and conscious creatures receive their *salaam*. That is, they exchange greetings with invisible creatures as well. Until now, no other people have extended this circle of greeting to such a degree as have the Muslims. Islam consists of performing such principal duties as fasting, giving alms, performing the Hajj, and striving to profess the faith. This means that they set sail on the sea of safety and security by obeying the command: *Enter safety (Islam) whole-heartedly* (2:208). Those who throw themselves into that sea emanate safety and Islam in every condition. No one sees anything but goodness in the actions and behavior of such people.

Why the Tongue and Hand?

As in every statement of our master, peace and blessings be upon him, every word in the hadith mentioned above was chosen carefully. Why did he choose the hand and the tongue to speak about? Of course there are many subtle points related to this choice. A person can harm someone in two ways: either directly or indirectly. The hand represents physical presence (directly), and the tongue represents absence (indirectly). People

---

[2] Bukhari, *Iman*, 20; Muslim, *Iman*, 63.

either attack others directly, physically, or indirectly, through gossip and ridicule. Real Muslims never engage in such activities, because they are supposed to always act justly and generously, whether they are acting directly or indirectly.

The Prophet mentioned the tongue before the hand because in Islam one can retaliate for what has been done with the hand. However, the same is not always true for damage done indirectly through gossip or slander. Thus, such action can easily cause conflict between individuals, communities, and even nations. Dealing with this type of harm is relatively more difficult than dealing with the harm caused by the hand, and this is the reason why the Prophet mentioned the tongue before the hand. On the other hand, the value of Muslims before God has been indicated. Being a Muslim has such a great value before God that other Muslims must control their hands and tongues in their actions toward them.

Another important moral dimension of Islam is that Muslims must keep at bay things that will harm others, whether physically or spiritually, and they must do their best not to harm others. Let alone not causing harm, every segment of Muslim society must also represent safety and security. Muslims can be real Muslims to the extent that they carry within themselves a feeling of safety and that their hearts beat with trust. Wherever they are or wherever they live this feeling that derives from *al-salaam* is revealed. They wish for safety upon departure, adorn their prayers with greetings, and send *salaams* to other believers when they end their prayers. In all probability, it is inconceivable that people who lead their whole lives in such an orbit of *salaam* would embark on a path that is contrary to the basic principles of safety, trust, soundness, and worldly and other-worldly security, thus causing harm to themselves or to others.

It would be useful to examine the very essence of these points: True Muslims are the most trustworthy representatives of universal peace. They travel everywhere with this sublime feeling, nourished deep in their spirits. Far from giving torment or suffering, they are remembered everywhere as symbols of safety and security. In their eyes, there is no difference between a physical (direct) or a verbal (indirect) violation of someone's rights. In fact, in some cases the latter is considered to be a greater crime than the former.

IDEAL SPIRITS AND HEROES OF LOVE

Only those who overflow with love will be able to build the happy and enlightened world of the future. Their lips smile with love, their hearts brim over with love, their eyes radiate love and the most tender human feelings—such are the heroes of love who continuously receive messages of love from the rising and setting of the sun and from the flickering light of the stars.

Those who attempt to reform the world must first reform themselves. In order for others to follow them on the way to a better world, they must purify their inner worlds of hatred, rancor, and jealousy, and adorn their outer worlds with all kinds of virtue. The utterances of those who are far removed from self-control and self-discipline, those who have failed to refine their feelings, may seem attractive and insightful at first, but they will not be able to inspire others—or, if indeed they can, the sentiments they arouse will soon die away.

Goodness, beauty, truthfulness, and being virtuous are embedded in the essence of the world. Whatever happens, the world will one day find this essence, and no one will be able to prevent that from happening.

Those who strive to enlighten others, those who seek happiness for them and extend them a helping hand have such a developed and enlightened spirit that they are like guardian angels. They struggle with the disasters that befall society, they stand up to "storms," they hurry to put out the "fires," and they are always on the alert for possible shocks.

Devotees of Love

Bediüzzaman said, "We are devotees of love; we do not have time for antagonism." This is a very important principle for us. However, it is not enough to say just this; the crucial matter is to represent it. As a matter of fact, many speak beautiful words about loving humankind, and these are indeed pleasant words. But, I wonder how many of those who speak such words are able to put into action and represent in themselves, in their characters, what they have verbalized? I think it would be difficult to find a satisfying answer to this question.

Representing what he preached is one of the important characteristics of our Prophet. He practiced whatever he said and implemented in his life whatever words he spoke. Words that are not put into practice, regardless of how beautiful or perfect they may be, are doomed to be spoiled, to be wasted, and to lose their influence with time. It will be understood by their impact on hearts how stagnant, not only human words, but even Divine Words can become if they are not put into practice. Not even one letter of the Qur'an has been changed and it has maintained the same freshness and originality that it had at the moment it was first revealed. It is a blessed and celebrated book, but it has become a victim of not being seen clearly through the foggy atmosphere of weak human representation and emptiness, and consequently is subject to the delirious ravings of deficiency that are not a characteristic of the Qur'an itself, but rather attributable to the societies that have failed to carry it over into life. Religion and the Qur'an should be vital to life and must be fully understood so that we can remain dynamic. The Qur'an should be fully represented so that it can perform the function that is expected from it. In short, what I want to say here is this: it is not enough to say that you are a devotee of love and a representative of peace. There are a number of obstacles that must be overcome. The crux of the matter is to put that beautiful expression of words into practice.

Love and affection are among the most important principles of Islam. We must represent these throughout the world. However, certain recent negative events in particular have lead people to think of Islam as being other than it really is. Of course, it would be completely wrong to attribute to Islam the mistakes that some people have made. It is true that a serious change has occurred in a neighboring country which has severely harmed the Muslim world, although many of the problems there could have been solved through reconciliation. This did not spread because it did not go beyond mere slogans. Moreover, that is not the only country that has incorrectly reflected the image of Islam in the world. There are many other countries and leaders that continually portray negative images through their attitudes and behavior and, of course, in so doing it is the opponents of the Qur'an who always benefit. Moreover, we must be insistent on what we say and we must be fully determined to implement it. Our inner world should overflow with love and affection for humankind; there should be no place at all in our heart for hostility. Let there be no doubt, this new century is going to be an age when love and dialogue will flourish. Antagonism will be eradicated and love and tolerance will spring up everywhere. This is not a remote probability, especially at a time when the world is experiencing globalization. God willing, when the time comes, the holy ones will carry out this mission.

People of Love

The people of love, like Rumi, Yunus, Yesevi, and Bediüzzaman were attached to God at a much greater degree than us, and their fallibility was much less than ours. For this reason, they made tremendous efforts regarding love, affection, and tolerance, and they greatly influenced those around them on this matter. But, if we evaluate them within the period they lived, none of them saw the level of dialogue and tolerance that has been attained today by believing people as a result of their efforts. In fact, each of them had to face unbecoming treatment; in comparison with what they suffered, the treatment we face is almost nothing. Bediüzzaman says in concerning the suffering they had to bear:

> Do they think I am an egotist who is only concerned for myself? In order to save the faith of the community, I have sacrificed my whole life and have had no time to think about my afterlife. During my life of over 80 years, I have tasted no worldly pleasure I have spent my life on battlefields, in prisons or in the jails and courts of this country. They have treated me like a criminal, banishing me from one town to another, keeping me under constant surveillance. There has been no persecution I have not tasted, no oppression I have not suffered. But if I were able to see the faith of my community secured, then I would not care about even being burned in the flames of Hell. For while my body is burning my heart will blossom like a rose-garden. (*Bediüzzaman Said Nursi, Tarihçe-i Hayatı*[Biography])

In spite of all these difficulties, none of these men of love saw the degree of acceptance in their own time that is received by today's representatives of dialogue and tolerance. Their messages did not have the same impact on the public that the messages of today's heroes of tolerance have. I think that if they were to live in this century and were to see today's trend toward dialogue and tolerance, they would ask, "How have you been able to be successful with dialogue all over the world? What is your secret?"

Such a distinction was not destined for these giants of light because the conditions of the time were not appropriate; in order to attain this distinction, it is necessary to persist on this way. Yesterday an eminent person said to me, "Some circles that were strongly opposed to believers until yesterday are now greatly supporting and commending them." In fact, these are all indications of the feeling of welcome for these devotees of love that God has put into the hearts of other people. Ignoring this would be sheer ingratitude, and witnessing it, but neglecting to give thanks for it would be another dimension of unbelief.

WHAT IT TAKES TO BE A BELIEVER

Today, above all else, we are in need of a generation that is conscientious in fulfilling their duty toward God and we need ideal people who can guide society; we are in need of ideal guides who will save humanity from the accursed abysses of atheism, ignorance, error, and anarchy and who will lead them to faith, insight, the correct destination, and peace. In each and every era of depression, there have been minds that have enlightened the masses suffering from religious, intellectual, social, financial, and moral depression; these minds have reinterpreted human beings, the universe and existence in its entirety, and they have even reinterpreted the background to existence, removing obstacles in our thought processes. Many times have people made a new shirt from their death shroud; they have reinterpreted things and phenomena many times. They have recited the book of existence—a book which in the perceptions of shallow minds had lost its color and luster and taken on a dim hue—as if it were music, feeling it to its very depths; they have observed it like an exhibition. They have unraveled the truths hidden in the heart of the universe by analyzing things season by season, paragraph by paragraph.

The most important characteristics of such auspicious people are their faith and the efforts they make to cause others to experience that faith. With this faith and these efforts they believe that they will be able to surmount everything and reach God, and they believe that they can attain true peace, be able to turn the world into a paradise and raise their standard in Eden. The joy of their destination makes them perceive life and the service of good deeds as a journey along the valleys of heaven.

In truth, whatever its peculiarities or complexities, no other system, doctrine, or philosophy has had such a positive influence on the faith of humanity. When faith enters the hearts of people within its own frame, the thoughts of these people concerning the universe, objects, and God all suddenly change, deepening and reaching a vastness which allows them to evaluate all existence as if it were the pages of an open book. All that such people have seen around them, things which to that date have aroused no interest in them, everything that has been lifeless and meaningless until that day, suddenly become vitalized and now appear as friends, companions and these things embrace them. In this heart-warming atmosphere, people feel themselves to be a degree of their own value; they understand that they are a conscious and unique part of existence; they attain the mysteries of the long, winding paths between the pages and lines of the universe; they feel that they are close to grasping the secret that lies behind the veil of all things; and then they are set free from the narrow prison of this three dimensional world, finding themselves in the stretches of eternity.

Indeed, all believers, through the thoughts which flow in the depths of their identity and in accordance with the degree of their faith, become boundless within their bounds; even though they are bound by space and time, they become paragons of unrestricted beings, reaching the ranks of beings that are above and beyond the concerns of space, listening to the angels' melodies. These beings, created from water, from what appears to be a shapeless pulp—what seems to be an insignificant creature, but what is in reality truly great—gains such importance that the Earth becomes the stage for the discovery of the divine breath contained in his or her soul. And, they become such creatures that they no longer fit between the skies and the Earth, becoming transcendent being reaching between the two poles.

They walk amongst us; sit with us; their feet step where our feet step and they place their head when praying on the same spot that we do, but they manage to unite their feet and their head, thus becoming a sphere; they prostrate themselves before God, putting themselves in front of Him like a ramp on the way to being close to Him and attain the horizon of becoming one of the closest to God in one step. They beat their wings in the same skies as the spirits and live like celestial beings in a human state. Such hearts always surpass individuality with the development and expansion of humane feelings; they become, in a way, a collective personality and embrace all believers; they lend a hand to everyone and salute creation in its entirety with the sincerest of feelings. They see colors, watch shapes, and are aware of the sounds of holy visions in everything and everyone that they encounter; they listen to the sounds of heaven on every possible frequency and feel as if they can hear the beating of angels' wings. They see, feel, and listen to such a vast ceremony of beauties: from terrifying bolts of thunder to the revelatory songs of the birds, from the crashing waves of the seas to the gentle sound of the rivers which inspire feelings of eternity, from the magical reverberation of the solitary woods to the accents of the awe-inspiring summits that seem to be reaching to the heavens, from the magical breezes that seem to caress the green hills to the enrapturing scents that pour out of gardens and spread everywhere; they say "this must be life." They try to give their breath its due value with prayers and by verbalizing and contemplating the Beautiful Names of God.

They open and close their eyes, their foreheads are always touching the floor, anticipating a familiar look from the threshold of a door which they hope will open; and they observe the other side of the door with longing, waiting for that happy hour when loss and longing will withdraw and peace and closeness will envelope their soul like a holy talisman. They try to find satisfaction for the desire of reunion in their soul. They keep running toward Him, sometimes flying, sometimes limping on the ground, unified with everyone and everything. They experience the joy of a "wedding night"[1] in the shadow of reunion at every station, extinguishing another one of the many fires of longing at every turn and at that very moment they are alight with a new flame, and start to burn. Who knows how many times they will find themselves surrounded with the breath of "divine intimacy" and how many times their hearts will be wounded by the aspect of the loneliness and tragedy of those who cannot feel this inspiration.

Indeed, souls that have such broadened horizons feel themselves to be always on the ramp toward new realms, always tensed with a resolution and determination to transcend human norms. They think of what further abilities they will be able to attain and what successes they will achieve with faith and the power behind that faith. They keep running without feeling exhausted, with their horizon and prospect always open, and their hearts at peace. At every station their relationship with their environment grows and deepens. They may or may not be aware of it, but when they listen to their souls, they see themselves on a never-ending mountain side of peace; despite the numerous motifs of longing and loneliness that they witness in other people, they never feel the agony of the

---

[1] The term Rumi uses for death.

road or homesickness because they know where they have come from, and why and where they are headed, and they are aware of all the harvesting and dispersion in the world, and they are aware that they are running on a particular track with a fixed purpose and aim. They feel neither the weariness of the road, nor experience the fears, worries, or agonies that other people do. They trust in God, striding with hope and tasting the joy of reaching the summit that holds the sky-blue dreams of tomorrow.

Indeed, on the roads along which the world strides, these chivalrous heroes of faith make their way to the degree of their faith as if they were strolling along the valleys of Heaven, breathing nothing but peace; on the other hand, through their affiliation with God, they can challenge the whole universe, they can surmount any difficulty, and they do not fall into despair even if they witness destruction everywhere. They do not recoil in terror even when hells appear before them. They always hold their head high and never bow except before God. They concede nothing to anyone, they expect nothing from anyone, nor do they make themselves indebted to anyone. When they are victorious and attain one success after another, they shake with fear at the comprehension that this is in fact a test of their loyalty and submission to God, while at the same time they are humbled with gratitude and shed tears of joy. They know how to be patient when they lose and are tensed with determination. They start their journey anew with a sharpened will. They do not become arrogant or ungrateful in the face of bounty nor do they fall into despair when they suffer deprivation.

They carry a prophet-like heart in their exchanges with people. They love and embrace everyone; they turn a blind eye to the faults of others, while at the same time they are able to question the smallest faults of their own. They forgive the faults of those around them, not only under normal conditions, but also at times when they feel angered; they know how to live peacefully with even the most irritable of souls. In fact, Islam advises its followers to forgive as much as possible, and not to fall prey to feelings of rancor, hatred, or revenge; in any case, it is inconceivable that those who are conscious of being on the path toward God should or could be any other way. To behave in any other way or to think in any other way is out of the question; on the contrary, in all their acts they seek the means by which they can benefit others, they wish for the good of others, and they try to keep alive the love in their hearts, waging a never-ending battle against rancor and hate. They feel the heat of their own faults and sins, burning with penitence, and they grasp the evil thoughts inside themselves by the throat a few times each day. They start their work willingly and prepare the ground for the seedlings of good and beauty everywhere. In the footsteps of Rabi'a al-'Adawiya they accept everyone and everything as a sweet syrup, even though it may be poison; even when they are approached with hatred, they welcome with smiles, and they repel the greatest armies with the indefatigable weapon of love.

God loves these people, and they love God. They are always stirred by the excitement of love and experience the dazzling delights of the feeling of being loved. Their wings of humility always rest on the ground and they need to become the soil in order to attain the joy of giving birth to roses. As much as they are respectful to others, they also value their honor; they never allow their indulgence, affection, gentleness, and refinement to be interpreted as a weakness. They never heed the censure or appraisal of other people, as they live according to their faith; they take care only not to let their own thought-atlas lose its luster, for they have resolved to be good believers.

SPIRITS DEVOTED TO GOD

The most remarkable feature of those who have devoted themselves to the bestowal of God's consent and to the ideal of loving and being loved by Him is that they never expect anything—material or spiritual—in return. Things like profit, wealth, cost, comfort, etc., things to which people of this world pay great attention, do not mean much; they hold no value, nor are they considered as criteria.

To devotees, the value of their ideals transcends that of the earthly ones to such an extent that it is almost impossible to divert them from what they seek—God's gratuitous consent—and lead them to any other ideal. In fact, stripped entirely of finite and transient things, devotees undergo such a transformation in their hearts to turn to God that they are changed because they recognize no goal other than their ideal. Since they devote themselves completely to making people love God and to being loved by God, dedicating their lives to enlightening others, and, once again, because they have managed to orient their goal in this unified direction, which in a sense contributes to the value of this ideal, they avoid divisive and antagonist thoughts, such as "they" and "we," "others" and "ours." Neither do such people have any problems—explicit or concealed—with other people. In contrast, all they think of is how they can be useful to society and how they can avoid disputes with the society of which they are members. When they detect a problem in society, they take action like a spiritual leader rather than a warrior, leading people to virtue and lofty spirituality, abstaining from any sort of political dominance or thought of rule.

What composes the depths of these devoted spirits is knowledge, the use of this knowledge, a strong and sound understanding of morality and its application in every aspect of life, faithful virtue and the awareness of its indispensability, among other factors. They seek refuge in God from fame and interest-based cold propaganda and ostentatious acts and deeds, things which indeed do not promise anything in the name of their future, that is, for their afterlife. Furthermore, living in accordance with their principles, they ceaselessly endeavor to lead those who watch and imitate to be in awe of sublime human values. Doing all this, such people do not ever expect any interest or kindness from anyone, and they try hard to evade any kind of personal interest or profit; they avoid this as they would a snake or a scorpion. After all, their inner richness has a centripetal power that does not allow any acts of advertisement, boasting, or ostentation. Their amiable behavior, also reflections of their spirits, is of such a quality that it fascinates and makes discerning people follow them.

For this very reason, these devotees never desire to boast about themselves or to advertise or spread propaganda about themselves, nor are they ambitious to be well-known or appreciated. Instead, they endeavor, with all their might and strength, to reach the spiritual life and they depend all their acts in this regard on sincerity, intending merely to please God. In other words, they aim to attain God's consent with each and every act and they ceaselessly strive to achieve this sublime goal, not contaminating their prophet-like determination with worldly expectations, ambition, or the appreciation or fondness of others. Because faith, Islam and the Qur'an are criticized and questioned in today's world, these people must spend all their energy countering these attacks. It is essential that individuals be supported in their Islamic thoughts and feelings, and that the people be rescued from aimlessness in order to be linked to some sublime ideals. Meeting such a need to the extent that people will never feel obliged to seek anything else is only possible with the revitalization of faith in the hearts of its own patterns and its own style. One may also call this a redirection of people to a spiritual life. Such an approach is extremely important, particularly at a time when some people are relying everything on a change and transformation of social life, trying to reshape it into new patterns. When one tries to redirect toward a spiritual life there will always be consensus, agreement, and solidarity, whereas, if one is to rely merely on change, then one is likely to witness disputes, divisions, and even fights.

Devotees do not experience emptiness in their mental lives and reasoning thanks to this understanding of a unified direction. On the contrary, they remain open to reason, science and logic, regarding this as a prerequisite of their beliefs. Having been melted in the depths of closeness to God, a closeness which depends on one's merit, and in the ocean that is like divine unity, their earthly desires and corporeal passion, take on a new shape (spiritual enjoyment as a result of God's consent) with a new pattern, a new style. Thus, devotees can breathe the same air as the angels at the peaks of spiritual life while conversing with terrestrial ones, fulfilling the licit requirements of life on Earth. For this reason, these devotees are considered as being related with both the present and the future worlds. Their relation with the present world is due to the fact that they apply and comply with physical forces. What ties them to the next world is the fact that they evaluate every matter in the light of their spiritual life and that of the heart. Any inhibitions in the worldly life that are imposed by the spiritual life do not necessarily entail a complete abandonment of the worldly life; it is for this reason that these people cannot entirely despise the world. In contrast, they always stand in the center rather than on the periphery of the world and rule it. This stance, however, is not one for or in the name of the world, but rather one in the name of complying with the physical forces and an attempt to connect everything to the Hereafter.

As a matter of fact, this is the way to keep the body in its own frame and the spirit on its own horizon; it is the way to lead life under the leadership of the heart and the spirit. The finite and restricted corporeal life must be to the extent that corporeality deserves, while the spiritual life, always open to eternity, must seek infinitude. If one thinks only supreme and transcendent thoughts, if one leads a life as the Life-Giver demands, if one regards illuminating others as the fundamental of one's life and if one always seeks the zenith, then one naturally becomes a practitioner of a supreme program, and, thus, to a certain extent, one limits personal desires and passions.

Of course, it is challenging to lead such a life. Yet, this arduous mission is quite simple for those who have devoted themselves to God, for those who aim to glorify His Name, for those who zealously commute to and from the gate of God trying to make people aware of Him, with one hand on the doors of the hearts of people and the other on His gate. Actually, there is nothing that counts as hardship for those who feel in their bosoms the heat of closeness to the Creator, and who try to inculcate belief from their hearts to the community—sometimes with awe and sometimes with friendly love. God confers His favor on the apostle of the heart, who, in the first place, confines his or her glance to Him and thinks only of Him, seeking ways to find Him and taking advantage of every means to reach Him. Presenting this position in His Holy Presence, God, in return, reminds everybody that they should respect such people, and rewards this tiny piece of terrestrial loyalty with a great deal more of His celestial loyalty. Here is what is squeezed in a drop from that vast ocean of celestial compliment:

> Repulse not those who call upon their Lord in the morning and in the evening, desiring His face; they have no reckoning against you at all, and you have no reckoning against them at all. (Al-Anam 6:52)

The people mentioned here whom God warned His Prophet not to "repulse" were the very people frequenting the meetings of the Messenger of God, people who devoted themselves to God's consent.

Provided this devotion is wholehearted and sincere, it is always likely that God will bestow His blessings onto these kinds of people. The more that people aim to please God and the more wholeheartedly that they are attached to God, the more likely they are to be appreciated, rewarded and the more likely it is that they will become the subject of supreme conversations. The every thought, word and act of such people will become a luminous atmosphere in the next world, an atmosphere which can also be called "the smiling face of fate." Such fortunate people, who filled their sails with the white winds of their fortune, sail with special blessing toward Him, not attaching themselves elsewhere. What the Qur'an presents as a depiction of these people is worth seeing:

> Men whom neither merchandize nor selling divert from the remembrance of God or steadfastness in prayer or giving alms, who fear a day when hearts and eyes shall be upset; that God may recompense them for the best that they have done, and give them more out of His Grace; for God provides whom He pleases without measure." (An-Nur 24:37-38)

Having been stripped of all dejection and sorrow, and also having surrendered to God, and, therefore, being free of all troubles, this kind of free spirit has nothing more to discover. In comparison with such achievements, all the earthly blessings, passions, and pleasures are no different from empty plates left on filthy tables. With regard to the world and its contents, the beauties they aspire to in their spiritual worlds are beyond comparison. After all, what blooms or grows green in the spring and then grows pale in the summer cannot be conceived of as being any different. Being aware of this reality, eternity-oriented spirits disregard everything that does not signify any eternal content and walk along the corridors of their heart toward the vineyards and gardens, never ever attaching their hearts to the world or to other terrestrial trivia.

TODAY'S DEVOTEES

Sublime ideals, high objectives, influential and universal projects can only be realized by those who soar high, who remain firm, who proceed on their route steadily, who present a determined stance, and who are motivated by heavenly ecstasies. What we need now is not ordinary people, but rather people devoted to divine reality who think to a lofty degree; people who by putting into practice their thoughts lead, first of all their own nation, and then all people, to enlightenment and help them find God—in other words, dedicated spirits, people who think what needs to be thought, who know what needs to be known, who without hesitation practice what they know and who wander like Israfil, who is on the verge of blowing the last trumpet in order to prepare dead spirits for the Day of Resurrection, and who instill hope in everybody. These are people whose hearts beat with sincerity, who cry out the inspirations of their hearts by speaking if they are capable of expressing it, by writing if they can, by means of the magic of poetry if they are poets, and with the fascination of music if they are lovers of music.

When it comes to exemplifying these heroes on the stage, they journey throughout the world, ultimately with a spirit of sacred emigration, they whisper with the language of their hearts to those they visit, they promote love throughout their surroundings; they inculcate love in the spirits they meet and establish thrones of love in their bosoms. Through these people, those spirits that thirst for love and friendship are revitalized and it is to them that these revived spirits lend an ear. Both those who emigrate with this kind of feeling and those that welcome them are aloof from all waywardness and are sincere. There are no vested interests between the ones that speak and those that listen, between the ones that display the essence and meaning in their nature and those who observe, between the ones that support and the supported ones, between the ones that bring the bowl of life and those who are awakened to the reality. Nor is there any consideration other than that of God's consent. These profound and sincere relations emanate entirely from universal human values and from the common respect that is felt for them.

The roses blooming all over the world today take on their hue from the enlightened faces and the comprehension in the spirits of these people, the social geography is being embroidered with their thinking and it is as if all of humanity is humming these ageless melodies. Considering their sources, these pure feelings and thoughts may seem to be mere droplets. Nonetheless, for those who can conceive, the profound meaning held within them are like boundless seas, foaming with inspiration.

As is required by the task itself, this cavalry of the light, which appears to illuminate only their surroundings for a fleeting moment, are now competing, in the same way that rain clouds pour down on us bliss, joy, love, and hope, to turn those dry hearts that crave tolerance and love into the gardens of Paradise. It can be claimed that the Earth, from one end to the other, is heavy with the seeds they have scattered and is impatiently expecting a blessed birth. In the same way, all human beings are exhilarated to see the signs of this blessed event. Though the voices and tunes may vary, what is felt deep in the hearts is always the same. And the winds of dawn are bringing a voice from the river of life to Job and wafting the Abrahamic scent from Joseph's shirt to Jacob.

This can be regarded as our final attempt, our advancing to our true position, as well as being seen as an alternative message of revitalization addressed to humanity. As a matter of fact, nations that have been wrung with various crises have also been awaiting such a breeze of hope. How fortunate are the blessed cadre to be the fuse to such an event. And, again, how fortunate are the ones whose breasts are receptive to this breeze.

We sincerely believe that the hue and design of the world are going to change and that humanity will relax with these heroes who are dedicated to upholding the monuments of human values. In the future world, human thought will most probably intensify its light through these people; human goals will be reached and many of our ideals will be realized through them. These ideals will be realized to such an extent that they will transcend our most utopian dreams. Indeed, all these will certainly take place one day and, when the time comes those with empty hearts and gloomy fortunes will repent, weep, and ask for forgiveness from these enlightened spirits. However, it will be too late for them to compensate for opportunities missed. If only these evil-feeling harsh and rough spirits could be a bit more grateful and honest before the day arrives, a day when they will desperately feel regret, then they would not blacken their future.

Endeavoring to enlighten every part of the world with a devotion that is suitable for the companions of the Prophet, peace and blessings be upon him, disregarding their own desires and acting in order to live for others without ostentation—on the contrary, always acting humbly—these legendary heroes are displaying today, despite many negative factors, a generosity rarely matched in history; they have come to serve humanity. They are whispering something from the bottom of their hearts, creating a Paradise on Earth by planting new saplings everywhere, trying to express themselves and inviting everybody to eternity—always faithful, determined, decisive, and hopeful for the future. The path on which they walk may seem hazardous. They, however, are aware of this. They have already taken into account that the roads will be difficult and treacherous, that the bridges will be impassable and their roads will be blocked. They are also awaiting turmoil of hatred and enmity. It is true that they have an unshakable belief in the path that they follow. Yet, they are always aware of the possibility that they may encounter obstacles that they have not conceived of before. For this very reason, they take on these hardships as being peculiar to the divine path and they keep up their pace, never losing any enthusiasm. Against these hardships, they surrender to God, taking refuge in the unshakable fortress of belief, endeavoring to comprehend the era and the events in which they live and to walk to the horizon of God's consent, depending on His promise of achievement.

In fact, it is detrimental for anyone to dissuade these righteous people who live with a reconciliation of heart and intellect to give up the values in which they believe. Nor can anyone prevent them from acting in accordance with God's consent and from trying to inculcate their feelings and their Creator into the world. With this sense of responsibility and duty they have managed to stand like mountains and challenge storms and tempests, to struggle with the elements and, having discovered the secret of growing fruits in all seasons, to grow roses and to sing songs of roses.

As far as their acts are concerned, they are always as reliable as clockwork, and they are exemplars of renewal, freshness, and righteousness. They lack neither harmony in their behavior nor bitterness in their expressions. Their hearts are as pure and clear as those of the angels and their tongues are faithful interpreters of their inner profundity. In this sense, their attitude and acts are almost always objects of envy, and their expressions arouse excitement. What they incessantly think of in their inner realms is the consideration of God; in their expressions there is an evident profound love of God, a love of existence and tolerance, affection, care and forgiveness. Their unique objective is God's consent. Their indispensable passion is to study and interpret the universe and phenomena correctly. The virtual hue of their nature is love and the bearing of their breasts to people.

The moment they present their stance toward God with their deepest love, they melt and are able to penetrate the most solid of hearts and the harshest of natures with the magic key of love; there they try to live up to the distinction of the blessings of the Sublime Creator. They love and are loved; with a prophet-like ambition they stand like mountains against the most pitiless attacks. When looking around, they look with divine eyes. Neither do they collapse in furious storms, nor do they shake during the strongest quakes. They bear their breasts to the waves and the downpour that come, and always display generosity.

These valiant ones are aware of what it is necessary to undertake this enormous task of seeking attainment of God's consent and, therefore they are ready to receive it, no matter what the circumstances. In terms of their personalities, they are as minute and modest as a candle, designed to burn and to enlighten, and yet always motivated and ready to compete with saintly ones, even if they do not appear to be competitive. Even when they appear to be still, they are always lively, determined, and feverish in their inner activities. At times, they, like the seas, water their environment with their waves or make distant places cool with clouds composed of their vapor. Near or far, they provide the elixir of life everywhere, and they wander as they inspire revival in listless bodies that have suffered over the ages. They tirelessly relate the tales in their hearts to others and keep aloof from any gossip or disputes that might bring about hatred in society.

As always, they dream of being beneficial to people, they feel sincerely in the depths of their spirits the agony and depression of others, they adopt a welcoming stance to whoever visits them, listening to their problems and grieving for them; they seek out the grief-stricken ones and rush with people who share the same passion to relieve the pain of others. At times, they bravely face difficulties, and plant roses with determination, even in the midst of thorns. They are constantly singing of roses.

Sometimes, under the influence of great pain and grief, these people turn the hue of blood, like a rose that is mourning the seeds that it has sent out into the world. At other times they become nearly exasperated and their melodies turn into wails. Despite all this, they place their hands over their hearts, and murmuring "All is with God," they walk toward their purpose, smiling and turning the places they frequent into green gardens. The people to whom they give a hand, whom they have revived, feel as if they have drunk from the elixir of life. Their helping hands are luminous, like the White Hand of Moses. Their striving undoes all the spells of magicians, making all the pharaonic thoughts surrender.

They have such inspiration and wealth that the wealth of Croesus is trivial in comparison. They can even reserve the entire world with this wealth and richness if they wish. The scales of charity—which is their life—is always tipped on the generous side; so much so that it infuriates the devils.

They well know where to invest their lives. As a result, they are extremely good at bartering transient things for everlasting ones. Never do they waste their time, nor do they accept falling behind in service. Their moral exertion is elevated, their will power is strong, and their resolution constant. Belief and action are an important discipline of their hearts and behavior. They fear no one save God and are always upright. They stand upright and walk humbly toward their goal of enlightening the whole world. They breathe out their holy thoughts like the winds, sometimes scattering seeds around them, and at other times letting them rain down, distributing life over the surface of the Earth. Neither setbacks in their activities nor consecutive crises can shake them. They frequently renew their oaths and spend all the blessings God confers upon them on the reinforcement of their monumental spirits. Wherever religion, piety, and the approval of God can be found, it is there that they endeavor to stay; they race toward the fulfillment of His orders. They take such great pains to succeed in worldly affairs that people who see these valiant ones take them to be people of the world unaware of the Hereafter. When they see the love in them, however, they think of them as being of those of the highest rank.

They abhor being idle or wasting their lives. They are always active in restoring religious life by composing something if they are literate, or by presenting a pen to those who are literate; they always strive to continue to make their contributions in the caravan of service. They love knowledge, respecting the wise ones, making friends with sensitive people, and continuously mentioning the Beloved One in their conversations.

Even if there were no real people left on Earth, even if all the horizons were obscured by dust, even if the streets had been invaded by total depravity, even if the thorns were to outnumber the roses, even if the avenues were peopled with magpies and their singing drowned out that of the nightingales, even if wasps were to fly around the honey bowls, even if a terrifying jungle wilderness were to dominate the streets, even if there was no respect left for knowledge, even if knowledge had been driven from every door, even if humanity had become a victim of disloyalty, even if friendships had been forgotten and friends had become enemies, they would still stand unshakable and say, "I stand even though all the others have collapsed! Everywhere may turn to desert. But since I have my tears for moisture, it is not a problem. God has given me two feet on which to walk and two hands with which to work. I have belief as my capital, and my territory is as vast as my heart. Opportunities to restore the world are awaiting me. With these opportunities, I can turn the whole world into a heaven, God willing. Why worry about the future when this land is so fertile? Moreover, does not God promise to make one into a thousand in the other world?" And thus they advance, despite collapsed bridges and blocked roads. Like a river, they bring life to everything, extinguishing the fires that are in everyone and that are found everywhere. Or like fire, even though it puts itself out, they protect people against the cold. Like candles, they melt, yet, they provide light for thousands of eyes. The very road that they walk on is a common route for saints and it has never been witnessed that the walkers on this road have failed to arrive at their destinations.

They are constantly faithful and enthusiastic, and they are generous enough to spend freely from all their belongings in the name of God. They spend their lives at feasts of giving, hoping to find that what they have given of in this world has been multiplied. In their eyes, there is no rank higher than that of preserving the religion and representing it across the world. They take this goal as their raison d'etre and live accordingly. All they are aware of is this thought; they come together for the purpose of projecting it and for deepening their togetherness by connecting it with God. The residents of the highest heavens applaud them too and ease their way on the roads in verification of their holy mission.

Never do they consider their own comfort and they always have God in their minds. They uphold "virtue," promote human values, open their hearts to everyone in a prophet-like manner, and they live for others. In return for their generosity, God honors them with surprising privileges on a day when our feet and hands are of no use; He bestows them with feathers from the wings of the angels and awards them with a meeting with His holy Presence. God also includes them among the blessed ones, treating them as His special guests, and crowning all these blessings with His consent.

HUMAN BEINGS AND THEIR NATURE

Humans, the greatest mirror of the names, attributes and deeds of God, are a shining mirror, a marvelous fruit of life, a source for the whole universe, a sea that appears to be a tiny drop, a sun formed as a humble seed, a great melody in spite of their insignificant physical positions, and the source for existence all contained within a small body. Humans carry a holy secret that makes them equal to the entire universe with all their wealth of character; a wealth that can be developed to excellence.

Humans are the signs and interpreters of the Most Sublime One in that the qualities given to them in the name of God in this transient world are open to development, and in fact have already been developed. Humans are the brightest mirrors of their Master, mirrors that reflect significant expressions. All of existence becomes a legible book only with their understanding and foresight, and these are the true qualities that are exhibited. It can be said that "God" is the mere source of all the wealth of the entire universe; humans—together with everything in and around them—on the other hand, are the royal witnesses of their Master.

People who have truly found their paths to God through their essence act also as guides for others, as they have attained the title of being witnesses of God. Should you have a chance to meet such people, it means you can avoid confusion and avoid sin. If you have a vision, or in other words, if you are aware of His holy secret, it means you are able to experience everything in a different dimension. Of course, humans whose thoughts are as clear as their beliefs, whose behavior and manners are intended to please God, remind everybody of God whenever and wherever they appear. Such people arouse, unconsciously and unknowingly, the feeling that they are "witnesses of God."

Prophet Muhammad, the Pride of Humanity, peace and blessings be upon him, has achieved horizons beyond that of the angels with his abilities, which he later developed to an even higher level, was both the seed and the fruit of the tree of existence. However much humanity thanks

God for this family tree and its choice fruit, it is not enough. Essentially, the first to be remembered when the word "human" is pronounced is the Messenger of God, because there is no one that ranks higher than he. And yet, this exalted being was a fruit of the tree of life as well. In short, while the human being is the most honorable of those created, the Prophet is the pride of humanity.

When this entire boundless universe, with all of its riches, components, and history, is connected to humanity it becomes clear why the value of humankind transcends all. It can also be said that God created not only this world, but also the next, in the name of the realization of human perfection. God's Messenger sensed the other world as he was leading his life in this world, softening his pain here with expectations from the other world, experiencing heavens through the width of his faith even before he actually headed for Paradise, while also sharing with his companions whatever he sensed. It must be once again stated that despite his vastness, he was a human, the brightest and luminous fruit of the tree of humankind.

Humans, however, are far from accomplishing such an achievement due to their corporeality and sensuality. Moreover, it can also be claimed that when humans are unaware of themselves or of their existence then they are lower than other creatures. Yet, humans, with their intellects, beliefs, consciences, and spirits are observers and commentators of the holy secrets that are found hidden between the lines of life. So, humans, no matter how insignificant they appear they are the "highest example," they are more beloved than all others. Islam does not evaluate humankind without going to extremes. It is the only religion among all the belief systems which sees humans as being exalted creatures directed toward a special mission, equipped with superior potential and talents. According to Islam, humans are superior merely because they are human. "Truly We created human with real honor." Through their surrender to God and His Messenger, humans irrevocably secure this station. "Glory belongs to God, to His Messenger, and thus, to Muslims." With their striving and struggle on the Earth, they too become God's favorite. "Undoubtedly, We show those who strive on Our path the way to success and satisfaction; God is, of course, with those that worship Him as if they see Him." "The Most Merciful God creates love in the hearts of people for those that believe and act accordingly." The Qur'an exemplifies the superiority of humanity in all its various aspects with the above statement. Everything that humans are granted, namely their faith, good deeds, and creation, is built upon human values, like lacework woven on the threads of human nature. Humanity is conferred upon humans as a gift; no price is asked and nothing is expected in return.

All these human relations are built up within this significance and in this context and these relations are always affected by these. A human being, be they man or woman, young or old, white or black, is respectable, protected and inviolate. Their belongings cannot be taken away, nor can their chastity be touched. They cannot be driven out of their native land, and their independence cannot be denied. They cannot be prevented from living in accordance with their principles, either. Moreover, they are prohibited from committing such crimes against others as well. They do not have the right to inflict harm on this gift that is presented to them by God, for they only are in temporary possession of this bounty; God is the true owner of everything. Humans are only charged with protecting this transient trust. Humans are to defend and keep safe this gift. It is holy for them; they will not harm it, nor allow it to come to any harm. When necessary they will fight for it and die for it. Stressing the significance of the inalienable rights of humanity and emphasizing the superiority of humanity, the Sultan of the Word, peace and blessings be upon him, put it thus:

> He who is killed in the name of protecting his wealth is a martyr. He who is killed in the name of protecting his life is a martyr. He who is killed in the name of protecting his relations is a martyr. And he who is killed in the name of protecting his native land is a martyr.[1]

How close is humanity today to this level of understanding? I think that to answer this question would be outside the scope of this article.

In terms of faith and connected matters, humanity has been blessed with distinction. Truly, when compared to the entire universe, humanity is superior to the heavens and to the angels too. Everything on the Earth and in the sky is at its service, and they have the right to make use of these bounties. God confers this gift upon humanity because of its impo-

---

[1] Tirmidhi, *Diyat* 22, (1418,1421); Abu Dawud, *Sunna* 32, (4772); Nesai, *Tahrim*, 22, (7,115,116); Ibn Maja, *Hudud*, 21, (2580).

tence and neediness; God regards human beings as guests in this world. Only those who believe can appreciate such a gift. Believers who are aware of the true meaning of existence would thankfully accept all the universes as a palace for them, and they take all things, living and non-living, as their servants.

One step further, when talking about one who acts with the conscience and will power, and also delves into the depths of the heart and the spirit, then it becomes difficult to describe such a person. The only way to praise such a human being, a person who has developed their potential values and reached the peaks, is to quote Akif[2]:

He is created more exalted than even the angels,
All the worlds are hidden within him and the realms are contained in him.

Now, after God has bestowed all these on us, what is expected from us as humans? This is what is really important. Whether we discuss such an issue or not is a separate matter. If only everybody were aware that such a great responsibility has befallen them.

---

[2] Mehmed Akif Ersoy: The renowned Turkish poet who also wrote the Turkish National Anthem

THE INNER PROFUNDITY OF HUMANKIND

The human being is the essence and the vital element of being, the index and core element of the universe. Human beings are at the center of creation; all other things, living or non-living, compose concentric circles around them. It could be said that the Exalted Creator has oriented every creature toward human beings, and He has oriented human beings toward His Divine Attraction by making them aware of the fact that this is the point where support and expectation of help can be found. Taking into account all the honor that has been granted to humanity, compared with all the rest of creation, humanity must be seen as the voice that expresses the nature of things, the nature of events and, of course, the nature of the All-Powerful One Who is behind everything, as well as being understood as a heart that encompasses all the universes. With human beings, creation has found its interpreter and matter has been distilled through the cognition of people, finding its spiritual meaning. The monitoring of things is an ability peculiar to human beings, their being able to read and interpret the book of the universe is a privilege, and their attribution of everything to the Creator is an exceptional blessing. Their quiet introspection is contemplation, their speech is wisdom, and their conclusive interpretation of all things is love.

Humans are the ones who have been granted the privilege to rule and make use of creation; and humans are the ones who reveal all the aspects of the truth behind natural phenomena, offering these to the Creator. Humans sense and discern the relationship between humanity, the universe, and the Creator—a relationship which leads them to knowledge. They discover their potential and depths, surpassing the angels as they are granted the ability to reflect the grandeur of the ocean in a single drop and to reflect all the suns within a single atom. Having honored the Earth, humanity's heels have become the crowns of those who were previously created, and their being created on the Earth has been the pride of this physical world related to the spiritual beings in heavens. If we think of the whole of existence as an immense ocean, then the human being is its most precious pearl. If the universe is an exhibition hall, with all its glories on display, then the human being is its appreciating visitor. If things and events are a captivating harmony of balances, then the human being is the sensitive spectator. In the light of faith-oriented thought and the healthy consciousness of humanity, existence, which used to seem quiet and surrounded by darkness, has been illuminated, and it has gained beauty—making our hearts feel as if we were in Paradise. Until the time when humanity ascended to their throne on Earth, the angels and other spiritual beings bore the flag that proclaimed the truth on the horizons of the spiritual realm. The flag, honored by the advent of humanity, started to wave in the heights of the mortal realm, and this globe—so small when compared to the skies—has become equal with the heavens by becoming the horizon of the realms beyond. Humanity has always been the crown of creation; this has been true for as long as faith has been the source of joy, for as long as Islam has been the code of life,[1] for as long as the knowledge of God and love have been the inner dynamics. The Earth is dependent on the light that is diffused by humanity . . . this light has been granted by the Almighty, out of His special favor. This special favor has honored humanity, making it the rarest of roses in this garden of beauty. Imam al-Ghazali[2] described this elegance in the following way; "the present creation cannot be more aesthetic, beautiful, or fascinating." Humanity can be seen as the sole nightingale of this world, a world which is but a shadow of Paradise.

It would not be an exaggeration to say that these galleries—nestled one within the other—have been arranged and designed solely for humanity. It would not be an overstatement to say that this world has been created as the garden for this rarest of roses, or that the sea of existence has been created as the womb of this pearl; rather it would be a modest expression of the true state of things. As a matter of fact, the whole of existence, in a way, has been interpreted and voiced in unison via humanity, for humanity, and at humanity's service; it is virtually dependent upon humanity; and in terms of humanity's dependence upon the Creator

---

[1] The faith revealed to humankind starting with Adam has always been the same; the faith has been perfected with Prophet Muhammad and the Qur'an, and it was given the name *Islam* by God.

[2] Imam al-Ghazali (1058-1111): An important Muslim jurist, who came to be known as *Hujjat al-Islam* (Proof of Islam). He is considered to be the Reviver of the fifth Islamic century. *Ihya' 'Ulum al-Din* [Reviving the Religious Sciences] is his most celebrated work.

Who has yielded everything to the command of humanity, such an intense relationship is felt between humanity and God that the purpose of all of creation can be nothing other than humankind and their servanthood to God.

In fact, the needs of humanity are so extensive that they cover all of creation, and are so deep that they extend to eternity. Above all, human beings have been created for eternity, and they long for it. The wishes and demands of human beings are boundless and their expectations are infinite. Even if the whole world were to be given to humanity, its appetite would not be satisfied nor would its ambitions cease. Explicitly or not, human souls expect another eternal abode, not to mention the fact that they hanker for the continuation of this transient world. Anybody who owns a heart that is open to the truth wishes to see Paradise—which is no more than an insignificant shadow of His Grandeur, and they wish to see the Exalted Creator in all His magnificence and beauty.

People who can feel and sense the truth in the facet of things and occurrences, and who are aware of their position in the universe are on this journey. At the same time, these people are appreciative of themselves and are open to showing respect for their Lord. As for those in opposition, they cannot be said to feel respect for either themselves or for their Lord. Moreover, they cannot even recognize their Lord as they should. Even if they should do so by chance, they are not able to glorify Him as His Greatness requires. Attaining true humanity depends on the recognition of the relationship between the Lord and His servants. Paradoxically, human beings, who are considered to be more blessed than the angels in terms of their potential, are likely to sink lower than the most contemptible of beings if they do not sense or appreciate this relation; this is stated in the verse: . . . *those are like cattle, or rather are even more misguided.* (Al-Araf 7:179)

The recognition of this association, which is generally phrased as belief, is a position through which a human being can attain virtual humanity, and from which they can ascend above all other creatures. As for disbelief, another term that indicates the lack of such an association, it turns human beings into beasts. Societies formed by such individuals suffer from severe resentment, fury, lust, greed, mendacity, hypocrisy, envy, deception, and intrigue; that is, disbelief creates societies in which everyone must be on alert. In any case, the people who have yielded to these evil habits can never be recognized as being a nation or a society, rather they can merely be described as being non-conscious masses. When Diogenes was searching for a human being in the street during the daytime with the aid of a lantern, he was probably trying to counsel or show his reaction against such people. Mark Orel, the author of *Thoughts*, another person who reflects the same idea from a different perspective, says "Every morning, when I join other people, I think to myself: 'Today, I will meet some beasts in human form again. If I reach the evening without startling them or without being bitten by any of them, I will consider myself happy." Rabi'a al-'Adawiya took a more serious and reactionary approach to the matter: "I hardly ever see a human on the street. What I see are some foxes in front of shops, some wolves and other creatures snarling at each other. . . . For a moment, I saw a half-human and I arranged my veil regarding him," Obviously, these people do not intend to condemn all members of humanity. Rather, they are trying to depict the inner worlds of those who have turned their inherent human values into selfishness. If people do not control their behavior according to the purpose of their creation or control their inner worlds with respect to their outward appearance in an effort to eliminate inconsistencies, then they are quite likely to appear as those described by Mark Orel and Rabi'a al-'Adawiya.

Among these people you can sometimes come across people whose visage appears to be cheerful even though they are miserable inside. They, too, are another type. One philosopher has compared them to a building with two different sides. Its facade is clean, splendid, and impressive, whereas the side facing the rear is dirty, shabby, and derelict. When we see such a building on the street, we say "very nice," making a prejudgment. When we examine the other side, however, we condemn the building that we so eagerly praised a few minutes before. The same is true for people. We will always be misled if we evaluate them from a single aspect. What matters is to see them as they really are and to make some efforts to improve their rear walls, as well as considering them in accordance with their good sides.

Human beings are the children of their own attributes and attitudes. We can judge which characteristic or attribute is dominant according to the behavior that a person demonstrates, good or evil. Sometimes people can turn into monsters, ready to bite those closest to them. Sometimes people turn into "Josephs," their faces shining like the moon, illuminating the dungeon, and rendering it a corridor to Heaven. Sometimes they become so pure that even the angels envy them. And sometimes they are so wicked that even the devils feel ashamed.

Human beings can sometimes become so heavenly that they reach the height of the skies; yet sometimes they are so mean that they become worse than snakes or venomous insects. Human beings are creatures who can demonstrate such a wide range of behavior that they can possess corrupt qualities alongside their merits; and they can be readily tempted to evil, in spite of possessing lofty virtues. Faith, wisdom, love, and spiritual pleasures are as much a part of them as their own hearts are; loving others, embracing everyone, living with feelings of kindness and making others live with the same is the ultimate goal of their lives. Eliminating evil through goodness, loving "love," and being in a constant struggle against feelings of enmity are as sweet to them as the whisper of their own soul. Evil feelings, such as greed, resentment, hatred, lust, slander, mendacity, hypocrisy, corruption, opportunism, egoism, cowardliness, and ambition stalk them stealthily, waiting for a weak moment. They might be seized by evil feelings and passions, becoming enslaved by them, making them evil to the utmost degree, in spite of the fact that the same people have the potential to be the masters of the universes through their virtues and good behavior. Even if such a person may seem to be free, in reality they are the most enslaved; freedom can only be achieved by success in the inner struggle—a struggle termed "the greater jihad" in Islam. Improvement of the inherent potential and the attainment of a second nature that is open to a relationship with the Almighty depend on success in this struggle, a struggle that takes place deep in the soul, on whether or not those undergoing the struggle appreciate this victory, and on whether or not they bend their heads to the level of their feet, forming a circle in their modesty and humility.

The weak-willed, who are unable to pass beyond superficiality to look into their inner depths, to see the gaps and defects within their nature as well as the merits of their souls, and who are unable to restore themselves every new day, can never progress in their inner worlds. Even if they continue to talk about making progress, whenever they try to step forwards they slide ever backwards. Such people cannot manage to rid their eyes, ears, tongues, lips, hands, or feet of their captivity to their own egos; they live as slaves throughout their lives without even being aware of this tragic fact. To tell the truth, these people, mere slaves of their corporeal desires, are in a pitiable condition.

To love and care for those who preserve and improve their humanity is to give them what they deserve. As for the rest, they should be shown love and sympathy so that they can be saved from the grasp of their evil feelings and passions. Such an attitude is an expression of caring for human beings, whom God created as worthy of respect . . . and the human being is an entity created to be loved.

HUMANITY
AND ITS RESPONSIBILITIES

If humanity is the vicegerent of God on Earth, the favorite of all His creation, the essence and substance of existence in its entirety and the brightest mirror of the Creator—and there is no doubt that this is so—then the Divine Being that has sent humanity to this realm will have given us the right, permission and ability to discover the mysteries imbedded in the soul of the universe, to uncover the hidden power, might and potential, to use everything to its purpose, and to be the representatives of characteristics that belong to Him, such as knowledge, will, and might. While people are involved in existence and fulfill their title of vicegerent, they will not run into any obstacles that they cannot surmount, they will not experience contradictions in their relationships with things; they should roam freely in the corridors of events, not experiencing stress when they discover the abilities that are stored within their nature, not being held back by unexpected hindrances when realizing their hopes.

It is clear that with the success and accomplishments that have been achieved up until today that people have been sent to the world with specific instruments and opportunities. Indeed, despite all the problems caused by human weakness, if we consider the point that we, as humans, have reached and the successes we have achieved so far, it is obvious that nothing hinders us. Even if we make mistakes in some acts, we have produced many successes; we have been given will power and have tried to transform existence, We have changed the world by developing it, and wittingly or not, we are the mirror that reflects the new cadre described when the Great and Just One stated *I will create a vicegerent on Earth* (Al-Baqara 2:30).

It is true that people have at times justified the fear of the angels who at the time of human creation predicted the bloodshed; but alongside this partial evil, the good deeds with broad, lasting, and heavenly results achieved by humanity are not insignificant, either. Indeed, countering the comparative evil, there have always been relative good deeds in the actions of humanity. The righteous subjects of God are the moons and suns of humanity; in order to counter evil and injury, the pious and those close to Him, the sincere ones and the prophets, have spread good deeds around them; these deeds have been experienced in every place. The right to bear the title of vicegerent—given into the safe-keeping of humanity—has been given its due and more, especially by those who are conscious of what the aim of creation is. Believers who have grasped the spirit of creation understand that they have been sent to this world endowed with a different way of thinking and believing and with different responsibilities; thus they must accord their behavior and attune their attitude with this way. That believers have to behave like this is understood through their apparent and hidden abilities and also through the Qur'an, which frequently stresses the relationship between due value and the attitudes and behavior of the believer. In the Qur'an, Almighty God emphasizes the most important goal of being created in the human form, of deserving the status of vicegerent and of being given these abilities by saying *I have created jinn and humans for no other reason than to act as my subjects (through knowing Me)* (Adh-Dhariyat 51:56). That is, such a primary, clear statement is both a call for communal responsibility and a call for giving thanks for the things that have been bestowed on humanity, as well as being an important caution that focuses our attention on the basic duty of being a vicegerent on Earth.

Submission, the state of being a subject of God in its broadest sense, is the celestial title of being in harmony with existence and things, of being well-adjusted to the world and all that is in it, of making one's way through the mysterious hallways of the universe without getting lost, in short, of protecting the balance of one's inner harmony with existence. The righteous person should put up his standard at the point where the fundamental principles of existence and the orders for rules of conduct meet; without providing such a balance it would be impossible to continue on the way, respecting and protecting human values.

The success of humankind in protecting their relationship with existence and the physical world can be determined by the degree to which they act in accordance with the purpose of all of creation. In contrast, those who do not act according to this purpose, and those who may partially neglect their duties, always clash with the gyrating spheres and grinding wheels of the universe, in addition to suffering from their own purposelessness and lack of supervision. In this way, they are able to turn this world, which is their home, and which could be like a palace, into a hell. Even today, some tremble in fear of the near future, as they are aware that it is possible to turn the world into such a hell.

It is an indisputable fact that God alone, who has prepared the universe as if it were a series of galleries, like a book, and Who then put it at the convenience of humanity, can know the nature of the compatibility between mathematical laws—the laws under which existence operates—and the general, deliberate behavior of humanity. Within the framework of these messages that emanate from this source of knowledge, obeying orders that are concerned with the rules of conduct is a unique way to comprehend the secrets of the principle of existence; it is also a way to ensure complete harmony with these principles. Indeed, it is only in this way that humanity can escape coming into conflict with laws that apply to all existence without experiencing feelings of loss, and feel the peace of being at home, being in a palace. On the other side of the coin, the separation of people from their Creator, their alienation from Him will only lead them into a vicious circle of separation and alienation where they will be in conflict with existence and phenomena. It is not possible for such a person to recover.

Humanity's vicegerency for the Creator takes place in an unusually broad sphere that encompasses acts ranging from believing in Him and worshiping Him to understanding the mysteries within things and the cause of natural phenomena, and therefore being able to interfere in nature. Throughout their lives, genuine human beings first arrange their feelings and thoughts, regulating their individual and social life through various forms of worship, balancing familial and social relationships by their actions and by carrying the standard of their species from the depths of the Earth to the expanse of the Heavens, doing what is necessary to be a genuine successor. At the same time, these genuine human beings try to exercise their freewill in a constructive manner, working with and developing the world, protecting the harmony between existence and humanity, reaping the bounties of the Earth and the Heavens for the benefit of humanity, trying to raise the hue, form and flavor of life to a more humane level within the framework of the Creator's orders and rules.

This is the true nature of a vicegerent and at the same time this is where the meaning of what it is to be a servant and lover of God can be found. Again, at one and the same time, we can find here the point of convergence between the slightest effort and the most generous gift. The action that will lead people to this point in one step is worship. Worship is not simply the performance of a set of particular movements, as some believe; it is what we call complete submission and the acceptance of a broad responsibility . . . and along with the title of vicegerent it is the clearest expression of the relationship amongst humans, the universe, and God. If worship is the placing of a consciousness of being bound to God into one's heart, if it is the liberation of one's self from all types of slavery, if it is the title of seeing, hearing and feeling the beauty, order and harmony that belong to Him in every molecule of existence—and there is no doubt that it is this and nothing else—then worship is the most immediate way to turn our face to God, with everyone and everything, the soundest and most immediate way of associating everything with Him; it is also a way in which we can renew these apparent and genuine bonds at every minute of the day. No one who consciously walks upon such a road will doubt for a moment that they are a servant, and that their sole duty is to give the bestowed honor of vicegerency its due value. Such people will try to live and let the fleeting life of this world be lived to the full; they will try to inscribe their names in the ink of effort and sincerity wherever they go. They will try to inspire similar feelings in all the places where their hands and their name reach. They will try to reach such a depth that it will fill all the worlds, while inscribing their thoughts on every bit of time and space—thoughts that are bound to Him. They will try to live with a greatness of intention that will be great enough to enable them to appreciate eternity and thus imbue them with an inner peace that comes from being connected to eternity. They will walk in the greatest spiritual ecstasy, overstepping the boundaries of existence and reaching Eden.

And if such people can reflect this duty of service and responsibility in the work and service that they carry out, if they are able to pursue the essence of the fundamental principles of existence and obey the orders concerning rules of conduct, rather than binding themselves to the consequences of their actions, then any unexpected outcome will not cause them to feel defeated, nor will their enthusiasm wane. Instead, they will carry out all deeds of service with a joy of worship and be aware of the gratitude of having reached the apex of true believers, an apex which is considered to be the highest level of existence. Such people will never fall into despair, never panic and never feel exhausted due to troubles encountered on the road. Such people are far removed from despair, panic, or exhaustion; they rush forward, feeling the intense flavor hidden in the essence of the deed, saying in echo of Rumi:

I have become a slave,
I have become a slave, I have become a slave;
Slaves are happy when they are set free,
But I am honored and happy to become a slave.

These people measure and evaluate the work and the deed not through the result attained, but rather directly by how the duty was performed, whether it has been performed with a pure heart and whether it corresponds to the approval of God. In this manner, they do not limit the vastness of their subjection by connecting it to any price or reward, they do not adulterate divine and holy deeds with deeds that are bound to the Earth; and these people assess their deeds as being naught before the infinite power of the All-Mighty, and lead their lives in this expansive dimension that they feel in their hearts.

People who feel this breadth and depth with all of their emotions and thoughts, and who feel it in the deepest depths of their heart reach the contentment of being a subject of the All-Mighty, and are freed from various pressures. Not only are they freed, but they have saved their humanity by being aware in their conscience that they are a servant at a gate that will not crush or block out the light; that is, this is where a person attains real freedom. While one's behavior on route to the appreciation of the blessings from God, blessings that come even if one rejects them, is a duty, the fact that God continues to send these gifts through other various wavelengths is a second blessing.

If human beings are the vicegerent of God on Earth—they are unique in the fact that they have the potential to be the candidate—then they will work for God, start everything with the mention of God, be offended for God, love for God, and intervene in existence only within the framework of what has been granted by Him, performing every duty with the aspiration of being His deputy. Thus, people will not take personal pride in their success, they will not fall into despair in defeat. They will not boast of their abilities, nor will they deny the benevolence of the All-Gracious; they will know that everything comes from Him and will consider all deeds done as their duty. Their confidence will be renewed with every success and they will turn toward their Lord, call out their trust and loyalty in God and will, in the words of Akif, repeat to themselves a few times each day:

> *Trust in God, hold tight to effort, and unify with the Celestial Will,*
> *If there is a path, this is it; I know of no other that leads there.*

This will be their hymn. They will always be tensed, always determined, always enthusiastic and comprehending of their duty, because they tie their behavior and actions to the purpose of being a subject of God; they will not become arrogant with their victories and successes, nor will they feel the desperation of defeat. They will be of the same determination and resolve whether they walk along a straight path or down an incline or climb the steepest slopes.

Indeed, while such people are able to put on a performance that inspires all their mental, spiritual, and emotional abilities to take action, action which surpasses the imagination, in order to fulfill the duty of deputy, they are also pensively expectant, immersed in submission, full of hopes for alternatives and always in expectation of connecting themselves with God.

Here is the genuine believer and the best model of the votary of truth! So many who have made this connection have come and gone, and they have transformed the paths on which they have crossed the hallways of heaven . . . and still many walk on these paths toward the days promised by All-Merciful. Those who have come and gone and those who follow in their footsteps have all lived and are living as heroes of these characteristics that are peculiar only to themselves.

AN IDEAL SOCIETY

G roups formed by disorganized and sinful (disobedient) individuals are merely crowds with no moral or esthetic values, people
who are far removed from the thought of doing good. On the
other hand, ideal, or complete, people carry the qualities of angels, and
are monuments of human foresight and comprehension.

We see these qualities in the following Qur'anic verse, as well as in
many others:

> We have indeed created man in the most perfect form and nature. (At-
> Tin 95:4)

The people to whom this verse refers understand it to mean that they
are the most adorned and beautiful forms of creation, material or spiritual. They enjoy the perfect state of creation, and are conscious of the
unlimited gifts that they have received.

Let us try to understand this verse: Humanity took on the responsibility that the Earth, the sky, and the mountains rejected, in fear that they
would not be able to shoulder this duty. They perceived that humanity
was the sole candidate for reaching immortality.

Humans may be considered as traveling on the path to becoming a
complete person as long as they continue to develop the gifts with which
they were adorned and to live according to divine inspiration.

Such mysteries, like the meaning of life and death, the reason of existence, and our responsibilities, are always on the minds of such people.
They think deeply concerning sins, doing good, and being pious. The
meaning of catastrophes that harm humanity agitates their minds; the
light of divine wisdom shines in their hearts; the rays of this light are
reflected on their souls.

All of this allows them to see behind the curtain. Their astonishment
and amazement turns into love and affection, and they turn to the Creator of their souls and feel contentment. Souls at this level do not let Divine benevolence go to their heads, nor are they shaken by its loss, for

they see benevolence and loss as one and the same thing, and understand that reward and punishment are also the same. While others are spoiled by such favors and descend into pessimism at the first sign of trouble, ideal people gain even when they seem doomed to lose. They manage to grow roses in the desert, to produce sugar from a dry cane.

Ideal people know that they are being continually tested and refined so that they may attain bliss. Even though they face fatal catastrophes and fall into the most terrible whirlpools, even in the most helpless and distressing moments, they hear comforting and consoling whispers from the other world; whispers that come from their innermost soul, and they bow in gratitude and admiration.

Such people have absolute confidence and trust in God, because they believe and trust in that omnipresent and omnipotent Immortal Power. The pure belief dwelling in the depths of their hearts, their perception that gives them unbelievable perspectives, and their knowledge and thoughts raise them to such a point that they can almost hear a voice say: "Fear not, nor be grieved, and receive good news of the garden which you were promised!"[1] and then they witness the most wonderful pleasures of all.

Ideal people try to remain removed from sin, for they have designed their lives according to the Divine Law in which they believe so sincerely. And, because they always struggle against their egos they have no time or energy to engage in ignorant pastimes or bohemian lifestyles. They are always on the look out for the beauty of their Friend, their minds are on the Hereafter, their hearts are bright and colorful gardens open to visits from spiritual beings, and they themselves are travelers in and explorers of this mystic land and atmosphere.

Worldly people who are enslaved by their egos live only to fulfill their carnal desires. Never content, they feel no tranquility. But ideal people are always at peace with themselves. They are content and, furthermore, they place their knowledge and understanding at the service of humanity. They courageously devote themselves to ridding the world of injustice and tyranny, and are not afraid to protect their land and honor. And, at times, they gracefully spread their wings of forgiveness over their brothers and sisters.

---

[1] Fussilat 41:30.

Knowing that everything but God is mortal and will fade away, ideal people do not bow before anything or anyone other than God. They resist the seductive attractions of the material world . . . they assess and use in the way of God that which has been bestowed upon them, just like heavenly beings . . . they examine all that occurs like a scientist in a laboratory . . . they dedicate their lives to humanity and leave a much better world for coming generations.

Ideal people constantly pursue God's blessing and strive to be true. Neither their bodily passions nor spiritual goals cast doubts on their sincerity. They value all servants of God as being the greatest of people, and appreciate each as their peer. In their hearts, they melt any harshness or bad feelings that emanates from others, thus showing how kindness defeats wrong.

In their bright atmosphere, spears of lightning fade away. . . Nimrod, a merciless emperor who ordered Prophet Abraham to be thrown into the fire, saw his flames die down and turn into a green garden that soothed harsh and ill-tempered souls.

Most of us have not reached this level yet. We cannot confront wrong-doing with kindness. We confront harshness with harshness and hate with hate. We convince ourselves that our thoughts are objective and not really our own selfish desires. Thus we besmirch our struggle in the way of God and lose, although we set out to win. If it were not for the beauty, attractiveness, and life-giving rays of the Qur'an, the misconceptions we have caused and the bad examples we have set would have prevented us from seeing this day.

SUFISM AND METAPHYSICS

THE MEANING OF LIFE

Are all of life's hardships worth enduring? The answer depends on what our goal is in living. In fact, understanding the purpose of life is a slow and absorbing process. We sense its mystery while reflecting upon our existence and humanity. Therefore, our concept of life evolves gradually throughout our lives.

The purpose of our creation is obvious: to reach our utmost goals of belief, knowledge, and spirituality; to reflect on the universe, humanity, and God, and thus prove our value as human beings. Fulfilling this ideal is possible only through systematic thinking and systematic behavior. Thought will provoke action, and thereby start a "prosperous cycle." This cycle will produce more complex cycles, which are generated from between the spirituality of the heart and the knowledge of the brain, thereby developing ever-more complex ideas and producing more ambitious projects.

Carrying out such a process calls for strong belief, consciousness, and understanding. People with these characteristics can perceive and analyze the unreflective lifestyles of others. Such people reflect, do what they believe to be right, and then reflect upon their behavior, thereby continually deepening their thoughts and acquiring new ideas. They believe that only those who reflect deeply are productive, and that the pain and suffering they endure make their belief stronger and more acceptable.

They live a life of reflection by observing creation every day, sometimes reading it like a book or embroidering their minds with the wisdom they acquire. Believing that the universe was created to be "read" and understood, they see the purpose of our creation as nothing less than that.

On its own, existence is the very bounty that leads us to a prosperous path of bounties. Given this, we should appreciate its value. Since we have been created along with an entire universe of bounties, we must then use these gifts and benefit from them.

To reach this goal, we must use our will power, a voice noticed and attached a value only by the All-Powerful One, and develop our abilities and skills to their furthest extent, thus proving ourselves to be willful beings. Our duty is to reflect upon our place in life, our responsibilities, and our relationship with this vast universe. We should use our inner thoughts to explore the hidden side of creation. As we do so, we will begin to feel a deeper sense of our selves, see things differently, witness that events are not what they seem, and realize that they are trying to communicate something to us.

I believe that this should be the real purpose of life. We are the most important living creations in this universe. In fact, we are more like its soul and essence, from which the rest of the universe develops. Given this, we should reflect upon and observe the universe so that we may realize and fulfill the purpose of our creation. Our duty is to hunt for insights and divine joys in our hearts and souls, for only this way of life can move us beyond the frustrating endeavors of a totally materialistic and painful life.

What makes this painful life worth living is the joy we feel while moving along the path and receiving these gifts. Those who walk this path are constantly delighted with various insights. They run enthusiastically toward their final goal like a river flowing to the sea.

We do not believe that happiness comes from temporary exterior sources. True happiness comes from within, deepens along with our relationship with God, and turns into an eternal life in heaven . . . yes, this is how joyful we are. Our inner world is a realm of Divine insights, and our consciousness is a follower of these insights. As we beckon and wait all our lives for the slightest glimpse, our souls sing in utter pleasure:

> Our hearts are your throne, O King! Welcome to our hearts!
> M. Lutfi[1]

Our generation needs guides to teach us how to achieve such belief, thought processes, and happiness. Their guidance will allow our youth to enjoy being young and live upright lives. They will experience existence

---

[1] Muhammed Lutfi Efendi (1868-1956): Also known as Alvarlı Efe, as he served as imam in Alvar village of Erzurum for 24 years, he was one of the most famous scholars, poets, and a spiritual persons of Turkey.

and non-existence as the same thing once they feel immortality in their souls; they will be able to realize that they can do more than they thought in only a couple of seconds. They will see the afterlife reflected in everything and thereby witness endless life; they will discover that life is worth living; they will witness that all creation rises and sets in their souls; and they will journey through the dimensions of their souls, just as if they were traveling through galaxies, observing infinity within the dimensions that they have reached during this mortal life.

FAITH: A PARTICULAR PERSPECTIVE

The word "faith," "*iman*" in Arabic, in the framework of descriptions or from the point of view of science and epistemology, comes from the root "*emn ü eman*," which means to be safe from fears, to believe, to promise, to trust, to procure the safety of others. It is a word that has the meaning of being safe and sturdy. Believing in God, attesting to His existence, making a confession in the conscience and making a proclamation from the heart, these are some of the meanings that are conferred upon this word from the point of view of linguistic tradition.

A person who puts faith in God is called a "*mumin.*" A *mumin* is the attester and representative par excellence of all the characteristics that we have seen above—here we could also talk about the issue of the relationship of deeds and faith, and whether deeds are included within the description of faith, but for the moment we shall not dwell on these topics. *Mumin*s are indeed heroes of attestation, proclamation and representation with their common sense, their ability to see and perceive, their pure intellect that has been enlightened by revelations, their vast and objective comprehension, their strong and encompassing vision, their fastidiousness and sensitivity in matters of responsibility, their determination and resolution against evil, their pursuit of greatness throughout their entire life and the safeguarding of these high ideals, the ability to keep alive their feelings, awareness and will, their curiosity that leads to the penetration of the essential meaning of things and their deep understanding in interpreting phenomena, their believing and trusting in God and being known among people as people of trust, their attestation to the existence of the Just One and their ability to always stay true to Him, their being known as people who can be trusted with anything and being remembered as people of credibility to whom one can turn at all times, their being remembered thus and being accepted by the all as thus, their being the means for the remembrance of God and also being understood as people who direct those who around them toward Him. They are heroes of attestation, proclamation, and representation, in the true sense of the word.

Even if every believing person is not a hero of faith and Islam to the same degree, it is clear how significant the feeling of belief is for each individual. For a start, this feeling is of the highest value in the nature of humanity, with regards to creation. Even though those who do not believe try to be fulfilled, satisfied, or more precisely, try to find distraction, they feel themselves to be in a vacuum. All time and space is a vacuum for them, today and tomorrow are all the same. Such people feel this vacuum deep down in their soul, they voice the smothering feelings that turn to senseless ravings thus:

> *All is emptiness; the ground is a void,*
> *the skies are a void, the heart, the conscience is a void;*
> *I want to hold on, but there is no where in sight to hang on.*
>
> Tevfik Fikret[1]

And a believing soul, giving expression to the chilling nature of the denial of truth and any attempt to conceal it, yet at the same time, expressing the peace that faith promises, simply calls out thus:

> *A rusted heart which has no faith is a burden for the breast.*
>
> Akif

A votary of the heart who is determined to dissolve the corrosion of these rusted hearts, on the other hand, will say: "Genuine pleasure, enjoyment without pain, happiness with no sorrow is possible only within the sphere of faith and its truths," so "those who want to enjoy the pleasures of life should enliven it with faith, adorn it with the deeds that God has prescribed for humanity and protect it by avoiding deeds that He has told us not to commit," for "when one manages to direct oneself toward the path of eternal life, however miserable and troublesome one's life may be, as one considers this world to be the waiting lounge for Heaven, one accepts everything contentedly and gives thanks" (paraphrased from Bediüzzaman). Such people would enlighten our horizons with their healing words and cause our hearts to feel the magic of faith.

---

[1] Tevfik Fikret (1867-1915): One of the leading poets of *Edebiyat-ı Cedide* [New Literature] at the turn of the twentieth century.

With regards to its content and essence, faith is a fruit which has been picked from the realm of life and presented to our souls; it is the heavenly river of *Kawthar*, from which our hearts have been made to drink, a meaning soaked in by the lips of our hearts, a monument of divine light in our hearts, shaped by the ruler and compass of meaning, feeling, conscience and understanding. Heroes of faith who repair and restore their hearts and feelings with faith and understanding have already discovered the secret of turning their world of the mind into the heavens; they have entered the route of eternal happiness and have been freed from all other quests. Since "there is always the existence of a spiritual heaven in faith, and a spiritual hell in blasphemy and sins . . . then indeed, just as faith carries the spiritual seed of the Tree of Heaven, so too does blasphemy store the spiritual seed of Hell" (paraphrased from Bediüzzaman).

In fact, if a soul has taken wings by means of faith, it will not loiter in any other doorway, nor will it stoop so low as to beg from another; a person with such a soul will not bow their head before anyone else; they will act bravely in the face of everything, to the degree of the strength of their faith. Indeed, "faith is both light and power. Those who attain true faith can challenge the universe and, in proportion to their faith's strength, be relieved of the pressures of events."[2] This is because "faith leads to testifying to God's uniqueness, this testimony leads to submission, submission leads to putting oneself in God's hands, and this last leads to happiness here and in the hereafter." Such monuments of faith use their hearts like spiral staircases that lead to the realms beyond the heavens and with this, they beat their wings in the direction of the angelic heights where angels and spirits[3] meet. At times, the angels and spirits whisper things in the ears of these people, and at times they present the spirits with garlands of comprehension and become people of distinction in that realm. And if such people have been able to deepen their faith with learning and have adorned that learning with spiritual tastes, then, indeed, it is then that they start to fly to horizons that even angels yearn for; they are always on the look out for destinations that Lord would approve of . . . spending their time with those deserving in Heaven and dreaming of the "highest Heaven." To be of a value great enough to be lifted to the highest Heaven with the light of faith and to attain a value

---

[2] Nursi, Bediüzzaman Said, *The Words*, Twenty-third Word.
[3] Martyrs and the ones who are believed to live in a different dimension.

befitting Heaven is the destiny of those who have faith; to stoop down to the level of dark denial and to become one of the people of Hell is the unfortunate end of the blasphemer; the latter is a topic unto itself, but it would take too many pages to make this analysis here.

Those who can see people of faith with their particular depths, remember God through them. Those who feel their breath find life as if they have been visited by Messiah and those who listen to the voices coming from their heart become intoxicated on the wine of the words, as if they have reached the company of the Sultan of Eloquence. Indeed, a soul which has completed its garments with faith and what faith promises is no longer in need of anything else. Through being elevated toward God, such a person is still powerful in weakness with the will of God, rich through His wealth in their poverty, and despite being small, is one of greats. This is due to the fact that such people depend on the eternal will of their Master when their powers of choosing and will are not sufficient. They trust in His will upon matters which surpass their abilities; when shaken in matters of this life, they take refuge in the orchards and gardens of life eternal. When the anxiety of death envelops their horizon, they throw themselves onto the open climate of eternal life. Faced with matters which they cannot resolve with their intellect and understanding, they resort to the glowing climate of the Qur'an, which finalizes the solution. They never experience despair, never feel emptiness; they never come face to face with everlasting darkness. Their experiences and lives are like a song of pleasure and they turn their face toward the Creator with thanks, just like bountiful ears of corn.

Perfect people with faith are not dependant solely on their own consistency or personal states; such people open up to everyone with a prophet-like resolve, embracing everyone and binding their life to the earthly and other-worldly happiness of others to such a degree that they will neglect themselves and live like a friend of the Prophet; scattering light onto their surroundings with the internal light that is like a candle, and maintaining a route which at times may be contrary to personal benefit...indeed, such people always look for places that are dark, like the night. They fight with darkness and oppression, always burning, as they burn, they feel the pain inside, and while their heads may be bowed, neither the continuous glow of their flame, nor the gradual expiration of the flame prevents such people from enlightening others.

Devotees of faith who have managed to raise their flags at the entrance to the way of faith tread the whole world in one bound. They reach the heavens, hold conversations with the stars . . . they are in contact with the sun . . . they befriend the moon . . . and they walk through large stretches of space, toward the "Perfect Companion." As they walk, their faces are always looking at the ground in humbleness and their breath is that of humility. Indeed, it is as if they have donned feathers taken from the wings of angels, they soar at inconceivable heights; but neither the dizziness of such heights, nor the fact that they are on a par with spiritual ones confuses their thoughts—the purest of the pure. Their heads are always inclined toward their breast, with the feelings of Prophet Adam, with a never-ending sigh and hope on their lips, they are like a red rose of the deepest hue. And they glow with varying colors when they turn toward the Just One, as if they are looking toward the sun; when they feel His majesty; they sweat like dew-laden leaves of the morning. It is as if they have heard the sounding of the *Sur*,[4] the fanfare of the Judgment Day.

Those who watch such people find a window through which to gaze upon All-Clement in all His actions, to turn toward eternity and to transform their worlds into nests of love. They display a variety of lights in the darkest night, in those nights where one awaits the dawn and in gardens swept by autumn. They present bunches of roses and flowers to those around them gathered from the emotions in their breasts.

Such people sometimes shape their feelings with majesty and benevolence, they sometimes cool their scorched breasts with tears; their tears flow as if to make the path more welcoming to their wishes and expectations, and they experience approaching happiness with the hope and faith that these aspirations will soon come true. They are always ready to go beyond distances, in accordance with the vastness of their faith. They keep time with the rhythm of their heart, making wings for their reason with feathers from the wings of their heart; they overcome in one step the seemingly insurmountable obstacles in which reason and earthly comprehension are embroiled, and they reach the apex of the world of meaning.

The adherents of truth are always at peace, even when they are surrounded by motifs of grief and sorrow. They do not suffer long from grief, nor are they familiar with unending sorrow. With their bond to

---

[4] Israfil, one of the Archangels, will sound *Sur*, the trumpet at the Day of Resurrection.

God and their intimacy with Him they are able to break the grip of grief with ease; they smother sorrow in its own sorrowfulness and if they have troubles, they adorn them with "sacred sobriety" and watch the pink hues of the spiritual beauty without distress, binding anguish to pleasure, and pain to the glory that is promised by trouble. They are able to transform the groans of pain to joyful sighs, and even when they are most distressed they are able to recite poems of happiness to those around them with the language of their hearts. When they capture the essence of this way and thus sanctify their first breath, with their second breath they bind their hearts to their minds, making their intellect speak with the tongue of the heart and making their voices heard even on the remotest stars and beyond, thus making all the spiritual ones listen to these calls to prayer, a song not heard before. Even believers can hear and enjoy them; as long as the believers keep their horizons free from the stain of sin.

THE HORIZONS OF FAITH

There are two sides to the love of truth; one is constituted by knowledge while the other is constituted by faith. Indeed, while on one side of the relationship is the discovery and determination of the truth, i.e., what creates the link between human knowledge and consciousness, on the other side is the attitude adopted in relation to the truth. The former is pursued by the sources of knowledge of religion and by science. The latter is determined by religion itself. Science which does not possess a love or purpose that is intent on analyzing and explaining existence and discovering the truth is blind, and the determinations of such types of scientific endeavor are not free from contradictions. It is always true that any scientific pursuit based on considerations of personal, familial, or social interests will run into some obstacles, and it is unavoidable that any knowledge attained with such a mentality, thought, or doctrine should lead to a very tortuous path. Religion, being a bountiful basin for science with its sources of knowledge, is an essential element, an important dynamic, a guide that has a clear method in matters that go beyond the horizons of knowledge; it is a guide that has a profound benevolence that does not mislead.

It is always possible to turn science into a punishing, spectral and frightening ghoul standing in the way of truth by leaving it at the disposal of a particular thought, a particular happening, or a particular doctrine, and thereby limiting its horizons; it is also possible that religion, which is a celestial truth, can be presented by some as possessing feelings of resentment, hatred, fury, and revenge. What a great contradiction that something can be twisted into appearing as its total opposite!

Now try to imagine a science—which in truth should be considered as holy as a temple—that has one way or another linked itself to a particular philosophical current, and has even become subservient to it. This means that science is now a slave to a bigoted thought; it is in no way free, and thus is so cursed as to make the greatest ignorance appear favorable in comparison. And try to imagine a religion which has been sought to be made into a vehicle for the interests of some political or nonpolitical parties; then, the temple becomes the fortress of that party, and the prayers that take place there become some sort of political ritual. In this case there is no doubt that both religion and the holiness of religion have been sacrificed.

Indeed, if in a society some people speak of "knowledge" and then use the dwelling places of this knowledge as their own villas, as showcases for their desires, fancies, and ideologies, then these abodes for science have long ceased to be temples and have become arenas where desires, ambitions, and hatred are sharpened. Again, if in a society some people speak of "piety," and then are able to call those who do not think like them and who do not share the same political considerations "heathen," "atheist," or "infidel," then the fault lies with those who have assumed the position of representatives. They have turned religion into a phobia that alienates people from God, which blackens their hearts, and closes the doors of hope in their faces; this is an image that is in total contradiction with why religion was sent down in the first place. Just as the enmity toward religion that emanates from mouths foaming with resentment, hatred and fury and from pens which blacken the soul constitute bigotry and are gifts presented to the Devil, quoting "religion" and then raising one's fists in the air in protest of a particular view or thought is equally bigotry and ignorance; such things sadden the inhabitants of the heavens.

Whatever a person's appearance may be, to consider someone who does not know what true faith is, who does not know with what the conscience calls, who has not partaken Divine love and affection, and who does not accept things that are petty in God's consideration as being petty, or notable things as being notable, as a pious person would be to show great disrespect to the celestial and universal nature of religion. The greatest harm we can do to religion and science is to accept our fancies, aspirations and desires as reasonable thoughts, and to present these as piety. This is a deep wide cavity in every human being and the source of this emptiness is their weakness. One of the greatest weaknesses is wishing to seem better than we are, and having expectations above our capabilities. It is this weakness that needs to be cured with certain values, values which are accepted by the collective conscience as being pious and that pertain to science and religion. In other words, some people want to use religion as if it were something to fill in the cracks of their emptiness. The most powerful weapon of conscience—which is indivisible from justice—against such human weaknesses is the love of truth and the struggle toward knowledge. If there is indeed an elixir which will wipe away the corrosion from the minds of those who appear learned, and the rust from the thoughts of those who seem to be siding with religion, it is undoubtedly the love of God, and the love for all existence and the love for truth, all due to Him. When hearts are imbued with love and souls are moved into action with affection, all human emptiness and weaknesses are smothered or are transformed into an elixir of life.

The world came to know and accept the love of truth that leads people to the love of God and brings them into close encounter with existence through the prophets. From the very first day, every prophet has guided people on his way as a lord of love and has embroidered his dealings with them with adornments of love; this Divine love has melted in its basin, reaching its true value. The Holy Messiah composed a poem out of his life that was based upon love for humanity and he continued his mission, voicing this feeling in various ways. If we examine how it was expressed through Fuzuli's poetry, the Pride of Humanity said "My word is the flag bearer of the army of lovers" and thus honored the world and continued as the breath and voice of love. When this divine love reached a transcendence, its eye upon transformation, it walked toward the hereafter. When the Qur'an is read with faith and concentration, apart from being vocally and musically enchanting, it is also seen to be the voice and breath of love, the point of convergence for longing and reunion. The passion for truth, the love of knowledge, the effort for research and serious investigation, and the attempt to get close are issues that are stressed in the Qur'an often in order to attract the attention of believing hearts. They are like brilliant quarries where attentive souls discover new gems each time they visit. Each traveler in thought who pursues the Qur'an attentively will most certainly find themselves in an artery which will take them to one of those brilliant reserves, and who knows what sort of delightful scenes will greet the traveler when they arrive.

But quite curiously, its spotless purity has a shadow thrown over it and doubts are cast in wavering souls because this book, which is richer than the richest tome in content, this book, which has been created to release us from all our pain and to provide the antidote for ancient wounds, is being misrepresented by deficient souls, people whose passion and love lie in opposing ways. Their search is superficial and they are skewed in their evaluation. Their investigation is always directed at others whose feelings are eternally linked to ambition and interest, whose intellect and reason block their feelings, whose judgment yields to fancies and who dart between "showcase" and "vision" rather than concerning themselves with inner depth and content. They are partly to blame for the fact that some of those who look on this glory see it with a little less luster. In truth, though they may seem to be on a path that leads to the world beyond and on the valleys of the metaphysical, since material interest has blinded their eyes, they are unable to comprehend or reflect a world that has been shaped by the soul and meaning. Moreover, examining the worlds of others founded upon human weakness, they fall into the trap of arming themselves with the same weapons, of using the same material and, in other words, of sharing the same things with the people whom they call "the others." By so doing, they will, in a matter of days, be imitating the evil they used to reprimand in others, and will follow exactly in their footsteps. To date, no one has ever benefited from such an aimless and purposeless struggle. On the contrary, in a struggle in which all express a multitude of regrets, it is our collective personality that is defeated and it is we who are damaged.

The Qur'an descended to the Earth with a deep understanding of balance; it has balanced the relationship between individuals, families, society, and with all creation and has heralded to its followers a path that leads to universal harmony. However, we have imprisoned the Qur'an in the tight confines of our own reason; first we have limited that great vastness, localizing the universal, and then we have demeaned its love to the base of the commonplace, subjecting its brilliant face to one eclipse after another. People of high ideals, like Said ibn Jubayr,[1] Abu Hanifa,[2] Ahmad ibn Hanbal,[3] Imam Serahsi,[4] never were party to inflicting oppression, on the contrary, they did not yield one inch, always deciding in

---

[1] Said ibn Jubayr (d. 721): An imam of great renown, whose father Jubair ibn Mut'im an-Naufali was a Companion acknowledged as a traditionist.

[2] Abu Hanifa (700-772): The Imam of Hanafi sect. A great Muslim jurist whose doctrines are widely accepted in the Muslim world.

[3] Ahmad ibn Hanbal (780-855): The Imam of Hanbali sect. Author of *Musnad*, which contains more than 30,000 traditions, Imam Hanbal acquired a high reputation from his profound knowledge of both the civil and spiritual law, and particularly for the extent of his erudition with respect to the precepts of the Prophet.

[4] Imam Serahsi (d. 1090): He expounded the jurisprudence of Abu Hanifa in his work *Al-Mabsud*.

accordance with the voice of their conscience that is ever open to God. They chose the agony of dark places—may God forgive us—instead of the delight and pleasure of palaces and they found the true depths by worshiping the All-Wise and thus they chose freedom of thought and conscience.

Indeed, those who live with an aim, or die with an aim live on. When they die, their tombs live like hearts, or even like a collective conscience, for eternity. Standing opposite these lofty souls are the unfortunate ones; slaves to their personal interests and thinking of themselves as being so clever that they do not need to concern themselves with anything in this world, yet they remain slaves enchained in their own desires and fancies—thus their lives are slavery, what they leave behind is cursed, and what they attain is disaster upon disaster.

Faithful students of the Qur'an—you can call them people of ideal—are the riders of eternity, who take up others onto their saddles, carrying them to eternity. They are able to transcend their own ardor, aspirations, and passions. As students of the Qur'an ride toward the horizon, idealized according to their inner world of contemplation, they gallop over many things that others call reality, while some who have long suffered from their ideals and have even lost these ideals think them to be fools.

In truth, purpose and aim are like catapults which hurl us into the midst of the realm of souls, a metaphysical atmosphere beyond this world, surrounded by matter which blocks our way and holds us to our feelings, interest, gain, and reputation. Everyone who is placed within that catapult one way or another, if not today, then one day, will go into orbit around the sphere of God; while they are waiting they are like a satellite waiting on the launch pad. Religion, in its entirety, is a bountiful source which feeds this ideal and the Prophet is the affectionate attendant of this source, the sincere representative and commentator who provides the most comprehensible explanations that are in keeping with its celestial origins. In that respect, he is an innovator, a revealer, a revolutionary who recommends the best, the excellent and the most human interpretation for those who come after him, and the one who is open to the most distant future with the principles that he preaches. Those who cannot see the Qur'an with their own inner depth and those who do not accept the person of the Prophet as the most skilful navigator of the depths of the Qur'an are unfortunates who have drowned in their own depths—if indeed we can call this a depth. They are sometimes shaken and stopped in their tracks by the echo of their own shallowness as reflected in the Qur'an, they sometimes seek refuge in historical murmurs, voicing their own emptiness. In their interpretation and representation, religion—more precisely Islamic theology—is either a monstrosity which has been riddled with fairy tales, or a non-contemporary system which has been defeated by time and which is vainly still trying to struggle against it.

In fact, the Qur'an is a source which has an enigma so deep and a purity so vast, a source with such richness that all those who address it can see that it is beyond the horizon of the sphere of their understanding, and they can experience the security of having such a source. Then with the discovery of their own horizon of understanding, they watch like a rainbow, a triumphal arch that is always just beyond the point that the follower has reached. Piety is such a transcending interpretation of the source of light that pours into life through a chrysolite prism, molding and shaping it, that those who feel it witness an inimitable "ease of flawless expression," even though they can see their level of understanding always expressed in the Qur'an.

THE HORIZONS OF THE SOUL:
METAPHYSICAL THOUGHT

The modern Western world view is said to be founded almost entirely on materialistic notions that exclude or even deny the spiritual or metaphysical dimensions of existence. This is a controversial point, but many so-called Muslim intellectuals who blindly imitate and import what they see as Western, despise and reject their societies' traditional modes of thinking and living. This is largely because they no longer have any awareness of the spiritual dimension of existence and life. Indeed, those who reduce existence to matter and think only in physical terms can hardly perceive and understand what is metaphysical and spiritual. Moreover, since those who can only imitate are more radical in their borrowed attitudes than the originators, and since imitation often obscures reality, those so-called intellectuals become more radical in rejecting what is spiritual and metaphysical, and lack adequate knowledge of matter and what is material.

Since the spiritual, metaphysical dimension requires us to go beyond our sensations and instincts into deep and vast horizons, materialists neither understand nor like it. In other words, they restrict their thinking only to what they can perceive and experience. Deceiving themselves and others that existence consists only of the material dimension, they present themselves as true intellectuals.

Despite their claims and the assertions of their Western counterparts, it is difficult to accept that Western scientific thought, although primarily materialistic, has always been separate from spirituality and metaphysics. Modern Western civilization is based on the trinity of Greek thought, Roman law, and Christianity. This latter, at least theoretically, contributes a spiritual dimension. The West never completely discarded Platonist thinking, although it failed to reconcile it with positivistic and rationalistic philosophy. It also does not pretend that such thinkers as Pascal and J. Jeans never existed, or exclude Bergson's intuitivism. Bergson, Eddington, J. Jeans, Pascal, Bernhard Bavink, and Heisenberg are just as impor-

---

This article originally appeared in *Yeşeren Düşünceler*, Kaynak, Izmir, pp. 155-58.

tant in Western thought as Comte, Darwin, Molescholt, Czolba, and Lamarck. Indeed, it is hard to find an atheist scientist and philosopher before the mid-nineteenth century.

In contrast, metaphysical thought and spirituality have been almost entirely discarded by many Muslim intellectuals. In the name of certain notions that have been reduced to such simplistic slogans as "enlightenment, Westernization, civilization, modernity, and progress," metaphysical thought and spiritual life have been denigrated and degraded. Such slogans have also been used to batter traditional Islamic values.

We use "the horizon of hope" to mean traveling beyond the visible dimension of existence, and considering existence as an interrelated whole in the absence of which things and events cannot be perceived as they really are. Nor can its essence and relation with the Creator, as well as the relation between Him and humanity, be grasped. Scientific disciplines that conduct their own discourse largely in isolation from one another and the prevailing materialistic nature of science that has compartmentalized existence and life cannot discover the reality of things, existence, or life.

When such investigations are seen in medicine, for example, people are viewed as being composed of many discrete mechanisms. The consequences are easy to see: Existence is stripped of its meaning and connectedness, and is presented as discrete elements consisting only of matter. However, the only way to fully comprehend and value life and existence is to experience existence through the prism of spirit and metaphysical thinking. Neglecting to do so means forcing reason to comment on things beyond its reach and imprisoning intellectual effort within the confines of sense-impressions. But when we heed the sound of our conscience, or inner world, we perceive that the mind is never content or satisfied with mere sense-impressions.

All the great, enduring, and inclusive modes of thinking developed upon the foundations of metaphysics and spirituality. The whole ancient world was founded and shaped by such sacred texts as the Qur'an, the Bible, the Vedas, and the Upanishads. Denying or forgetting such anti-materialistic Western thinkers, scientists, and philosophers as Kant, Descartes, Pascal, Hegel, and Leibniz means ignoring an essential strand of Western thought.

We can only imagine a new, better world based on knowledge or science if we look at the concept of science through the prism of metaphysics. Muslims have not yet developed a concept of science in its true meaning, namely, one derived from the Qur'an and Islamic traditions primarily shaped by the Qur'an and the hadiths. The application of science or technology by an irresponsible, selfish minority has engendered more disasters than good.

If Muslims want to end their long humiliation and help establish a new, happy world at least on a par with the West, they must replace old-fashioned positivistic and materialistic theories with their own thoughts and inspirations. Aware of their past pains and troubles, they must exert great efforts to define these problems and cure them.

A true concept of science will join spirituality and metaphysics with a comprehensive, inclusive view that affirms the intrinsic and unbreakable relation between any scientific discipline and existence as a whole. Only a concept embracing the whole in its wholeness can be called truly scientific. Seeing existence as discrete elements and trying to reach the whole from these will end up getting swamped in multiplicity. By contrast, embracing the whole and then studying its parts in the light of the whole allows us to reach sound conclusions about the reality of existence.

Spirituality and metaphysics also provide art with their widest dimensions. It fact, art only attains its real identity through spirituality and metaphysics. An artist discovers the inner world of humanity, with all its feelings, excitement, expectations, frustration, and ambitions and discovers how it relates to the outer dimension of existence. The artist then presents these in forms suitable to the medium being used. Art expresses our inner essence, which is in continuous movement to return to its source. In other words, artists unite the inspirations flowing into their spirit from things and events, from all corners of existence. Bringing together all nomena and phenomena, they then present things to us in their wholeness.

Remember that the most important source of science, thinking, and art, even virtues and morality, is metaphysics. All of existence can be perceived with a sound mode of thinking based on pure metaphysics. This allows us to view all of existence as a whole, and to travel through its deeper dimensions. Without spirituality and metaphysics, we cannot build a community on sound foundations; such communities are forced to beg continuously from others. Communities that lack sound meta-physical concepts suffer identity crises.

To build a new, happy world wherein human virtues and values are given due prominence and are effective in shaping policies and aspira-tions, all people, regardless of religion, must rediscover and reaffirm the spirituality and metaphysics taught in the God-revealed religions.

CHAOS
AND THE MYSTICAL WORLD OF FAITH

Today, everyone breathes resentment, swallows hatred, curses all that is deemed to be an enemy with a fixed and determined passion, as if programmed for fury. The ink that flows on the pages of newspapers, the pictures that are broadcasted over the television, the electromagnetic waves that resonate on the radio scratch our ears like ill-omened screams emitting from a variety of places—in the mountains or on the water, in the valleys or up in the hills; they strike our eyes like photographs that make us shudder and they open wounds in our hearts. These epics of hate that we hear of day and night and that startle us, all these ill-omened screams, make us sick at heart, and yet the people who seek a cure for these ills are few indeed. Their thoughts go in different directions, but they always seem to arrive at the same point: money, financial prosperity, and success.

> . . . *emotions base, desire consuming*
> *The meaning that flows over from the gaze is full of contempt for the subject of God.*
>   Akif

Very few are exempt from such a turbulent point of view; no difference remains between what is collective and what is not, between capitalism and communism and no difference remains between these and liberalism. The distance in nature—between those who attach their lives to the considerations of eating and drinking, resting, and earning money, having a good time in general, and, other beings who are obliged due to the unchanging character of their nature—becomes smaller day by day. The basic differences between the two sides vanish into thin air one by one, and humanity seeks new directions, despite its own nature.

Religion, piety, morals, free thought, our own perceptions of art are thought little of; power has become so ulcerated as to be unrecognizable, fantasy has taken on the image of ideas and these disagreeable ideas are being forced upon others. Indeed, I have to say that I have a hard time

This article originally appeared in *Işığın Göründüğü Ufuk* [The Horizon Where the Light Has Appeared], Nil, Istanbul, 2000, pp. 21-28 understanding the inner drama of such a terrible fanaticism. Nowadays, when enlightenment has become widespread, when intellectualism is at its apex, the fact that science and ignorance should meet at the same spot, contrary to the distance that one would expect to exist between them, suggests a dark complicity and makes the existence of a serious problem obvious. Such a contradiction gives us the impression that the emotional will of some people is miles ahead of their intellectual and logical will.

I believe that in such a dark period, when opposites have become intertwined, when in different sections of society chaos is heaped upon chaos, when dark acts of different origins have darkened the face of the Earth, when what is underground reigns over what is above, when polemics and dialectics have become so popular with so many, when hearsay, especially through the use of media, is welcomed as acceptable merchandise, when the lives of others has begun to be the sustenance of our existence, when the soul of unity has been shaken and different groups are scattered everywhere, when hopes are shattered and wills are paralyzed, when souls give up the fight against desire, there is a burning need to turn toward our own spiritual sphere and listen to our own inner world, to tear ourselves from the dark atmosphere of the bodily realm and sail into the magical atmosphere of a hearty and spiritual life. Those who do not fall into lethargy and return to themselves as soon as possible will feel the magic and charm of their own inner world; the unfortunate who fail to return and remain in between, or who remain on the other side, continue to resent, hate, slander, lie, and feel contempt, they continue in the dissolution and obstinate disagreement which they have practiced until this day, and even in climates where the sun continues to shine they will dream of dark things, they will mutter dark thoughts, always seeking dark places in which to hide and dark corners in which to live.

One hopes that they would be able to feel the joy of the blessed days and nights that we experience, when showers of light reach everywhere. One hopes they too would abandon the heresy, atheism, dissension, and sedition in their hearts and that they would be able to respect the chosen understanding and stance of every single soul! Maybe one day these wishes will be fulfilled, but the self-proclaimed enemies of God, the prophets, religion and piety—once having breathed nothing but materialism, having gone into a frenzy denying divinity, and having plunged into the quicksand of anarchy and nihilism—will never be able to breathe this reviving air. Oh dear Lord, had you only made yourself known to them and released the chains from their hearts!

In every community and society there are people who are inclined to abandon their faith and there have been many times when such people have spun out of control; other communities and societies do not have such powerful places to seek refuge when faced by these abysses and weaknesses as we have. Indeed, they have thoughts which soothe, beliefs which reconcile, days and nights which tremble with joy, festivals and carnivals; but, these days, these nights, these festivals, these carnivals are devoid of any holiness. They are like fireworks, shining for a moment and then are gone, giving only instantaneous pleasure; they are ephemeral and physical, not promising anything in the way of spiritual joy. Indeed, in their worlds you cannot feel the greatness of faith to God, nor can you feel that souls are free from the boundaries of time and space; everything starts with a false and transitory happiness, and takes place in a delirium of flesh. All is then transformed into painful memories, regrettable dreams, and disappointed hopes, and finally everything simply disappears.

In this spiritual atmosphere where we are closely bound to God, every sound, every word, every action is felt like a nursery rhyme and listened to like a melody. These shower down upon us like the rain; we soak up the bounties of these showers. The moon changes its form every night, as if signaling particular times and happy hours, the sun moves to a new spot on the horizon at every dawn, awakening our feelings and thoughts in a new period of time, causing our dreams to follow it, presenting memories to us that resemble the river *Kawthar*, promised to us in Heaven. The past becomes like a veil of many colors draped before our eyes, the happy future is the apex of our dreams, waiting for us with open arms and we, who have been freed from the narrow confines of time, live the multiplicity of yesterday-today-tomorrow simultaneously and, like the angels, feel all the joys of surpassing time. It is impossible for those who are not fed from the same source as we, those who do not share the same feelings and thoughts as us, to feel and understand the holy depths in which we lose ourselves or the happiness and joy that we sip like the rivers of Paradise.

Our faith, our horizons of thought, and our manner—characteristics of the fortunate, but at the same time belonging to a little-wronged nation of this part of the world—have become, through being formed and re-formed in the mold of the collective personality, greatly refined and adorned with universal values; this is a situation that exists in no other community; this is so much so that those who spend time with us need not stay long to be aware of this difference. The truth is that in these differences, the holy sadness of our hearts and the enthusiasm of our souls, like water running between the rocks, is felt and heard. Indeed, those who listen to what we have to say always hear the melodies of the pain of separation voiced along with hope; they hear the notes of reunion, of the sweet and eternal search for home in our intonation and manner. Indeed, while on the one hand we murmur "Oh, cup bearer, I have burnt in the flames of love, give me a cup of water," on the other we say "I have dipped my finger in and tasted the honey of love, give me a cup of water," and thus we are able to turn our grief into smiles. Our tongues speak sometimes of love and sometimes of weariness; though love and weariness cause pain to others, in them we always hear, like Rumi, the poem of longing for the realm that we have left to come here. Love and weariness to us are like a plea from the tongue of the soul, stemming from a sorrowful desire for eternity. Since our beliefs and feelings take us to the magical worlds of beyond, we almost always feel sadness and joy intertwined; we hear the sounds of crying and laughing as different notes of the same melody. We respond to the troubled heaving of our breasts with smiles on our faces, as our eyes overflow with tears, our conscience takes upon a red hue with the roses of the *Iram*[1] gardens.

Even though it may not be easy for every individual, our connection to God is the most natural attitude that we can adopt; our relation with Him is like a spell that transforms all the moments of our life into enthusiasm and joy. Our hearts that beat with feelings toward Him fill and refill with the dream of this gaze; we are able to live through the bitterest autumns in our hearts because we have the joy of spring. Our souls adopt the most enviable attitudes with instincts of particular feelings and joy that are the result of our connection with the All-Glorious One; thus transformed, they make us feel a refreshed enthusiasm, a new opening and revelation, even at moments when we are filled with sadness and grief. Pleasure or sadness, revelation or sorrow, all these emotions undergo metamorphoses in our hearts that beat with faith and speak to us of

---

[1] A place mentioned in the Qur'an (al Fajr 89:7-8), ". . . the city of Iram, with lofty pillars; the like of which were not produced in all the land."

the most natural pleasures and the most realistic expectations. It is a fact that we, too, experience interconnected moments of ease and hardship, sweet weeks and bitter days, light and darkness which come and pass, like day and night. However, we sip the unsurpassable benevolence and joys from the hands of all these tribulations, because we have our beliefs, our connection to the Just One and our hopes! Those who do not recognize the trials and pleasures to be the product of the same will writhe in never-ending agony, while in our own atmosphere we see clearly that everything will be transformed into deep compassion. Taste a whole life, with its bitter and sweet facets like *Kawthar*, in everything that we eat and drink, at every place that we inhabit, with all the beautifully divine discoveries of our own inner world, with all of their different wavelengths, feel our sorrows shrink in the face of happiness, feel our pain melt away in pleasure and feel how our lives flow into glazed cisterns in a spectrum of colors. Our mortality is transformed into eternity; we exude smiles even when we cry.

In our world, the beliefs and the expectations that emerge from the heart of those beliefs are so intertwined with our lives that each chapter of our lives lends us the wings of the station of prayer and takes us to the gate of the Hereafter. It takes us there and lets our hearts drink of the beauties of heaven. In this way, we feel as if we are inhaling the scents of heaven. Even if we should let ourselves be swept along by our daily lives, the calls for prayer, songs that exalt God, the various sounds of prayer, the recitation of the names of God, those who give Him thanks, calling out His Uniqueness, letting this spill from the windows of the mosques, all draw us to their climate; they paint our souls with their hues, they give a tambour-like voice to our hearts, they make them sigh like a flute and excite them with the happiness of music. These sounds excite our souls and we are charmed by the mysteries pertaining to God, the charm of these mysteries which comes galloping from the depths of our inner world and which spreads to all our senses, this charm which tints the gardens of heaven in our thoughts and which flows past our lips like cascades of inspiration. Thus charmed, we stand awe-struck.

This charm, this recognition of the mysteries pertaining to God, reaches a higher level on the blessed days and nights when limitless abundance and bounty are showered upon us. This is true to such an extent that everything around us ascends in a state of joy, every corner takes on a

spiritual hue and the excitement of our souls, aiming at metaphysical destinations, reaches its apex, or in Sufi terms, our souls reach the highest
heaven of maturity. To the degree that we can hear and listen to what is
all around us, we too, rejoice like children who feel as if they are in the
fair grounds of joy; thus we experience the happiness and joy of a feast
day.

In such a world, the dawn flows into our houses from the doors and
windows like an awaited guest; the evening comes into our private cham-
bers like a lover and sits by us; the night clings to us with its associations
of reunion with the Confidant; and in every valley hands are raised up
toward Him in prayer, ready to receive the gifts that will come from
Him, assuming a state of metaphysical tension with the power of the
soul, sighing, saying "Hold my hand dear Confidant, hold it, for I cannot
do without You."

In such a world, the prayer roars like the booming voices of *Gulbang
hymns*[2] and echo like the voice and breath of the divine depths; the warm
solitude of the night envelopes our souls like silk; our pulses beat with the
excitement of one who has received good tidings. Perhaps some of us
keep singing His praises, come rain or shine, like the nightingale that
breaks its heart in an effort to express the ideal rhythm for its emotions
with the most touching of sounds. In a word, everyone is humming a
melody with never-ending agony and joy, never-fading love and excitement, listening to the shivering of their souls and letting others hear it
too. Everyone sighs with the fever of love and makes other people feel it
too. Yes, as they reflect on the excitement in their souls and the inspiration of their hearts, expressing themselves one last time, they become the
mouthpiece for the feelings shared by all and they are able to speak of the
hidden meanings that they want to speak of but fail to verbalize.

The horizon of living yesterday-today-tomorrow at the same time
with such a degree of faith and hope, of love and recognition of the mysteries that pertain to God gives such a depth to life that each heart in the
orbit of the hereafter finds itself wrapped up in the melodious harmony
of emotions and ideas and is freed from the limiting, stifling effects of
matter. I believe that the strongest basis of all human relations, the purest
source of all pleasures, and the fountain of all love, longing, attraction,
and gravity is this faith and hope. Every disciple of the heart who attains

---

[2] Hymns sung in the mosque in unison by the congregation.

this faith and hope can experience and feel the state of being outside of time, with the ability to sense all of its depths.

Indeed, to the extent that one can attain this view, one can feel existence in a different manner, evaluate things in a different way and melt in on oneself with the color, taste, aroma and accent of manifestations from the Eternal; these attributes pervade everything and people can reach a second existence with a new "birth after death."[3] During such joyful hours, when the internal gaze is focused on that which is behind the visual scene of existence, one feels all the joys of being. One feels as if one has taken a shower in wisdom, as if one is freed from the weight of all things that are alien to one. The distant heavens shower blessings down upon these hearts, hearts thirsty for love and galloping with longing and affection; all hearts that live in fear of drying up are quenched. Celestial flowers flourish in these showers adorned with dreams!

Some of us may not be able to comprehend the state—a state which becomes a succession of struggle (to come over the darkness with its all connotation) and dawn—of these people of faith and horizon; but all these are phenomena of the heart, soul and emotions. Living through the countless revelations of life, no one but the active heroes of the dawn and of the great strife can understand this love, enthusiasm, poetry, and music poured into our souls by the Eternal One. Those who do not understand this will not be able to understand us, either. Those who remain distant to this fine and delicate life live in the darkness of this distance, while the comprehension of those who have found a position from where they can view the truth in such a way that it appears as obvious as it really is always feel this gift in all its wavelengths, sip it like the rivers of Paradise and live their earthly lives as if in Heaven.

Who knows how many more times we will speak of this never-ending pleasure and joy, in the delight of a festival, of a feast day! How ever many more times we may speak of it—the faults of the speaker's mode of expression aside—we will still listen with pleasure and try to share it with others.

---

[3] The change communicated along these lines is not to be related to reincarnational notions.

THE HORIZONS OF TRANQUILITY

People have always dreamed of attaining peace of mind since the day the first foot was set on the Earth; people have longed for peace of mind, pursuing and struggling in a multitude of ways to obtain it. Sometimes people have connected tranquility to working hard and earning financial wealth; sometimes they have tied it to living to their heart's content and to boundless freedom; at other times, peace of mind has been seen as being in the possession of advanced technological means and the achievement of physical comfort; or at times it has been connected to eating and drinking and the satisfaction of carnal desires. People have bound their lives up in the attainment and possession of these means. On this misty, dusty road people have sometimes lived in hope, have sometimes experienced disappointment and writhed in despair, but never have they reached the longed for expectation; it is impossible via these routes, as the peace of mind that they are in pursuit of is the fruit of virtue within faith and can only be attained through perfect faith. This has also been the essence of the call of the prophets.

The essence of this call for peace and peace of mind can be instituted when individuals turn toward God and submit themselves to Him with all of their being: it is impossible for a person of faith who has achieved submission to this degree to continuously be a slave to bodily desires, nor is it possible such a person to fear anything but God or feel any anxiety. For now, just as these people have found the One that they have been searching for and as they find the beloved toward whom they have directed their love, they also find themselves at peace, for they have been sheltered in the refuge of Eternal Omnipotence in front of whose majesty they will always feel awe and respect. They are at peace, for they know that the Endless Omnipotence and Grace never abandons those who have turned their faces toward Him, whoever they may be, and He never lets them wallow in misery.

For this reason, people of faith are always at peace and always feel secure. They know that they will reach the desired destination if they con-

This article originally appeared in *Işığın Göründüğü Ufuk* [The Horizon Where the Light Has Appeared], Nil, Istanbul, 2000, pp. 240-245.

tinue walking, associating everything with Him. They will be safe all along the way and will, in the distance, experience "the wedding night" of being in close proximity; they will walk toward the purpose of existence with the guidance of the Qur'an, with the trust that the faith in their hearts promises, with breezes of submission wafting through their emotions and conscience and with the supervision of the Divine Master. With all of these they can overcome all the hellish pits of corporeal attachments and the insatiable appetites of their desires and fancies. Indeed, those who enter the atmosphere of the Qur'an and who take refuge in His guidance always feel a deep contentment and an unshakable trust in their hearts when they breathe of safety. As they listen to their conscience, as they gaze upon objects, as they contemplate the tomorrows of both the near and far future, i.e. the future stretching until eternity, as they take into consideration the *Barzah* (the place where the souls will wait till Judgment Day), *Mahshar* (the place where all the dead and living will meet on Judgment Day), *Sirat* (the very narrow bridge which leads to Heaven), Hell, and Heaven, they carry a remarkable awareness of their duty and a feeling of responsibility, and they are also filled with a deep feeling of hope. This feeling of hope is directly proportional to the depth of the faith in their breasts. They gaze upon objects through such a specific window of benevolence, given unto them as befits the breadth of their faith, that should the curtain of physical existence be completely drawn back, they will find the things that they see and the experiences beyond that window akin to the things that they feel and experience here. Due to the nature of earthly confinement, they will come face to face with what they have felt briefly on the Earth beyond this window in fine detail, and they will smile at their good fortune.

Indeed, faith is the magical key to happiness in this world and the Hereafter and promises a virtuous end to those who pass their lives under its banner. Faith promises a bright time of *Barzah*, giving glad tidings of a gentle and warm resurrection, whispering an octave of the Divine Scale that is pleasant to our souls, making our hearts feel our approaching adventure on the *Sirat* Bridge with its depths of hope and poise. Heaven opens its doors with content and comprehension, with surprises that exceed all expectations and presents us with blessings from the Tree of Heaven, blessings that make us forget even the most trouble-laden and painful moments of this life!

In fact, when people of faith turn toward God with all their being, everything else disappears from sight. All false powers and desires deflate like pricked balloons. All physical lights which have occasionally dazzled their eyes with their false glitter are attenuated in the face of His divine light that shines into our hearts; all around we hear, resounding: "Today all wealth and possessions belong to God, the Absolute Victor." A heart which has attained this level is free from the deceptive promises of all seductive powers, forces, kindness, and grace and turns only toward God and awaits help only from Him. When such people are in trouble or shaken by difficulties, they trust in and lean on Him. They seek protection against all threats, taking refuge in the sanctuary of His grace, benevolence and help.

When such people weaken, they enter the advice of His transcending power. When they are tainted by sin, they run to His basin of forgiveness to cleanse themselves, dispersing the fog and smoke that has occasionally enveloped their horizon by putting faith in Him and submitting themselves to Him. Thus, they walk toward the future without submitting to any phenomena that may appear in their way. They solve all their individual, familial, and social problems by connecting with Him and they never fear, or feel a loneliness that cannot be overcome in their souls. At times they may be subjected to temporary loneliness in public, but thanks to their faith and submission, they always feel the breeze of "divine companionship." Whatever befalls them, they take it as a warning sign from fate, and welcome such transactions with assent and patience.

Their faith in God and the characteristics of their faith open up the possibility of acquainting themselves with everything, and thus they see all existence—living or not—as a family. They make contact with the rest of creation, taking an active part in the life of things and in their conscience they feel the vastness of the title of vicegerent which has been bequeathed to them. They perceive that all things have been created for their benefit, and they bow in gratitude, realizing that they are hand in hand with the perception of angels and the souls of the universe. They find the ground that they walk upon, the lowland and the heath, as warm as ancestral residences, and they feel as at home there as if they were in their mother's cradle. They evaluate existence in a way that in no way resembles materialist and naturalist depictions, but with the eye of a person of faith who associates everything with God, and in response, they receive recognition from all that is around them. They receive messages of confidence from all the things with which they come into contact and respond with an attitude expressing the same confidence. They are not afraid of anyone and do not cause anyone to fear; they embrace all as their brethren. They shower smiles upon all things; they sip water, breath air and accept all manners of presents as blessings from God. They inhale the scent of the Earth and those that it gives birth to as if it were the sweetest of aromas. They salute the orchards and gardens, the mountains and valleys, the grasses and trees, the roses and the flowers with the language of their heart, as if these things too had senses. They caress all creatures that they encounter as if they were friends assigned to keep them company in this guesthouse. With every action they demonstrate that they have been sent to the Earth as a sign for agreement and reconciliation.

Thus, people of faith who, with this vast faith of theirs, see everyone and everything through this framework, feel themselves to be in an expansive atmosphere of peace, so much so that it would make all other people jealous if they were but aware. These people are overjoyed with the inexpressible pleasures of living with faith. Indeed, there are no fights, no disputes; they expend all their energy on making other people feel what they feel and enjoy, on sharing these sincere feelings with everyone; they strive to lead everyone to this song of joy by uncovering the horizons of others to whatever degree they can. They are always a few steps behind ordinary living because of their efforts to cause other people to experience these joys. In all of their acts, they have eternal trust in God; they take care never to posit themselves deliberately against other people. Indeed, on the one hand, they feed their own, relative, power with the omnipotence of God; on the other, they also try to attain the support of other people of faith who are like them. They transform all powers that may stand against them into a new depth of their capabilities, thus walking toward their goal as if they were flying. They walk toward the goal of reaching peace with faith, the goal of making other people believe, and toward the achievement of God's pleasure.

If truth be told, a society where individuals have reached such a state of satisfaction, where they love and respect one another and where they are connected with a bond of the heart is a society that is the perfect candidate for peace. It is the perfect candidate, because the factors that may lead its members to unease and the creation of factions have totally disappeared. Among these people, there are no considerations or privileges of nobility, ancestry, region, or status. These people, who see all people and all things as stemming from the same root, are brethren in the fullest meaning of the word. The Qur'an calls attention to this deep truth when it says, *the people of faith are only brethren to one another* (Al-Hujraat 49:10). This is not just a physical kinship; in the words of the Prophet, they are strongly bound to each other by love, affection, and sincerity, like organs of the same body, and they always feel the pain of other's in their hearts, and suffer the agony, share their joys, and experience the same happiness together.

Indeed, they are like each other's eyes and ears, tongue and lips, hands and feet. In this society, every individual has devoted themselves to facilitate another's life, to do all that they can for the happiness of others. Consequently, there is no abandonment or wallowing in despair among such people. When one is hurt, all the others feel this pain in their hearts. All join in the feast of happiness when one partakes of it. Again, in this society, parents are respected like saints, children are raised with diligent care, as if they were flowers. Spouses, even when they have grown gray together, treat each other with the joy of their first day, with contemplation of the eternal togetherness in the Hereafter. They try to live their lives following a route of the heart and mind, beyond the limits of emotional relationships. They are true to each other to the degree that no stranger's shadow is ever reflected in their eyes. This harmony in the family is also true for the nation, which is considered to be a larger family; in a nation composed of such families, all will love and respect one another, all will regard each other with affection, all will wish well for others and all will try to extinguish evil to the best of their ability. No one thinks bad thoughts about anyone, and no one holds another in suspicion. No one uses people as spies against one another. One section of society does not devote its existence to the destruction of another. No one, no one at all, engages in acts like complicity, mendacity, deceit, and slander; these are the habits of the lowest sort of people. In this society of peace, each individual is at battle with all that is negative; it is as if they have sworn to protect human values. As a result, this society becomes a society of conscience and peace.

SUFISM AND ITS ORIGINS

Sufism is the path followed by Sufis to reach the Truth: God. While this term usually expresses the theoretical or philosophical aspect of this search, the physical or practical aspect is usually referred to as "being a dervish."

What is Sufism?

Sufism has been defined in many ways. Some see it as God's annihilating the individual's ego, will, and self-centeredness and then reviving him or her spiritually with the lights of His Essence. Such a transformation results in God's directing the individual's will in accordance with His Will. Others view it as a continuous striving to cleanse one's self of all that is bad or evil in order to acquire virtue.

Junayd al-Baghdadi (d. 910), a famous Sufi master, defines Sufism as a method of recollecting "self-annihilation in God" and "permanence or subsistence with God." Shibli summarizes it as always being together with God or in His presence, so that no worldly or otherworldly aim will even be entertained. Abu Muhammad Jarir describes it as resisting the temptations of the carnal self and bad qualities, and acquiring laudable moral qualities.

There are some who describe Sufism as seeing behind the "outer" or surface appearance of things and events and interpreting whatever happens in the world in relation to God. This means that people regard every act of God as a window through which they can "see" Him, live their lives as a continuous effort to view or "see" Him with a profound spiritual "seeing" that is indescribable in physical terms, and with a profound awareness of being continually overseen by Him.

All of these definitions can be summarized as follows: Sufism is the path followed by individuals who, having been able to free themselves from human vices and weaknesses in order to acquire angelic qualities

This article originally appeared in *Emerald Hills of the Heart: Key Concepts in the Practice of Sufism* Vol. 1, The Fountain, New Jersey, 2004, Revised Edition.

and conduct pleasing to God, live in accordance with the requirements of God's knowledge and love, and experience the resulting spiritual delight that ensues.

Sufism is based on observing even the most "trivial" rules of the shari'a in order to penetrate their inner meaning. An initiate or traveler on the path (*salik*) never separates the outer observance of the Shari'a from its inner dimension, and therefore observes all of the requirements of both the outer and the inner dimensions of Islam. Through such observance, this person travels toward the goal in utmost humility and submission.

Sufism, being a demanding path that leads to knowledge of God, has no room for negligence or frivolity. It requires the initiate to strive continuously, like a honeybee flying from the hive to flowers and from flowers to the hive, to acquire this knowledge. The initiate should purify his or her heart from all other attachments; resist all carnal inclinations, desires, and appetites; and live in a manner reflecting the knowledge with which God has revived and illuminated the heart, always ready to receive divine blessing and inspiration, as well as in strict observance of the Prophet Muhammad's example. Convinced that attachment and adherence to God is the greatest merit and honor, the initiate should renounce his or her own desires for the demands of God, the Truth.

Sufism requires the strict observance of all religious obligations, an austere lifestyle, and the renunciation of carnal desires. Through this method of spiritual self-discipline, the individual's heart is purified and his or her senses and faculties are employed in the way of God, which means that the traveler can now begin to live on a spiritual level.

Sufism also enables individuals, through the constant worship of God, to deepen their awareness of themselves as devotees of God. Through the renunciation of this transient, material world, as well as the desires and emotions it engenders, they awaken to the reality of the other world, which is turned toward God's Divine Beautiful Names. Sufism allows individuals to develop the moral dimension of their existence, and enables the acquisition of a strong, heartfelt, and personally experienced conviction of the articles of faith that before they had only accepted superficially.

SUFISM AS A LIFESTYLE

Sufism is the spiritual life of Islam. Those who represent Islam according to the way of the Prophet and his Companions have never stepped outside this line. A *tariqah* is an institution that reaches the essence of religion within the framework of Sufism and by gaining God's approval, thus enabling people to achieve happiness both in this world and in the next.

As a life-style, Sufism was practiced at the most sublime level during the Age of Happiness, the Time of the Prophet and the Four Caliphs, upon them be peace and blessings. Later, this teaching was systemized according to the individual character, spiritual make-up, and understanding of men whom we can call "*tariqah* dignitaries." This is a completely normal occurrence. Now if I had the ability to read people's minds, that is, if I had the ability to know everyone with their particular characteristics, I would direct each person to the hill of perfection that is the most appropriate for them. I would recommend continuous reflection, contemplation, and reading; I would tell them to study the signs of God in the universe and in people themselves; I would advise people to busy themselves with the study of the Qur'an; I would advise others to recite a portion of the Qur'an and certain prayers on a regular basis; I would tell still others to continuously reflect on "natural" phenomena. That is, I would, in a sense, designate duties to people in the areas in which they have natural abilities. What the Sufi masters actually do is not any different from this. According to the character, general nature, and make-up of people, the Sufi masters assign them religious responsibilities in accordance with their spiritual capacities and enable these people to evolve spiritually according to their capabilities. The Sufi masters aim to take people to the horizon of perfection, which is the purpose of the creation of humanity.

JIHAD – TERRORISM – HUMAN RIGHTS

HUMAN RIGHTS IN ISLAM

Islam is balanced, broad, and universal on the subject of human rights. Except for those who strive to tear down the state or the legitimate administration, or who have willingly taken someone's life, the Qur'an teaches us that to take the life of a person unjustly is a crime against the whole of humanity (Al-Ma'ida 5:32). Such an evaluation cannot be found in any other religion or modern system, and such high value has never been attached on human life by any human rights commission or organization. Islam accepts the killing of one person as if all of humanity had been killed, for the murder of one person allows the idea that any person can be killed.

The son of Adam, Cain, was the first person to shed blood. Although their names are not mentioned specifically in the Qur'an or in the Sunna, we learn from previous Scriptures that a misunderstanding took place between the two brothers, Cain and Abel, and that Cain unjustly killed Abel out of jealousy, thereby opening an era of bloodshed. For this reason, in one of the hadiths, the Messenger of God said:

> Whenever a person is killed unjustly, part of the sin for that murder is credited to Cain, for he was the first to open the way of unjust killing to humanity.[1]

This event, with an important lesson, is expressed in the Qur'an:

> Explain truthfully to them the news of Adam's two sons: When they each offered a sacrifice, and one was accepted and the other rejected. He said: "I swear I am going to kill you." The other said: "God only accepts from those who are pious." He added, "I swear that even if you reach out your hand to kill me, I will not reach out my hand to kill you. I fear God, the Lord of the Worlds." (Al-Ma'ida 5:27-28)

The following judgment is given:

---

[1] Bukhari, *Diyat*, 2, *Anbiya*, 1; Muslim, *Kasamah*, 27.

Anyone who kills a person, unless it be for murder or for causing dissension and spreading corruption in the land, it would be as if he killed humankind all together; and if any one saves a life, it would be as if he saved the life of humankind all together. (Al-Ma'ida 5:27-32)

This principle is universal and therefore valid for all times. Another verse states:

If someone kills a believer intentionally, his (or her) recompense is Hell, to abide therein (forever): and the wrath and the curse of God are upon him (or her), and a dreadful penalty is prepared for him (or her). (An-Nisa 4:93)

In another hadith, our Prophet stated: "Whoever is killed while defending their property is a martyr. Whoever is killed while defending their blood (life) is a martyr. Whoever is killed while defending their religion is a martyr. Whoever is killed while defending their family is a martyr."[2] All the values mentioned in this hadith have been protected as separate principles in all legal systems. These matters are given importance in the fundamental books comprising our law as being "indispensable." From this respect, freedom of faith, life, reproduction, mental health, and personal property are basic essentials that must be preserved for all. Islam approaches human rights from the angle of these basic principles.

Only Islam honors humanity with the title of "God's vicegerent." No other system or religion does this. In addition, Islam states that everything in the heavens and the Earth is subservient, by God's law, for the benefit of humanity if used in a legitimate way. How could a religion that associates such a high importance upon human beings neglect the human rights of even one person? (Also see: *Islam as a Religion of Universal Mercy* in this book.)

---

[2] Tirmidhi, *Diyat*, 22; Abu Dawud, *Sunna*, 32.

LESSER AND GREATER JIHAD

What Is Jihad?

Derived from the root *j-h-d*, jihad means using all one's strength, as well as moving toward an objective with all one's power and strength and resisting every difficulty. This latter definition of jihad is closer to the religious meaning.

Jihad gained a special characteristic with the advent of Islam: struggling in the path of God. This is the meaning that usually comes to mind today. Jihad occurs on two fronts: the internal and the external. The internal struggle (the greater jihad) is the effort to attain one's essence; the external struggle (the lesser jihad) is the process of enabling someone else to attain his or her essence. The first is based on overcoming obstacles between oneself and one's essence, and the soul's reaching knowledge, and eventually divine knowledge, divine love, and spiritual bliss. The second is based on removing obstacles between people and faith so that people can choose freely between belief and unbelief. In one respect, jihad is the purpose of our creation and our most important duty. If the opposite were true, God would have sent Prophets with this duty.

There is an unbridgeable difference between those who remain behind without a valid excuse and those who continually engage in jihad:

> Not equal are those believers who sit (at home) and are not hurt, and those who strive and fight in the cause of God with their goods and their persons. God has granted a grade higher to those who strive and fight with their goods and persons than to those who sit (at home). Unto all (in faith) has God promised good: but for those who strive and fight has He distinguished above those who sit (at home) by a special reward. (An-Nisa: 4:95)

The Prophet says:

> Keeping watch one day to protect the border for God's sake is superior to this world and everything in it. The small place that your whip (used

This article consists of excerpts from Gülen's *Cihad veya I'la-yi Kelimetullah*, Izmir: Nil, 1998; *Asrın Getirdiği Tereddütler*, Izmir: T.Ö.V. 1997, 3:186-219.

in the way of God) occupies in Heaven is superior to this world and everything in it. An evening or morning walk made on God's path is superior to this world and everything in it.[1]

Types of Jihad

The lesser jihad is not restricted to battlefronts, for this would narrow its horizon considerably. In fact, the lesser jihad has such a broad meaning and application that sometimes a word or silence, a frown or a smile, leaving or entering an assembly—in short, everything done for God's sake—and regulating love and anger according to His approval is included. In this way, all efforts made to reform society and people are part of jihad, as is every effort made for your family, relatives, neighbors, and region.

In a sense, the lesser jihad is material. The greater jihad, however, is conducted on the spiritual front, for it is our struggle with our inner world and carnal soul (*nafs*). When both of these jihads have been carried out successfully, the desired balance is established. If one is missing, the balance is destroyed.

Believers find peace and vitality in such a balanced jihad. They know they will die the moment their jihad ends. Believers, like trees, can survive only as long as they bear fruit. As a matter of fact, when a tree stops producing fruit, it dries up and dies. Observe pessimists, and you will notice that they no longer struggle or explain the Truth to others. Thus, God cuts off His blessing to them, leaving their interiors dark and cold. But those who pursue jihad are always surrounded by love and enthusiasm. Their inner worlds are bright, their feelings are pure, and they are on the road to prosperity. Every struggle stimulates the thought of yet another one, and thus a righteous circle is formed. As every good deed becomes a vehicle for a new good deed, such people swim among good deeds. Our hearts are informed of this truth:

> And those who strive in Our Cause, We will certainly guide them to Our Paths: For God is with those who do the right. (Al-Ankabut 29:69)

---

[1] Bukhari, *Jihad*, 142; Tirmidhi, *Fada'il al-Jihad*, 25.

There are as many roads to God as there are creatures. God leads those who struggle for His sake to salvation on one or more of these roads. He opens each road to goodness and protects it from the roads to evil. Everyone who finds His road, the Straight Path, finds the middle road. Just as these people follow a middle path regarding anger, intelligence, and lust, they also follow a middle way regarding jihad and worship. This means that God has led humanity to the path of salvation.

The lesser jihad is our active fulfillment of Islam's commands and duties; the greater jihad is proclaiming war on our ego's destructive and negative emotions and thoughts (e.g., malice, hatred, envy, selfishness, pride, arrogance, and pomp), which prevent us from attaining perfection. As this is a very difficult and strenuous jihad, it is called the greater jihad.

During the Age of Bliss, people fought like lions on the battlefield and, when night fell, lost themselves in devotion to God through worship and *dhikr* (remembrance and invocation of God). These valiant fighters passed their lives in a corner in worship and solitude. They learned this from their guide, the Prophet, a man of the heart who was first in the material and spiritual jihad. He encouraged his followers to ask for God's forgiveness, and was always the first to do so.

Those who succeed in the greater jihad will succeed in the lesser jihad; those who fail in the greater jihad will fail in the lesser jihad. Even if such people obtain some degree of success, they cannot obtain the full results.

'A'isha related:

> One night the Messenger of God asked: "'A'isha, can I spend this night with my Lord?" (He was so genteel that he would ask for such permission. Nobility and refinement were important aspects of his profundity.) I replied: "O Messenger of God, I would like to be with you, but I'd like what you like even more." The Prophet performed ablution and began praying. He recited: *Behold! In the creation of the heavens and earth, and the alternation of Night and Day—there are indeed Signs for people of understanding* (Al-Imran 3:190). He recited this verse and shed tears until morning. (Ibn Kathir, *Tafsir*)

Sometimes in order not to wake up his wife, the Prophet would get up and worship without asking her. Again 'A'isha relates:

One night when I woke up, I could not find God's Messenger. . . . When I started to get up in the dark, my hand touched his foot. He was prostrating on the prayer rug and reciting something. I listened to his prayer. He said: "My God, I take refuge in Your compassion from Your anger and wrath. I take refuge in Your sparing me from punishment. My Lord, I take refuge in You from You (refuge in Your blessings from Your wrath, refuge in Your grace from Your grandeur, refuge in Your mercy and compassion from Your domination.) I am not capable of praising You (properly). You are as You have praised Yourself."[2]

This incident clearly displays the inner depth and the extent of greater jihad in the Prophet. In another hadith, the Prophet mentioned these two jihads:

There are two kinds of eyes that will never see the fire of Hell: those of soldiers who act as guards on battlefields and fronts, and those who weep because of the fear of God.[3]

The jihad of those who abandon their sleep and act as guards at the most dangerous times is material jihad. Their eyes will not be subjected to the fire of Hell. As for those who do the spiritual and greater jihad and cry for fear of God, they also will not see the torture of Hell. Instead of repeating what others have done, people should have good intentions and implant in their hearts and minds the consciousness of being sincere.

Jihad is a balance of internal and external conquest. Reaching spiritual perfection and helping others do so are of the utmost importance. Attaining internal perfection is the greater jihad; helping others attain it is the lesser jihad. When you separate one from the other, jihad is no longer jihad. Indolence is born from one and anarchy from the other. Thus, the Muhammadan spirit is the only way of settlement. As is always the case, this is possible only by following and conforming to God's Messenger. How happy are those who search for a way to salvation for others as

---

[2] Muslim, *Salat*, 22; Haythami, *Majma' al-Zawa'id*, 10:124; Tirmidhi, *Da'wat*, 81.
[3] Tirmidhi, *Fada'il al-Jihad*, 12.

much as they do for themselves. And how happy are those who remember to save themselves while saving others!

LOVE, TOLERANCE, AND JIHAD
IN THE LIFE OF THE PROPHET

The blessed life of the Pride of Humanity, peace and blessings be upon him, was interwoven with threads of peace and tolerance as if it were a beautiful piece of lace. To begin with, peace is fundamental to Islam. There are many verses in the Qur'an connected with this matter. For example, in one of these the Prophet is addressed:

> But if the enemy inclines toward peace, do you (also) incline toward peace, and trust in God: for He is the One that hears and knows (all things). (Al-Anfal 8:61)

Even in an atmosphere in which two armies have fought against each other and blood has been spilled, if the enemy forgoes fighting and wants to make a treaty, then the Muslims are commanded not to react emotionally, but to make a treaty, putting their trust in God. Thus, a universal principle regarding this subject has been established. Consequently, to talk about fighting or conflict is completely contrary to the basic spirit of a religion that enjoins treaties and reconciliation, not only in time of peace, but even during wartime.

The mission of the Prophet was to communicate the faith as he had been enjoined by God. He did this without any prejudice. This was true to such an extent that, the Prophet, this man of love and peace, visited even the most hard-hearted unbelievers, such as Abu Jahl and 'Uqbah ibn Abi Mu'ayd, many times without displaying any resentment. He desired that all people should be able to feel Paradise in their hearts. He often said:

> Pronounce there is no deity but God and be saved.[1]

What he meant by this was: "To attain fulfillment in your heart, help the seed of belief which has been sown in your heart to grow into para-

---

[1] Ibn Kathir, *al-Bidayah wa'l-Nihayah*, 3:62-63.

dise and secure your other world." Once Abu Jahl answered this invitation in a disrespectful and mocking way, "Hey, Muhammad, if you are doing this to make us witnesses of your call before God, do not invite me to religion again. I will bear witness there." This unbeliever always answered without respect. But in spite of Abu Jahl's insults, the Glory of the World, peace and blessings be upon him, talked about Islam every time they met and never changed his exemplary style; these insulting words, attitude, and behavior never affected him.

One event that is connected with the Pride of Humanity's vast love, compassion, and tolerance for humankind took place during the conquest of Makka. After the conquest was complete, everyone gathered around the Prophet and, looking into his eyes, they began to wait for him to make a decision concerning their fate. Up until the last moment a small group, among whom was Abu Jahl's son, Ikrimah, had opposed the Muslims' entrance to Makka. Once more their feelings of violence and revenge were inflamed. At a moment when the atmosphere was incredibly tense, the Messenger of God asked the Makkans who were waiting with anticipation and anxiety, "What are you expecting me to do to you?" Some of the Makkans who knew well what a noble, forgiving, and generous person he was did not refrain from showing their feelings and said, "You are the most generous of the generous, the noblest of the noble." The Prophet's goal was neither possessions nor property, neither sovereignty nor power, nor the conquest of land. His aim was to save people and conquer their hearts. This Man of Love and Affection gave his decision concerning his enemies, saying:

> I say to you as Joseph once said to his brothers. There's no blame for
> the actions that you have performed before. God will forgive you, too.
> He is the Most Merciful of the Merciful. Go, you are all free.[2]

What this approach actually meant could be expressed as follows: "Do not suffer any internal pain. I have no intention to punish anyone. Everyone's behavior displays his or her character. This is how I do things."

After the return to Madina, Ikrima ibn Abu Jahl, who had spilled blood even during the conquest of Makka, was convinced by his wife

---

[2] Al-Iraqi, al-Mughni an Haml a-Asfar, 3:179.

Umm Hakim to return from where he had escaped, and he was taken before the Prince of Prophets, peace and blessings be upon him. Before he entered the Prophet's presence, those around him said that if he asked for forgiveness, the Messenger of God would forgive him. In all probability, before Ikrima came into his presence the Prophet had warned those around him, "Ikrima is coming. Do not hurt his feelings by saying unbecoming things about his father." As soon as Ikrima stepped inside, the Messenger said warmly, "Welcome to the one who emigrated by boat." Never expecting words full of this much love and affection, Ikrima later said, "As long as I live I will never forget this behavior of the Prophet." Four years after Ikrima became Muslim, he was martyred at Yermuk. Murmuring the words, "O Messenger of God, have you found the goodness you expected as compensation for the evil done by the one who emigrated by boat?" he joined the other martyrs.[3]

As I stated above, the Messenger's call was his mission to represent the truths he told to others. In other words, it was his duty to practice in his life the things he said. He always practiced a thing before calling on others to do the same. The things we have explained so far comprise the general character of the Prince of Prophets, peace and blessings be upon him. However, some try their best to misinterpret the existence of and encouragement to jihad in the Holy Qur'an and the Sunna as being in conflict with our Prophet's universal love and affection. But jihad can mean an armed struggle as an action tied to special conditions that is sometimes necessary to carry out in order to protect such values as life, property, religion, children, homeland, and honor. It is also resorted to sometimes when it is necessary to remove obstacles from the path that leads to raising God's Word. Today these two situations are constantly confused; sometimes this is due to ignorance and sometimes it is done intentionally. Love, affection, and tolerance, in their broadest dimensions, were enjoyed during the Age of Happiness, a time full of peace and happiness, a time which in the words of the Prophet was, "the best of centuries." As a matter of fact, this period represented the apex of Muslim civilization; it was a golden time when peace, love, and understanding were given their true position in society.

---

[3] Ibn Athir, *Usd al-Ghabah*, 3:567-570; Muttaqi al-Hindi, *Kanz al-'Ummal*, 13:540-541.

REAL MUSLIMS CANNOT BE TERRORISTS

Islam literally means "surrender." Islam is the religion of contentment, security, and peace. These principles are so commonplace in the lives of Muslims that when they once start to perform the prayer they cut off all ties with the world, bow and prostrate before God and then stand with their hands clasped in respect. When they leave the prayer, it is as if they have started a new life. They end the prayer by greeting those to their left and right and wishing them health, security and peace, then go and join other people.

Greeting others and wishing them peace are considered to be among the most auspicious acts that can be performed in Islam. Indeed, when Prophet Muhammad, peace and blessings be upon him, was asked, "What is the most auspicious act in Islam?" he replied, "Giving food to others and greeting all those you know and do not know."[1]

Accusations of Terrorism

It is a great shame that Islam, which is based on those tenets, is seen by others to be equaled with terrorism. This is an enormous historical mistake; as we pointed out above, if a system based on peace and security becomes associated with terrorism, this only shows that the people making the accusations know nothing of the spirit of Islam and are unable to grasp it in their own souls. One should seek Islam through its own sources and in its own true representatives throughout history; not through the actions of a tiny minority that misrepresent it. The truth is that there is no harshness or bigotry in Islam. It is a religion made up entirely of forgiveness and tolerance. Such pillars of love and tolerance like Rumi, Yunus Emre, Ahmed Yesevi, Bediüzzaman and similar figures have expressed this aspect of Islam most beautifully and they have gone down in history as examples of this affection and tolerance.

This article originally appeared in *Turkish Daily News*, September 19, 2001.

[1] Bukhari, *Isti'zan*, 9, 19; Nesai, *Iman*, 13.

Jihad in Islam

Jihad is an element of Islam which is primarily defined as the inner struggle of a believer against all that stands between the believer and God. An aspect of jihad, on the other hand, is based on certain specific principles aimed at removing all the obstacles to the defense and exaltation of the name of God. We can cite numerous examples throughout history in connection with this topic. There will always be battles; this is an inescapable reality of human life. However, the verses in the Qur'an that specify conditions for jihad have been misinterpreted by others and taken as the fundamental aim of Islam. In essence, these people, who have failed to grasp the true spirit of Islam, have been unable to strike a balance between the broad and finer points and this, when coupled with the fact that they have been consumed with hatred, has led them to misinterpret Islam. The heart of a genuine Muslim community is full of love and affection for all of creation.

Love Binds Existence

Prophet Muhammad, peace and blessings be upon him, was a man of affection. He was also known as "Habibullah," which comes from the word "habib," meaning "he who loves God and is loved by God." Mystics such as Imam Rabbani, Mawlana Khalid, and Shah Waliyullah say that the highest degree is that of love.

God created the whole of creation out of love and Islam has embroidered the delicate lacework of this love. In the words of another great mystic, love is the raison d'être for the existence of creation. Of course, in spite of all this, we cannot deny that there is an element of violence in Islam; it is there in the name of deterrence. However, some people take these elements, which should be secondary, and consider them to be the fundamentals of Islam, whereas true Islam appeals to peace. Once a friend of mine who shared these sentiments told me, "You speak with everybody without imposing any restrictions. This in turn breaks the metaphysical tension we have, whereas we have been taught that according to Islam we should show our hostility to certain people in the name of God." Actually, this thought stems from an incorrect interpretation of this idea. In Islam, everything that is created is to be loved in the name of God. What is to be hated and what we must be hostile to are impure and immoral thoughts, feelings, and blasphemy. God intended humans as kind creatures (Al-Isra 17:70) and one can say that everyone is blessed with that quality to varying degrees. The Prophet of God was passing a Jewish funeral and he stopped to pay his respects. When reminded that the man being buried was a Jew, he replied, "He is still a human." He demonstrated the value that Islam gives to humanity.

Yes, this was the measure of our Prophet's respect for people. The reasons why certain Muslim people or institutions that misunderstand Islam are becoming involved in terrorist attacks throughout the world should be sought not in Islam, but within the people themselves, in their misinterpretations and in other factors. Just as Islam is not a religion of terrorism, any Muslim who correctly understands Islam cannot be or become a terrorist.

Even though there are naturally exceptions, the interpretations of Islam by Turkish scholars are tolerant. If we can spread the understanding of Islam held by the pillars of affection like Rumi and Yunus Emre throughout the world, and if we can get their message of love, dialogue and tolerance to those people who are thirsting for this message, then people from all over the world will come running into the arms of this love, peace, and tolerance that we represent.

The tolerance of Islam is so vast that the Prophet specifically forbade people to even say things that could be offensive. Despite all the self-sacrificing efforts by Muhammad, Abu Jahl failed to become a Muslim and died outside the religion. By the way, the name Jahl means ignorant. This ignorant and coarse man spent all his life as the enemy of the Prophet, and now, sadly, his nickname has become the second nature of today's Muslims. Shortly after the conquest of Makka Abu Jahl's Muslim son, Ikrima, started speaking in council against his father and was reprimanded by the Prophet for doing so.

Respect for Humankind

Another hadith explains why we should not be intolerant to others. The Prophet warned his Companions not to curse their own parents. His Companions curiously asked why one would curse one's parents. The prophet replied that if one curses the parent of another person, then the other person will retaliate; thus in effect one is cursing one's own parent.

While the Prophet always showed respect for others, the fact that today people are saying that Islam is offensive to others means that they have not properly understood the Prophet. There is no room for hate or hostility in either Islam or in the universal realm of its envoy Muhammad, peace and blessings be upon him.

Servants of God

The Qur'an is based throughout on forgiveness and tolerance.

> Those who spent benevolently in ease and straightness, and those who restrain their anger (swallowing their anger as if swallowing a thorn) and pardon men; and God loves those who do good to others. (Al-Imran 3:134)

It would be worthwhile to look at this in detail. You may encounter an incident that makes your blood boil; for example, people might curse and insult you. But, you should try your utmost to behave indifferently and without reacting. The Qur'an describes in the verse above how people of good morals should behave even at times when you may want to lose your temper. The Arabic words from this passage have much meaning. "*Kazm*" means swallowing what cannot be swallowed; while *Kazim* means someone who swallows his anger. In another passage, God tells believers to avoid vanity:

> And they who do not bear witness to what is false, and when they meet hollow words or unseemly behavior, they pass them by with dignity. (Al-Furqan 25:72)

An Islamic Style

The Prophet practiced everything that is taught in the Qur'an. For example, someone came and admitted to committing adultery, asking to be cleansed of his sins, whatever the punishment may be; the Prophet told him, "Go home, and repent. There is no sin God will not forgive."[2] Another hadith tells how a person accused another of stealing. Just when the penalty was about to be read, the man turned and forgave the thief, to which the Prophet said, "Why didn't you forgive him in the first place?"[3]

So, when all of these examples are looked at in detail, it can be seen that the style adopted by those who treat others with hatred and hostility

---

[2] Muslim, *Hudud*, 17, 23; Bukhari, *Hudud*, 28.
[3] Abu Dawud, *Hudud*, 14(4394); Nasai, *Sarik*, 4 (8, 68); Muwatta, *Hudud*, 28, (2, 834).

is not in keeping with Islam. As indicated above, Islam is a religion of love and tolerance. Muslims are the devotees of love and affection, people who shun all acts of terrorism and who have purged their bodies of all manner of hate and hostility.

ON RECENT TERRORIST ATTACKS

Muslims Should Say, "In True Islam, Terror does not Exist."

Today, at best we can say that Islam is not known at all. Muslims should say, "In true Islam, terror does not exist." In Islam, killing a human is an act that is equal in gravity to *qufr* (not believing in God). No person can kill a human being. No one can touch an innocent person, even in time of war. No one can give a *fatwa* (a legal pronouncement in Islam, issued by a religious law specialist, concerning a specific issue) in this matter. No one can be a suicide bomber. No one can rush into crowds with bombs tied to his or her body. Regardless of the religion of these crowds, this is not religiously permissible. Even in the event of war—during which it is difficult to maintain balances—this is not permitted in Islam. Islam states; "Do not touch children or people who worship in churches." This has not only been said once, but has been repeated over and over throughout history. What Our Master, Prophet Muhammad, said, what Abu Bakr said, and what 'Umar said is the same as what, at later dates, Salahaddin Ayyubi, Alparslan, and Kılıçarslan also said. Later on, Sultan Mehmet II, the Conqueror, also said the same. Thus, the city of Constantinople, in which a disorderly hullabaloo reigned, became Istanbul. In this city the Greeks did not harm the Armenians, nor did the Armenians harm the Greeks. Nor did the Muslims harm any other people. A short time after the conquest of Constantinople, the people of the city hung a huge portrait of the Conqueror on the wall in the place of that of the Patriarchate. It is amazing that such behavior was displayed at that time. Then, history relates that the Sultan summoned the Patriarch and gave him the key to the city. Even today, the Patriarchate remembers him with respect. But today, Islam, as with every other subject, is not understood properly. Islam has always respected different ideas and this must be understood for it to be appreciated properly.

I regret to say that in the countries Muslims live, some religious leaders and immature Muslims have no other weapon to hand than their fundamentalist interpretation of Islam; they use this to engage people in

---

This text has been excerpted from the interview Gülen gave to Nuriye Akman, published in *Zaman* between March 22–April 1, 2004.

struggles that serve their own purposes. In fact, Islam is a true faith, and it should be lived truly. On the way to attaining faith one can never use untrue methods. In Islam, just as a goal must be legitimate, so must all the means employed to reach that goal. From this perspective, one cannot achieve Heaven by murdering another person. A Muslim cannot say, "I will kill a person and then go to Heaven." God's approval cannot be won by killing people. One of the most important goals for a Muslim is to win the approval of God, another being making the name of Almighty God known to the universe.

The rules of Islam are clear. Individuals cannot declare war. A group or an organization cannot declare war. War is declared by the state. War cannot be declared without a president or an army first saying that there is a war. Otherwise, it is an act of terror. In such a case war is entered into by gathering around oneself, forgive my language, a few bandits. Another person would gather some others around himself. If people were allowed to declare war individually then chaos would reign; because of such small differences a front could be formed even between sound-thinking people. Some people could say, "I declare war against such and such a person." A person who is tolerant to Christianity could be accused as follows: "This man, so and so, helps Christianity and weakens Islam. A war against him should be declared and he must be killed." The result would be that a war is declared. Fortunately, declaring war is not this easy. If the state does not declare a war, no one can wage war. Whoever does this, even if they are scholars whom I admire, does not create a real war; this is against the spirit of Islam. The rules of peace and war in Islam are clearly set out.

An Islamic World, Indeed, Does Not Exist

In my opinion, an Islamic world does not really exist. There are places where Muslims live. They are more Muslims in some places and fewer in others. Islam has become a way of living, a culture; it is not being followed as a faith. There are Muslims who have restructured Islam in accordance with their thoughts. I do not refer to radical, extremist Muslims, but to ordinary Muslims who live Islam as it suits them. The prerequisite for Islam is that one should "really" believe, and live accordingly; Muslims must assume the responsibilities inherent in Islam. It cannot be said that any such societies with this concept and philosophy exist within Islamic geography. If we say that they exist, then we are slandering Islam. If we say that Islam does not exist, then we are slandering humans. I do not think Muslims will be able contribute much to the balance of the world in the near future. I do not see our administrators having this vision. The Islamic world is pretty ignorant, despite a measured enlightenment that is coming into being nowadays. We can observe this phenomenon during the Hajj. We can see this displayed during conferences and panels. You can see this in their parliaments through television. There is a serious inequality in the subject matter. They—these Muslims—cannot solve the problems of the world. Perhaps it could be achieved in the future.

Today, there is an Islam of the individual. There are some Muslims in different places of the world. One by one, all have been separated from one another. I personally do not see anyone who is a perfect Muslim. If Muslims are not able to come into contact with one another and constitute a union, to work together to solve common problems, to interpret the universe, to understand it well, to consider the universe carefully according to the Qur'an, to interpret the future well, to generate projects for the future, to determine their place in the future, then I do not think we can talk about an Islamic world. Since there is no Islamic world, every one acts individually. It could even be said that there are some Muslims with their own personal truths. It cannot be claimed that there is an Islamic understanding which has been agreed upon, approved by qualified scholars, reliably based upon the Qur'an, and repeatedly tested. It could be said that a Muslim culture is dominant, rather than Islamic culture.

It has been so since the fifth century AH (eleventh century AD). This started with the Abbasid Era and with the appearance of the Seljuks. It increased after the conquest of Istanbul. In the periods that followed, doors to new interpretations were closed. Horizons of thought became narrowed. The breadth that was in the soul of Islam became narrowed. More unscrupulous people begun to be seen in the Islamic world; people who were touchy, who could not accept others, who could not open themselves to everyone. This narrowness was experienced in the dervish lodges, as well. It is sad that it was even experienced in the *madrasas* (schools of theology). And of course, all of these tenets and interpretations require revision and renovation by cultivated people in their fields.

Al-Qaeda Network

One of the people whom I hate most in the world is [Osama] Bin Laden, because he has sullied the bright face of Islam. He has created a contaminated image. Even if we were to try our best to fix the terrible damage that has been done, it would take years to repair.

We speak about this perversion everywhere on many different platforms. We write books about it. We say, "this is not Islam." Bin Laden replaced Islamic logic with his own feelings and desires. He is a monster, as are the people around him. If there are other people similar to them anywhere, then they too, are nothing more than monsters.

We condemn this attitude of Laden. However, the only way to prevent this kind of deeds is that Muslims living in the countries seeming to be Islamic—and I stated earlier that I do not perceive an Islamic world, there are only countries in which Muslims live—will solve their own problems.

Should they think in a totally different way when electing their leaders? Or should they carry out fundamental reforms? For the growth of a well-developed younger generation, Muslims must work to solve their problems. Not only their problems in the issue of terror, an instrument that is certainly not approved of by God, but also those concerning drugs and the use of cigarettes, two more prohibitions made by God. Dissension, civil turmoil, never-ending poverty, the disgrace of being governed by others, and being insulted after having put up with government by foreign powers are all problems that could be added to the list.

As Mehmet Akif Ersoy said: slavery, a multitude of troubles, addiction, the acceptance of things out of habit, and derision are all commonplace. All of these are anathemas to God, and all of these have been placed primarily on our nation. Overcoming these, in my opinion, depends on being a just human being and a human being who is devoted to God.

Our Responsibility

It is our fault; it is the fault of the nation. It is the fault of education. A real Muslim, one who understands Islam in every aspect, cannot be a terrorist. It is hard for a person to remain a Muslim if he becomes involved in terrorism. Religion does not approve of the killing of people in order to attain a goal.

But of course, what efforts did we make to raise these people as perfect humans? With what kind of elements did we bind them? What kind of responsibility did we take in their upbringing so that now we should expect them not to engage in terror?

People can be protected against becoming involved in terrorism by means of some virtues originating in the Islamic faith, such as, fear of God, fear of the Day of Judgment, and fear of opposing the principles of religion. However, we have not established the required sensitivity on this issue. There have been some minor attempts to deal with this neglected subject to date. But, unfortunately there have been some obstacles put in the way, by our countrymen.

Some say the kind of activities that we need should not be allowed. That is, courses teaching culture and morality should be totally forbidden in educational institutions. At the same time we contend that every requirement of life should be met in schools. Health education should be provided, taught by doctors. Classes related to general life and life in the home should be comprehensively taught in schools.

People should be instructed in how to get along with their future spouses, and how to raise their children. But the issues do not stop here. Both Turkey and other countries that have a large Muslim population suffer from drug abuse, gambling, and corruption. There is almost no one left in Turkey whose name has not been involved in some type of scandal. There are some goals that were supposed to be reached that have been reached. Yet, there are many objectives that still cannot be reached. You cannot question anyone concerning this. You cannot call the people in charge to account. They are protected, sheltered, and thus they have been left alone.

These people are people who grew up among us. All of them are our children. Why have some of them become bad guys? Why were some raised as bullies? Why have some of them rebelled against human values? Why do they come to their own country and blow themselves up as suicide-bombers?

All these people were raised among us. Therefore, there must have been something wrong with their education. That is, the system must have some deficiencies, some weak points that need to be examined. These weak points need to be removed. In short, the raising of human beings was not given priority. In the meantime, some generations have been lost, destroyed, and wasted.

Dissatisfied youth has lost its spirituality. Some people take advantage of such people, giving them a couple of dollars, or turning them into robots. They have drugged them. This has become a topic on the agenda these days which can be read about in magazines. These young people were abused to an extent that they could be manipulated. They have been used as murderers on the pretext of some crazy ideals or goals and they have been made to kill people. Some evil-minded people have wanted to achieve certain goals by abusing these young people.

These people have been turned into robots. Once, many people were killed in Turkey. This group killed that person, another group killed another person. On March 12, 1971 everyone became involved in a bloody fight. The military came and intervened. On September 12, 1980 people were out for one another's blood. Everyone was killing one another.[1]

Some people were trying to reach a goal by killing others. Everybody was a terrorist. The people on that side were terrorists; the people on this side were terrorists. But, everybody was labeling the same action differently. One person would say, "I am doing this in the name of Islam." Another would say, "I am doing it for my land and people." A third would say, "I am fighting against capitalism and exploitation." These all were just words. The Qur'an talks about such "labels." They are things of no value. But people just kept on killing. Everyone was killing in the name of an ideal.

In the name of these bloody "ideals" many were killed. This was nothing less than terror. Everybody, not only Muslims, was making the same mistake. Since everyone did it, one after another, these killings came to be a goal that was "realizable." Killing became a habit. Everyone began to get used to killing, even though killing another person is a very evil action. Once, one of my dearest friends killed a snake. He was a theology graduate and he is now a preacher. As a reaction to this action, I did not talk to him for a month. I said: "That snake had a right to live in nature. What right did you have to kill it?"

But today the situation is such that if 10 or 20 people are killed, or if the numbers are not as high as was feared, then we say, "Oh, that's not so

---

[1] Turkey has suffered three military coups in the second half of the twentieth century. The given dates are the second and third, which took place due to unrest in society.

bad, not too many have died." This incredible violence has become acceptable by people at a horrible level. "It's good that the number of the death is only 20-30," we say. In short, society as a whole has come to accept this as part of our daily lives.

This situation could have been prevented by education. The laws and regulations of the government could have prevented this. Some marginal groups who are being shielded, and therefore who cannot be stopped, are exaggerating trivial matters, and making important matters insignificant. There is a remedy for this. The remedy is to teach the truth directly. It should be made clear that Muslims cannot be terrorists. Why should this be made clear? Because people must understand that if they do something evil, even if it is as tiny as an atom, they will pay for that both here and in the Hereafter.[2]

Yes, killing a human is a very significant thing. The Qur'an says that killing one person is the same as killing all people. Ibn Abbas said that a murderer will stay in Hell for eternity. This is the same punishment that is assigned to unbelievers. This means that a murderer is subjected to the same punishment as an unbeliever. In short, in Islam, in terms of the punishment to be dealt on the Day of Judgment, a murderer will be considered to be as low as someone who has rejected God and the Prophet (an atheist in other words). If this is a fundamental principle of religion, then it should be taught in education.

---

[2] Al-Zilzal 7-8.

EDUCATION

EDUCATIONAL SERVICES ARE SPREADING THROUGHOUT THE WORLD

Why Education?

Many things have been said and written about education. We will approach this subject from three interrelated angles: human-psychological, national-social, and universal.

We have been under the serious influence of contemporary Western thought, which undoubtedly has many superior aspects, for several centuries. However, within this thought there are also some defects, stemming in particular from the historical periods it has passed through and the unique conditions created by it. In the Middle Ages, when Europe was living under a theocratic order ruled by the Church or Church-appointed monarchs, Western thought came into contact with the Islamic world, especially through Andalusia and the Crusades. This was one of the factors that opened the door for the Renaissance and Reform movements. Some of the other factors, such as land shortage, poverty, the drive to meet ever-growing needs, and the fact that some nations, like England, were naturally inclined to sea travel, all culminated in Western thought leading to overseas discoveries.

The primary drive behind all these developments was the satisfaction of material needs. The accompanying scientific studies developed in opposition to the Church and medieval Christian scholasticism, and thus Europeans were confronted with a conflict between religion and science.[1] This caused religion to split off from science and many people to break with religion. This development eventually led to the development of materialism and communism. In social geography, humanity was faced with the most striking elements of Western history: global exploitation, unending conflict based on interest, two world wars, and the division of the world into political or economic blocs.

---

[1] This opposition was due to two factors: the Catholic Church refused to come to terms with new scientific discoveries and concepts, and the emerging new middle class wanted to be free of the disciplining rules of religion.

The West has held the world under its economic and military control for several centuries. In recent centuries, the conflict between religion and science has occupied many intellectual circles. Enlightenment movements that began in the eighteenth century saw human beings as consisting of the mind only. Following that, positivist and materialist movements saw humans as solely material or corporeal entities. As a result, spiritual crises have followed one after another. It is no exaggeration to say that these crises and the absence of spiritual satisfaction were the major factors behind the conflict of interests that enveloped the last two centuries and that reached its apex in the two world wars.

As possessors of a system of belief with a different history and essence, we have some basic values and concepts which can be given, not only to the West, with whom we have deep economic, social, and military relationships, but also to humanity at large. At the top of the list is our understanding and our concept of humanity. This view is neither exclusively ours, nor is it a subjective view; rather, it is an objective view that puts forward what humans really are.

Humans are creatures composed not only of a body and a mind, or feelings and a spirit; rather, we are harmonious compositions of all these elements. Each of us is a body writhing in a network of needs; but this is not all, we also possess a mind that has more subtle and vital needs than the body, and each of us is driven by anxieties about the past and the future in a search for answers to such questions as: "What am I? What is this world? What is the purpose of life and death? Who sent me to this world, and why? Where am I going, and what is the purpose of life? Who is my guide in this earthly journey?"

Moreover, each person is a creature made up of feelings that cannot be satisfied by the mind, and a creature of spirit; it is through the spirit that we acquire our essential human identity. Each individual is a combination of all of these factors. When a person around whom all systems and efforts revolve is considered and evaluated as a creature with all these aspects and when all needs are fulfilled then this person is able to attain true happiness. At this point, true human progress and evolution in relation to our essential being is possible only through education.

To comprehend the significance of education, we need only to look at one difference between us and the animals. At the beginning of the journey from the world of spirits that extends into eternity at the earthly stage, we are weak, in need, and in the miserable position of being dependent on everything from others.

Animals, however, come to this world as if they have gained perfection in another realm. Within two hours, two days, or two months after their birth, they have learned nearly everything they need to know, they have developed a full relationship with the universe and the laws of life. The strength to live and the ability to work that takes us 20 years to acquire is attained by a sparrow or a bee in 20 days. More correctly, they are inspired with this ability and strength. This means that the essential duty of an animal is not to become perfect through learning and evolving by gaining knowledge or by seeking help; these things imply a weakness that is not inherent in the nature of an animal. Rather, it is the duty of an animal to work according to its natural ability and it is in this way that it actively serves its Creator.

On the other hand, we humans must learn everything when we come into this world, for we are ignorant of the rules of life. In fact, in 20 years, or perhaps even throughout our life, we still cannot fully learn the nature and meaning of the rules and conditions of life nor can we completely understand our relationship with the universe. We are sent here in a very weak and helpless form. For example, we can stand on our feet only after one year. In addition, it takes us almost our whole life to learn what things are really in our interest and what are not. Only with the help of a social life can we turn toward our interests and avoid danger.

This means that our essential duty as a creation that has come to this passing guesthouse with a pure nature is to reach stability and clarity in thought, imagination, and belief so that we can acquire a "second nature" and qualify to continue our life in "the next, much more elevated realms." In addition, by performing our duties as servants, we must activate our hearts, spirits, and all our innate faculties. By embracing our inner and outer worlds, where innumerable mysteries and puzzles reside, we must comprehend the secret of existence and thus rise to the rank of true humanity.

The religion-science conflict and its product, materialism, have seen nature, like humanity, as an accumulation of material created only to fulfill bodily needs. As a result, we are experiencing global environmental disasters.

Let us consider this point: A book is the material manifestation, in the form of words, of a "spiritual" existence in the writer's mind. There is no conflict between these two ways of expressing the same truth and ideas in two different "worlds." Similarly, a building has a spiritual existence in the architect's mind; it has "destiny" or "pre-determination" in the form of a plan; the material form is in the form of a physical structure. There is no conflict among the ways of expressing the same meaning, content, and truth of these three different worlds. To look for conflict would be nothing more than a wasted effort.

Similarly, there can be no conflict among the Qur'an, the Divine Scripture, (coming from God's Attribute of Speech), the universe (coming from His Attributes of Power and Will), and the sciences that examine them. The universe is a mighty Holy Book (Qur'an) derived from God's Attributes of Power and Will. In other words, if we can be forgiven for using such a prosaic comparison, the universe is just a large Qur'an that has been physically created by God for our instruction. In return, as it is an expression of the laws of the universe in yet another form, the Qur'an is a universe that has been codified and written down. In its actual meaning, religion does not oppose or limit science or scientific work.

Religion guides sciences, determines their real goal, and puts moral and universal human values before science as guides. If this truth had been understood in the West, and if this relationship between religion and knowledge had been discovered, things would have been very different. Science would not have done more harm than good, nor would it have opened the way for producing bombs and other lethal weapons.

Claims are made today that religion is divisive and opens the way for the killing of others. However, it cannot be denied that religion, in particular Islam, did not lead over the last few centuries to merciless exploitation: in particular the wars and revolutions of the twentieth century that killed hundreds of millions of people and left behind even more homeless, widows, orphans, and wounded were not down to Islam. Scientific materialism, a view of life and the world that had severed itself from religion and a clash of interests caused this exploitation.

There is also the matter of environmental pollution, which has been caused by scientific materialism, a basic peculiarity of modern Western thought. Underlying the global threat of pollution is the concept, brought about by scientific disbelief, that nature is an accumulation of things that has no value outside its ability to meet physical needs. In fact, nature is much more than a heap of material or an accumulation of objects: it has a certain sacredness, for it is an arena in which God's Beautiful Names are displayed.

Nature is an exhibition of beauty and meaning that displays profound and vast meanings; trees taking root, flowers blossoming, the taste and aroma of fruit, the rain, streams flowing, air being inhaled and exhaled, and soil nurturing innumerable creatures. Thus, a person's mind and heart become like a honeycomb; the nectar presented is made up of judgments and the faculty of contemplation. This travels all over the world, like the pollen that attaches itself to the honeybee. The honey of faith, virtue, love of humanity and all creatures for the sake of the Creator, the nectar of helping others, sacrificing oneself to the extent that one foregoes the passion of life so that others can live, and providing service to all creation—this is what oozes from this honeycomb.

As stated by Bediüzzaman, there is an understanding of education that sees the illumination of the mind in science and knowledge, and the light of the heart in faith and virtue. This understanding, which makes the student soar in the skies of humanity on two wings and seek God's approval through service to others, has many things to offer. It rescues science from materialism, from being a factor that is as harmful as it is beneficial—both from material and spiritual perspectives—as well as preventing science from becoming a lethal weapon. Such an understanding, in Einstein's words, will not allow religion to remain crippled. Nor will it allow religion to be perceived as being cut off from intelligence, life, and scientific truth, nor as a fanatical institution that builds walls between individuals and nations.

Serving Humanity through Education

Due to rapid developments in transportation and communication, the world has become a global village. Nations have become like next-door neighbors. However, we must remember that in a world like this, national existence can be ensured only by protecting the specific characteristics of each nation. In a unified mosaic of nations and countries, those that cannot protect their unique characteristics, "patterns," or "designs" will disappear. As with all other nations, our essential characteristics are religion and language, history and the motherland. What Yahya Kemal, a famous Turkish poet and writer, expressed with great emotion in *The Districts without a Call to Prayer*, was that our culture and civilization had been brought from Islam and Central Asia and had been kneaded for centuries in Anatolia, Europe, and even Africa.

All people need one another. As mentioned above, we have more to give humanity than we have to take. Today, voluntary or non-governmental organizations have established companies and foundations and are enthusiastically serving others in the name of Islam. The large-scale acceptance of the educational institutions that have spread all over the world, despite the great financial difficulties that they have faced, and the fact that they are competing with, and frequently surpassing their Western peers in a very short period of time, should be proof that what we have said cannot be denied.

The Turkish people have accumulated many problems over the past few centuries. At the base of these problems lies our mistaken concentration on the exterior of Islam and the neglect of its inner pearl. Later on we began to imitate others and surmised that there was a conflict between Islam and positive science. We arrived at this conclusion despite the fact that the latter is no more than discoveries of Divine laws that manifest God's Attributes of Power and Will; it is nothing but a different expression of the Qur'an derived from God's Attribute of Speech. This neglect, in turn, led to despotism in knowledge, thought, and administration; a hopelessness that led to a disorder that encompassed all individuals and institutions; a confusion in our work; we no longer paid any attention to the division of labor.

In short, our three greatest enemies are ignorance, poverty, and an internal schism. Knowledge, work-capital, and unification can struggle against these. As ignorance is the most serious problem, it must be opposed with education, which always has been the most important way of serving our country. Now that we live in a global village, education is the best way to serve humanity and to establish a dialogue with other civilizations.

But above all else, education is a humane service; we were sent here to learn and be perfected through education. Bediüzzaman drew attention to possible solutions and the future by saying: "The old state of affairs is impossible. Either a new state or annihilation is needed." Saying that "controversial subjects should not be discussed with Christian spiritual leaders," he opened dialogues with members of other religions. Like Mawlana Jalal al-Din al-Rumi, who said: "One of my feet is in the center and the other is in seventy-two realms (i.e. in the realm of all nations) like a compass," he drew a broad circle that encompassed all believers. Implying that the days of brute force were over, Bediüzzaman said: "Victory with civilized persons is won through persuasion," thus pointing out that dialogue, persuasion, and discussion based on evidence are essential for those of us who seek to serve religion. By saying that "in the future humanity will turn toward knowledge and science, and in the future reason and words will govern," he encouraged knowledge and dialogue. Finally, by putting aside politics and direct political involvement, he drew the basic lines of the truly religious and national service in this age and in the future.

In the light of such principles, I have encouraged people to serve the country in particular, and humanity in general, through education. I called on them to help the state educate and help people to develop by opening schools. Ignorance can be defeated through education, poverty through work and the possession of capital, and internal schism and separatism through unity, dialogue, and tolerance. As the solution of every problem in this life ultimately depends on human beings, education is the most effective vehicle, regardless of whether we have a paralyzed social and political system or we have one that operates like clockwork.

Schools

After the government granted permission for the opening of private schools, many people voluntarily chose to spend their savings on serving the country instead of passing into the next world after having spent this life in pursuit of a frivolous existence. In fact, people have done so with the enthusiasm normally given to worship. It is impossible for me to know about all of the schools that have been opened both here and abroad. Since I have only recommended and encouraged such actions, I do not even know the names of many of the companies that opened schools or where the schools are located.

However, I have followed this matter to a certain extent in the press and in series of articles written by such worthy journalists as Ali Bayramoğlu, Şahin Alpay, and Atılgan Bayar. Schools have been opened in places ranging from Azerbaijan to the Philippines, from St. Petersburg to Moscow, and with the help of our Jewish fellow-citizen and prominent businessman Üzeyir Garih, and with reference to his knowledge, in Yakutsky. These schools have been opened in almost all countries, except for those like Iran, where permission has not been given.

Writers and thinkers who have visited the schools confirm that these schools have been financed by voluntary organizations in Turkey. In most or all of them, student fees are an important part of this financing. Local administrators contribute sizable assistance by providing land, buildings, principals, and teachers when necessary. The teachers, who are dedicated to serving their country, nation, and humanity, and who have found the meaning of life in serving others, work enthusiastically for a low salary.

Initially, some of our foreign affairs officials were hesitant to give their support, for they did not really understand what was going on. Today, however, most of them support the schools. In addition to Turkey's last two presidents, the late honorable Turgut Özal and the honorable Süleyman Demirel, as well as the former Chairman of the Parliament, Mustafa Kalemli and former Minister of Foreign Affairs, Hikmet Çetin, all gave their support to these efforts by actually visiting the schools.

Local administrators are just as aware of secularism, or even more so, than the Turkish government. It has been explained by enlightened journalists like Şahin Alpay, Atılgan Bayar and many others, in a way similar to Ali Bayramoğlu's observations, that these countries do not feel the slightest concern regarding these schools for the future. In fact, speaking at the opening ceremonies for the school in Moscow, the Head of the Moscow National Education Office said: "There are two important events in Russia's recent history. One of these is Gagarin's journey to the skies. The other is the opening of a Turkish school here." He described this as an historic event.

For some, this life consists of the few days passed in this earthly guesthouse in pursuit of the fulfillment of the ego's desires. Other people have different views, and so give life a different meaning. For me, this life consists of a few breaths on the journey that begins in the world of spirits and continues eternally either in Heaven or, God forbid, Hell.

This life is very important, for it shapes our afterlife. Given this, we should spend it in ways designed to earn the eternal life in Paradise and gain the approval of the Giver of Life. This path passes through the inescapable dimension of servanthood to God by means of serving, first of all, our families, relatives, and neighbors, and then our country and nation, with finally humanity and creation being the object of our efforts. This service is our right; conveying it to others is our responsibility.

EDUCATION FROM CRADLE TO GRAVE

The main duty and purpose of human life is to seek understanding. The effort of doing so, known as education, is a perfecting process though which we earn, in the spiritual, intellectual, and physical dimensions of our beings, the rank appointed for us as the perfect pattern of creation. At birth, the outset of the earthly phase of our journey from the world of spirits to eternity, we are totally impotent and extremely needy. By contrast, most animals come into the world as if mature or as if they have been perfected beforehand. Within a few hours, or days, or months, they learn everything necessary for their survival, as well as how to relate to their environment and with other creatures. For example, sparrows or bees acquire maturity and all the physical and social skills they need within about twenty days; we need twenty years or more to acquire a comparable level of maturity.

We are born helpless as well as ignorant of the laws of life and must cry out to get the help we need. After a year or so, we can stand on our feet and walk a little. When we are about fifteen, we are expected to have understood the difference between good and evil, the beneficial and the harmful. However, it will take us our whole lives to acquire intellectual and spiritual perfection. Our principal duty in life is to acquire perfection and purity in our thinking, perceptions, and belief. By fulfilling our duty of servanthood to the Creator, Nourisher, and Protector, and by penetrating the mystery of creation through our potential and abilities, we seek to attain the rank of true humanity and become worthy of a blissful, eternal life in another, exalted world.

Our humanity is directly proportional to the purity of our emotions. Although those who are full of negative feelings and whose souls have been influenced by egoism appear to be human beings, it is doubtful whether they really are human. Almost anyone can train their bodies, but few can educate their minds and feelings. The former produces strong bodies, while the latter produces spiritual people.

This article is a summary from Gülen's articles published in *Sızıntı*, March 1981–June 1982, Issue No: 26-41.

Our Innate Abilities and Education

Since the time of Ibn Miskawayh,[1] human faculties or "drives" have been dealt with in three categories: reason, anger, and lust. Reason encompasses our powers of perception, imagination, calculation, memory, learning, and so on. Anger covers our power of self-defense, which Islamic jurisprudence defines as something necessary to defend our faith and religion, sanity, possessions, life and family, and other sacred values. Lust is the name for the driving force behind our animal appetites:

> Decked out for humanity is the passionate love of desires for the opposite sex and offspring; for hoarded treasures of gold and silver; for branded horses, cattle, and plantations; and for all kinds of worldly things. (Al-Imran 3:14)

These drives are found in other creatures. However, whether in their desires, intelligence, or determination to defend life and territory, these drives are limited in all creatures, but not in humanity. Each of us is uniquely endowed with free will and the consequent obligation to discipline our powers. This struggle for discipline determines our humanity. In combination with one another and according to circumstances, our capabilities are often expressed through jealousy, hatred, enmity, hypocrisy, and ostentation. These too need to be disciplined.

Humans do not only consist of a body and a mind. Each of us has a spirit that needs to be satisfied. Without this, we cannot find true happiness or perfection. Spiritual satisfaction is possible only through knowledge of God and belief in Him. Confined within the physical world, our own particular carnal self, time, and place can feel like a dungeon. We can escape this imprisonment through belief and regular worship and by refraining from extremes while using our faculties or powers. We must not seek to destroy our drives, but rather to use our free will to contain and purify them, to channel and direct them toward virtue. For example, we are not expected to eliminate lust, but to satisfy it lawfully through repro-

---

[1] Ibn Miskawayh (c.930-1030): Muslim moralist, philosopher, and historian. His moral treatise *Tahdhib al-Akhlaq* [Gilding Morality], influenced by the Aristotelian concept of the meaning, is considered one of the best statements of Islamic philosophy. His universal history *Kitab Tajarib al-Umam wa Ta'aqub al-Himam* (Eclipse of the 'Abbasid Caliphate), was noted for its use of all available sources and greatly stimulated the development of Islamic historiography.

duction. Happiness lies in confining our lust to the lawful bounds of decency and chastity, not in engaging in debauchery and dissipation.

Similarly, jealousy can be channeled into emulation free of rancor, which inspires us to emulate those who excel in goodness and good deeds. Applying the proper discipline to our reason results in the acquisition of knowledge, and ultimately of comprehension or wisdom. Purifying and training anger leads to courage and forbearance. Disciplining our passion and desire develops chastity.

If every virtue is thought of as being the center of a circle, and any movement away from the center is thought of as being a vice, then the vice becomes greater as we move further away from the center. Every virtue therefore has innumerable possible vices, since there is only one center of a circle, but an infinite number of points around it. It is irrelevant in which direction the deviation occurs, for deviation from the center, in whatever direction, is a vice.

There are two extremes related to each moral virtue: deficiency or excess. The two extremes connected with wisdom are stupidity and cunning. For courage, they are cowardice and rashness, and for chastity, lethargy and uncontrolled lust. So a person's perfection, the ultimate purpose of our existence, lies in maintaining a condition of balance and moderation between the two extremes relating to every virtue. 'Ali ibn Abu Talib is reported to have said:

> God has characterized angels by intellect without sexual desire, passion, or anger, and animals with anger and desire without intellect. He exalted humanity by bestowing upon them all of these qualities. Accordingly, if a person's intellect dominates his desire and ferocity, he rises to a station above that of angels, because this station is attained by a human being in spite of the existence of obstacles that do not vex angels.

Improving a community is possible only by elevating the young generations to the rank of humanity, not by obliterating those who are on the wrong path. Unless a seed composed of faith, tradition, and historical consciousness is germinated throughout the country, new evil elements will appear and grow in the place of each eradicated evil.

The True Meaning and Value of Education

Education through learning and leading a commendable way of life is a sublime duty that is the manifestation of the Divine Name *Rabb* (Educator and Sustainer). By fulfilling this, we are able to attain the rank of true humanity and to become a beneficial element of society.

Education is vital for both societies and individuals. First, our humanity is directly proportional to the purity of our emotions. Although those who are full of evil feelings and whose souls are influenced by egoism appear to be human beings, whether they really are so is questionable. Almost anyone can train themselves physically, but few can educate their minds and feelings. Second, improving a community is possible by elevating the coming generations to the rank of humanity, not by obliterating the bad ones. Unless the seeds of religion, traditional values, and historical consciousness are germinated throughout the country, new negative elements will inevitably grow up in the place of every negative element that has been eradicated.

A nation's future depends on its youth. Any people who want to secure their future should apply as much energy to raising their children as they devote to other issues. A nation that fails its youth, that abandons them to foreign cultural influences, jeopardizes their identity and is subject to cultural and political weakness.

The reasons why we are able to observe the indulgence in vice in today's generation, as well as the reasons for the incompetence of some administrators and similar nation-wide troubles, can be found in the prevailing conditions and ruling elite of 25 years ago. Likewise, those who are charged with the education of the young people of today will be responsible for the vices and virtues that will appear in the next 25 years. Those who wish to predict a nation's future can do so accurately by taking full account of the education and upbringing given to its young people. "Real" life is possible only through knowledge. Thus, those who neglect learning and teaching should be counted as being "dead," even though they are living; we were created to learn and communicate to others what we have learned.

Making correct decisions is dependent on possessing a sound mind and being capable of sound thought. Science and knowledge illuminate and develop the mind. For this reason, a mind deprived of science and knowledge cannot make the right decisions; it is always exposed to deception, and is subject to being misled.

We are only truly human if we learn, teach, and inspire others. It is difficult to regard those who are ignorant and without desire to learn as being truly human. It is also questionable whether learned people who do not renew and reform themselves in order to set an example for others are truly human. Status and merit acquired through knowledge and science are higher and more lasting than those obtained through other means.

Given the great importance of learning and teaching, we must determine what is to be learned and taught, and when and how to do so. Although knowledge is a value in itself, the purpose of learning is to make knowledge a guide in life and to illuminate the road to human perfection. Thus, any knowledge not appropriated for the self is a burden to the learner, and a science that does not direct one toward sublime goals is a deception.

But knowledge acquired for a legitimate purpose is an inexhaustible source of blessings for the learner. Those who possess such a source are always sought out by people, like a source of fresh water, and are able to lead people to good. Knowledge limited to empty theories and unabsorbed pieces of learning, which arouses suspicions in minds and darkens hearts, is a "heap of garbage" around which desperate and confused souls flounder. Therefore, science and knowledge should seek to uncover the nature of humanity and the mysteries of creation. Any knowledge, even "scientific knowledge," is legitimate only if it sheds light on the mysteries of human nature and enlightens the dark areas of existence.

Family, School, and Environment

People who want to guarantee their future cannot be indifferent to how their children are educated. The family, school, environment, and mass media should all cooperate to ensure the desired result. Opposing tendencies among these vital institutions will subject young people to contradictory influences that will distract them and dissipate their energy. In particular, the mass media should contribute to the education of the young generation by following the education policy approved by the community. The school must be as perfect as possible with respect to its curriculum, the scientific and moral standards of the teachers, and its physical conditions. A family must provide the necessary warmth and atmosphere in which to raise children.

In the early centuries of Islam, minds, hearts, and souls strove to understand that which the Lord of the Heavens and the Earth approves. Each conversation, discussion, correspondence, and event was directed to that end. As a result, whoever could do so, imbibed the correct values and spirit from the surrounding environment. It was as if everything was a teacher which would prepare the individual's mind and soul and develop his or her capacity to attain a high level in Islamic sciences. The first school in which we receive the necessary education to be perfected is the home.

The home is vitally important for raising a healthy generation and ensuring a healthy social system or structure. This responsibility continues throughout life. The impressions we receive from our family cannot be obliterated later in life. Furthermore, the family's control over the child at home, with respect to other siblings and toys, continues at school with respect to the child's friends, books, and places visited. Parents must feed their children's minds with knowledge and science before their minds become engaged in useless things, for souls without truth and knowledge are fields in which evil thoughts are cultivated and grown.

Children can receive a good education at home only if there is a healthy family life. Thus, marriage should be undertaken to form a healthy family life and so contribute to the permanence of one's nation, in particular, and of the human population in general. Peace, happiness, and security at home establish mutual accord between the spouses in thought, morals, and belief. Couples who decide to marry should know each other well and consider purity of feelings, chastity, morality, and virtue rather than wealth and physical charms. The mischief and impudence of children reflect the atmosphere in which they are being raised. A dysfunctional family life increasingly reflects upon the spirit of the child, and therefore upon society.

In the family, older members should treat younger ones with compassion, and the young should show respect for their elders. Parents should love and respect each other, and treat their children with compassion and due consideration of their feelings. They must treat each child justly and not discriminate among them. If parents encourage their children to develop their abilities and be useful to themselves and the community, they have then given the nation a strong new pillar. If they do not cultivate the proper feelings in their children, they release scorpions into the community.

The School and the Teacher

A school may be compared to a laboratory; it offers an elixir that can prevent or heal the ills of life. Those who have the knowledge and wisdom to prepare and administer this elixir are the teachers.

A school is a place of learning, where everything related to this life and the next is taught. It can shed light on vital ideas and events, and enable students to understand their natural and human environment. A school can also quickly open the way to unveiling the meaning of things and events, thereby leading a student to wholeness of thought and contemplation. In essence, a school is a kind of place of worship; the "holy leaders" are the teachers.

True teachers sow the pure seed and preserve it. They occupy themselves with what is good and wholesome, and lead and guide the children through life and whatever events they may encounter. For a school to be a true institution of education students should first be equipped with an ideal, a love of their language and know how to use it most effectively; they should possess good morals and perennial human values. Their social identity must be built on these foundations.

Education is different from teaching. Most people can teach, but only a very few can educate. Communities composed of individuals devoid of sublime ideals, good manners, and human values are like rude individuals who have no loyalty in friendship or consistency in enmity. Those who trust such people are always disappointed, and those who depend upon them are sooner or later left without support. The best way of equipping oneself with such values is a sound religious education.

A community's survival depends on idealism and good morals, as well as on being able to reach the necessary level in scientific and technological progress. For this reason, trades and crafts should be taught, beginning at least at the elementary level. A good school is not a building where only theoretical information is given, but an institution or a laboratory where students are prepared for life.

Patience is of great importance in education. Educating people is the most sacred, but also the most difficult, task in life. In addition to setting a good personal example, teachers should be patient enough to obtain the desired result. They should know their students well, and address their intellects and their hearts, spirits, and feelings. The best way to educate people is to show a special concern for every individual, not forgetting that each individual is a different "world."

A school provides its pupils with the possibilities of continuous reading, and speaks even when it is silent. Because of this, although it seems to occupy only one phase of life, school actually dominates all times and events. For the rest of their lives, pupils re-enact what they have learned at school and derive continuous influence from this experience. Teachers should know how to find a way to the student's heart and be able to leave indelible imprints upon his or her mind. They should test the information to be passed on to students by refining their own minds and the prisms of their hearts. A good lesson is one that does more than provide pupils with useful information or skills; it should elevate them into the presence of the unknown. This enables the students to acquire a penetrating vision into the reality of things, and to see each event as a sign of the unseen world.

A MOVEMENT ORIGINATING
ITS OWN MODELS

In this article I would like to discuss a legend; to talk about it is a duty, and therefore it is difficult to put it into words. However, I wonder if it is possible to describe in the scope of such an article an important resurrectional movement, a movement that has thrived in every part of the world, budding, giving off shoots and seedlings. I think not. What I know about the issue comes only from the videos I have seen. My attestation relies on what I have heard. The limits of my pen are those of my comprehension. I do not know to what era the implication of all that has been happening belongs. Now tell me what can be told under these circumstances. All I can do in describing this will be like someone attempting to describe roses and flowers as they really are after only seeing a picture of a rose or a flower. But my task resembles more an attempt to describe the unique pattern, accent, and manner of each flower and rose in a garden by merely looking at the picture of a dead rose; the rose garden nor the flower garden cannot be described in this way. Even so, I believe that one should dare to talk on behalf of the phenomenon of the era to galvanize people of letters and conscience. If some people close to God will be inspired as a result of this article, I think then that my aim has been achieved.

No matter how expressive and stylishly it is told, what matters is that this important phenomenon of the era should be related. It should, after all, be related so that we add a footnote to history and show our respect for those devoted people who performed such heroic deeds. If, on the other hand, this soft breeze, this warm atmosphere, this fresh thought and this love, and the gentle winds felt across the globe were to be described very briefly, it would be disrespectful toward the noble traits, such as magnanimity and altruism.

The author has dedicated this article to countless educational activists who have gone all around the world, with a motivation to provide quality education and to promote peace between different nations and cultures. All throughout his life and career Gülen has preached the importance of education and directed his audience to participate in and support educational activities.

This movement is a phenomenon to be written about and under-scored. A few dozen passionate people set off in all directions for the sake of God without stopping to think about their longings or their feelings of separation and without uttering the words "foreign lands" or "unknown places" at a time when nobody could even fathom what lay ahead. They were full of determination, firm of intention, and self-reliant. They sup-pressed their love for their country and their homeland, replacing it with a love for mission. They were aware of their efforts for the cause of God as few have been, they lived as such, and they walked to the east and to the west saying:

We have entered the path of love,
We are lovesick.

Nigari[1]

At the most colorful period of their lives, when worldly pleasures and material objectives attract young people with an irresistible lure, and when physicality oppresses the hearts and minds of a person, they virtu-ally flew to all these places with a passion for accomplishment that sup-pressed the various desires and compulsions; the excitement of those in the first row was in their hearts. This flight abroad was not like the depar-ture of lovelorn youths who chased a false siren that had entered their lives at an unlucky time, those youths who pursued their dreams for a lifetime, who became lovesick, and who were strangers to their own na-ture, yet unable to reach the desired goal. The mission of these youths was from the heart and based on emotions, on consciousness, and deter-mination; it had a depth of good faith and sincerity. You could say that these were the usual dynamics of faith, the natural conditions of divine ambition, the ideals of the devoted, the guides of the Infinite Light, or the efforts of those who had abandoned their selves and their beloved ones in order to express themselves. Indeed, they were neither prevented by their own shortcomings nor did they surrender to the obstacles in their way; they walked to the far corners of the world, the only never-fading love in their hearts being God's favor and the ambition to meet Him. They walked; the roads took pride in this, the angels cheered them

---

[1] Seyyid Nigari: A famous poet of Azerbaijan. He was an important representative of nineteenth century mystical poetry.

on, and, naturally, the devils beat their breasts. They walked; they had neither horses nor cars, nor weapons, nor ammunition. Their source of energy was their incredible faith and the excitement in their hearts that seethed like magma; on the horizon was the happiness of humanity, consent, and pleasure. Their destiny equaled that of the Companions and the disciples. Soon after dawn they attained, with their chastity and purity, a manner that was tantamount to kinship with the angels. They became a theme for legends and a thing of never fading memory. They brought streams of light from eternity wherever they went. They lit a fire all around; the flame, ember, and smoke of this fire was happiness. The spell of tyranny and darkness gave way. The disbelieving bats were deprived of their sleep, and darkness unceasingly grumbled. Lies, calumny, and intrigue were hindered once again. All this made boorish thoughts and bigotry intolerably arrogant, making it want to tread on others' ideas and set up traps for faith. However, all opposition was in vain: the light shone everywhere. The light that radiated from eternity embraced the entire world. Now it was the time and the epoch of the bright souls, although the murky situation still prevailed and the horizons were foggy, but the magic of darkness and the boorish thoughts were already undone.

Now it was the turn of the bright souls to speak. Humanity would discover itself through them and take its true place in the hierarchy of creation. Therefore, it was a generation that had long been awaited. As people had been waiting for them, wherever they went they always bent double as a consequence of their reverence for God and their respect for humanity, their eyes fixed on the doorway of the Most Gracious, meekly and humbly, awaiting the time when showers of light would be unleashed, while their heads and feet touched the ground. No matter how the people of today assess the issue, these were the children of tomorrow; the bright future bore their secrets. These lucky people, who were the apostles of resurrection, each in their own way, held the flowers of friendship in their hands and the verses of brother and sisterhood on their lips. Their tongues, sharper than sharpest swords, were nourished by Qur'anic waterfalls and their words had divine dimensions. These words destroyed darkness, but did not harm anyone. They brought the sound of the rivers of Paradise within earshot, but they did not lead to a longing for Paradise. In fact, these people needed neither hands nor tongues. Their pure faces that reminded one of God wherever seen were so magical that words stumbled in the presence of the meanings that emanated from their manners, and tongues became mute. Even their shadows burned the night moths; not to mention their light, which dazzled anyone that came near. We rightfully say, "Tongues and words have nothing to say in the presence of actions. When manners speak, is there a need for speech?" They are the representatives of this truth. There have always been multitudes of good people on the Earth; however, the manners and words of this latest group are entirely different. I can hardly say that they were singular or unique, but were I asked to explain how they were, I would not be able to immediately reply. I would probably say, "They look like angels," and give up there.

Wherever these bright souls go, dry deserts turned into gardens of Eden thanks to the light they radiated. Much coal has been transformed into diamonds. Natures made of mud and stone have ascended to the rank of gold and silver. And everybody is talking about them now, waiting for the days when the love, brotherhood, and tolerance they promised will be realized. Today, only those who confuse darkness and light and who spend their lives in the realm of physicality are speaking against them. The bats are uneasy. The wolves and jackals are baring their teeth. The fools are restless. I find all these natural, and say, "Everybody exhibits his or her true nature."

Whatever happens, despite those who blow out the candles, these men have long illuminated the hearts that are thirsty for light wherever they go, they warn the pure natures of what lies behind things and events, and they announce the universal human values to unspoiled souls.

I firmly believe that, just as intercontinental obstacles were once overcome thanks to the Qur'an, and love, respect, and dialogue were permanently established, a new ground for agreement has been or will be founded by the efforts of these lucky people today. Humanity used to recognize our nation, with its smiling face and fortunate destiny. Why should this very fact not also be true today? A flood of love among the people has started overflowing in almost every place that these bearers of the mission visit. There have been breezes of happiness and gladness, one after another, that can be felt all around. Moreover, islands of peace, which we can call invulnerable castles of harmony and stability, are forming near and far.

Who knows, maybe in the near future, thanks to these volunteers who devote themselves to letting others live, the mind and soul will embrace each other once again; conscience and logic will become complementary depths of each other; physics and metaphysics will stop fighting and withdraw to their own realms, and everything will find the opportunity to express the beauty in its own nature through its own language, the intricacy of legislative rules and the principles of creation will be rediscovered, people will regret having fought each other over nothing, an atmosphere of peace that was not previously established in the marketplaces, in the schools and homes will be established, and breezes of happiness will blow, chastity will not be violated, honesty will not be oppressed, hearts will always breathe respect and esteem, no one will envy others, their property or their reputation, the powerful will treat the weak justly, the weak and the poor will have the chance to live humanely, nobody will be arrested on the strength of mere suspicions, no dwelling or workplace will be attacked, nobody's blood will be shed and the weak will not cry, everybody will adore God and love humanity. It is only then that this world, which is the hallway to Paradise, will become an Eden that is fascinating to live in.

GLOBAL PERSPECTIVES

REAL LIFE AND REAL HUMANITY

Since "real" life is only possible through knowledge, those who have neglected learning and teaching are considered to be "dead," even when they are biologically alive. We were created to learn and to communicate what we have learned to others.

Real life is lived at the spiritual level. Those whose hearts are alive, those who conquer the past and the future, transcend the restrictions of time. Such people are never overly distressed by past sorrows or overly anxious about the future. Those who are not able to experience full existence in their hearts, those who lead banal, shallow lives, are always gloomy and inclined to hopelessness. They consider the past as a horrifying grave, and see the future as a bottomless well. They live in agony, wondering whether they will live or die.

All of us are travelers, and the world is a multicolored exhibition and a rich and colorful book. We were sent to study this book, to increase our spiritual knowledge, and to uplift others. This colorful and pleasurable journey is a one-time event. For those whose feelings are alert and whose hearts are awake, this journey is more than enough to establish a Paradise-like garden. But for those whose eyes are covered, it is as if all goes by in a single breath.

The humble and modest are highly regarded by the created and by the Creator. The haughty and self-conceited, those who belittle others and put on haughty airs, are always disliked by the created and are punished by the Creator.

Humility is a sign of virtue and maturity, whereas haughtiness and self-conceit indicate an imperfect, low spirit. The most perfect human beings are those who are at ease and intimate in the company of others. In contrast, those who are too proud to join in with others and to form warm friendships are considered to be mere representatives of imperfectness. Humility makes people into true human beings. One sign of humility is that people do not change after they have obtained rank or wealth,

This collection of aphorisms was written in 1984 and recently appeared in one volume *Ölçü veya Yoldaki Işıklar*, Kaynak, Izmir, 2000; English edition *Pearls of Wisdom*, The Fountain, New Jersey, 2000, pp. 13, 23, 41, 42, 49, 50.

learning or fame, or whatever else may be publicly esteemed. If any of these circumstances causes people to alter their ideas, attitudes, and behavior, then they cannot be regarded as having attained true humanity or true humility.

When interacting with others, always use as a measure what you find pleasing or displeasing. Wish for others what you wish for yourself and do not forget that whatever conduct displeases you will also displease others. If you do this, you will be safe from misconduct and bad behavior, and will not hurt others.

Maturity and perfection of spirit mean that you should be just in your treatment of others, especially those who have done you an injustice. Return their bad action with goodness. Do not cease doing good even to those who have harmed you. Rather, treat them with kindness and nobility, for harming someone is cruel. Repaying evil with evil implies a deficiency in character; the opposite is nobility.

There is no limit of goodness that can be done for others. Those who dedicate themselves to doing good for humanity are so altruistic that they can even sacrifice their lives for others. However, such altruism is a great virtue only if it originates in sincerity and purity of intention; it should be far removed from racial or tribal superstitions.

Those who regard even the greatest favor they have done for others as being insignificant, yet greatly appreciate even the smallest favor done for themselves are perfected ones who have acquired the Divine standards of behavior and have found peace in their conscience. Such individuals never remind others of the good that they may have done for them, and never complain when others appear to be indifferent to them.

A COMPARATIVE APPROACH TO ISLAM AND DEMOCRACY

Religion, particularly Islam, has become one of the most difficult subject areas to tackle in recent years. Contemporary culture, whether approached from the perspective of anthropology or theology, psychology or psychoanalysis, evaluates religion with empirical methods. On the one hand, religion is an inwardly experienced and felt phenomenon, one that, for the most part, is related to the permanent aspects of life. On the other hand, believers can see their religion as a philosophy, a set of rational principles, or mere mysticism. The difficulty increases in the case of Islam, for some Muslims and policy-makers consider and present it as a purely political, sociological, and economic ideology, rather than as a religion.

If we want to analyze religion, democracy, or any other system or philosophy accurately, we should focus on humanity and human life. From this perspective, religion in general, and Islam in particular, cannot be compared on the same basis with democracy or any other political, social, or economic system. Religion focuses primarily on the immutable aspects of life and existence, whereas political, social, and economic systems or ideologies concern only certain variable social aspects of our worldly life.

The aspects of life with which religion is primarily concerned are as valid today as they were at the dawn of humanity and will continue to be so in the future. Worldly systems change according to circumstances and so can be evaluated only according to their times. Belief in God, the hereafter, the prophets, the holy books, the angels, and divine destiny have nothing to do with changing times. Likewise, worship and morality's universal and unchanging standards have little to do with time and worldly life.

Therefore, when comparing religion or Islam with democracy, we must remember that democracy is a system that is being continually developed and revised. It also varies according to the places and circum-

This article originally appeared in *SAIS Review*, 21:2 (Summer-Fall 2001):133-38.

stances where it is practiced. On the other hand, religion has established immutable principles related to faith, worship, and morality. Thus, only Islam's worldly aspects should be compared with democracy.

The main aim of Islam and its unchangeable dimensions affect its rules governing the changeable aspects of our lives. Islam does not propose a certain unchangeable form of government or attempt to shape it. Instead, Islam establishes fundamental principles that orient a government's general character, leaving it to the people to choose the type and form of government according to time and circumstances. If we approach the matter in this light and compare Islam with the modern liberal democracy of today, we will be better able to understand the position of Islam and democracy with respect to each other.

Democratic ideas stem from ancient times. Modern liberal democracy was born in the American (1776) and French Revolutions (1789-1799). In democratic societies, people govern themselves as opposed to being ruled by someone above. The individual has priority over the community in this type of political system, being free to determine how to live his or her own life. Individualism is not absolute, though. People achieve a better existence by living within a society and this requires that they adjust and limit their freedom according to the criteria of social life.

The Prophet says that all people are as equal as the teeth of a comb.[1] Islam does not discriminate based on race, color, age, nationality, or physical traits. The Prophet declared:

> You are all from Adam, and Adam is from earth. O servants of God, be brothers [and sisters.]"[2]

---

[1] Abu Shuja' Shirawayh ibn Shahrdar al-Daylami, *Al-Firdaws bi-Ma'thur al-Khitab* [The Heavenly Garden Made Up of the Selections from the Prophet's Addresses], Beirut, 1986, Dar al-Kutub al-'Ilmiya, 4:300.

[2] For the second part of the hadith see the sections "Nikah" (marriage Contract) in Abu 'Abdullah Muhammad ibn Isma'il al-Bukhari, ed., *al-Jami' al-Sahih* [A Collection of the Prophet's Authentic Traditions], Istanbul: al-Maktabat al-Islamiya, n.d., ch. 45; "Birr wa Sila" (Goodness and Visiting the Relatives) in Imam Abu Husayn Muslim ibn Hajjaj, ed., *al-Jami' al-Sahih*, op. cit., ch. 23; and for the first part see "Tafsir" (The Qur'anic Commentary) and "Manaqib" (The Virtues of the Prophet and His Companions) in Abu 'Isa Muhammad ibn 'Isa al-Tirmidhi, *al-Jami' al-Sahih*, Beirut, Dar al Ihya al-Turath al-'Arabi, n.d., chs. 49 and 74, respectively. The original text in Arabic does not include the word "sisters" in the command. However, the masculine form used refers to both men and women, as is the rule in many languages. An equivalent in English would be "humankind," which refers to both men and women. By saying "O servants

Those who were born earlier, who have more wealth or power than others, or who belong to certain families or ethnic groups have no inherent right to rule others.

Islam also upholds the following fundamental principles:

1. Power lies in truth, a repudiation of the common idea that truth relies upon power.
2. Justice and the rule of law are essential.
3. Freedom of belief and rights to life, personal property, reproduction, and health (both mental and physical) cannot be violated.
4. The privacy and immunity of individual life must be maintained.
5. No one can be convicted of a crime without evidence, or accused and punished for someone else's crime.
6. An advisory system of administration is essential.

All rights are equally important, and the rights of the individual cannot be sacrificed for the sake of society. Islam considers a society to be composed of conscious individuals equipped with freewill and having responsibility toward both themselves and others. Islam goes a step further by adding a cosmic dimension. It sees humanity as the "motor" of history, contrary to the fatalistic approaches of some nineteenth century Western philosophies of history, such as dialectical materialism and historicism.[3] Just as the will and behavior of every individual determine the outcome of his or her life in this world and in the hereafter, a society's progress or decline is determined by the will, worldview, and lifestyle of its inhabitants. The Qur'an says:

> God will not change the state of a people unless they change themselves (with respect to their beliefs, worldview, and lifestyle). (Ar-Rad 13:11)

---

of God," the Prophet also means women, because both men and women are equally servants of God.

[3] See Karl R. Popper, *The Poverty of Historicism*, trans. Sabri Orman, Istanbul, Insan Yayınları, 1985.

In other words, each society holds the reins of its fate in its own hands. The prophetic tradition emphasizes this idea: "You will be ruled according to how you are."[4] This is the basic character and spirit of democracy; an idea which does not conflict with any Islamic principle.

As Islam holds individuals and societies responsible for their own fate, people must be responsible for governing themselves. The Qur'an addresses society with such phrases as: "O people!" and "O believers!" The duties entrusted to modern democratic systems are those that Islam assigns to society and classifies, in order of importance, as "absolutely necessary, relatively necessary, and commendable to carry out." The sacred text includes the following passages:

> Establish, all of you, peace. (Al-Baqara 2:208)

> Spend in the way of God and to the needy of the pure and good of what you have earned and of what We bring forth for you from the Earth. (Al-Baqara 2:267)

> If some among your women are accused of indecency, you must have four witnesses (to prove it). (An-Nisa 4:15)

> God commands you to give over the public trusts to the charge of those having the required qualities and to judge with justice when you judge people. (An-Nisa 4:58)

> Observe justice as witnesses respectful for God, even if it is against yourselves, your parents and relatives. (An-Nisa 4:135)

> If they (your enemies) incline to peace (when you are at war), you also incline to it. (Al-Anfal 8:61)

> If a corrupt, sinful one brings you news (about others), investigate it so that you should not strike a people without knowing. (Al-Hujurat 49:6)

> If two parties among the believers fight between themselves, reconcile them. (Al-Hujurat 49:9)

---

[4] 'Ala al-Din 'Ali al-Muttaqi al-Hindi, *Kanz al-'Ummal fi Sunan al-Aqwal wa al-Af'al* [A Treasure of the Laborers for the Sake of the Prophet's Sayings and Deeds], Beirut, Mu'assasat al-Risala, 1985, 6:89.

In short, the Qur'an addresses the whole community and assigns it almost all the duties entrusted to modern democratic systems.

People cooperate with one another by sharing these duties and establishing the essential foundations necessary to perform them. The government is composed of all of these basic elements. Thus, Islam recommends a government based on a social contract. People elect the administrators and establish a council to debate common issues. Also, the society as a whole participates in auditing the administration. During the rule of the first four caliphs (632-661) in particular, the fundamental principles of government mentioned above—including free elections—were fully observed. The political system was transformed into a sultanate after the death of Ali, the fourth caliph, due to internal conflicts and the global conditions at that time. Unlike the caliphate, power in the sultanate was passed down through the sultan's family. However, even though free elections were no longer held, societies maintained other principles that are found at the core of liberal democracy of today.

Islam is an inclusive religion. It is based on the belief in one God as the Creator, Lord, Sustainer, and Administrator of the universe. Islam is the religion of the whole universe. That is, the entire universe obeys the laws laid down by God; everything in the universe is "Muslim" and obeys God by submitting to His laws. Even a person who refuses to believe in God or who follows another religion has to be a Muslim perforce as far as bodily existence is concerned. Our entire life, from the embryonic stage to the body's dissolution into dust after death, every tissue of the muscles, and every limb of the body follows the course prescribed for each by God's laws. Thus, in Islam, God, nature, and humanity are neither remote from one another nor are they alien to one another. It is God who makes Himself known to humanity through nature and humanity itself, and nature and humanity are two books (of creation) through which each word of God is made known. This leads humankind to look upon everything as belonging to the same Lord, to whom it itself belongs, and therefore regarding nothing in the universe as being alien. His sympathy, love, and service do not remain confined to the people of a particular race, color, or ethnicity. The Prophet summed this up with the command, "O servants of God, be brothers (and sisters)!"

A separate but equally important point is that Islam recognizes all religions that came before it. It accepts all the prophets and books sent to different peoples in different epochs of history. Not only does it accept them, but it also regards belief in them as an essential principle of being Muslim. In this way, it acknowledges the basic unity of all religions. A Muslim is at the same time a true follower of Abraham, Moses, David, all the other Hebrew prophets and Jesus. This belief explains why both Christians and Jews enjoyed their religious rights under the rule of Islamic governments throughout history.

The Islamic social system seeks to form a virtuous society and thereby gain God's approval. It recognizes right, not force, as the foundation of social life. Hostility is unacceptable. Relationships must be based on belief, love, mutual respect, assistance, and understanding instead of conflict and the pursuit of personal interests. Social education encourages people to pursue lofty ideals and to strive for perfection, not just to run after their own desires. Justified calls for unity and virtues create mutual support and solidarity, and belief secures brotherhood and sisterhood. Encouraging the soul to attain perfection brings happiness in both worlds.

Democracy has developed over time. Just as it has gone through many different stages in the past, it will continue to evolve and improve in the future. Along the way, it will be shaped into a more humane and just system, one based on righteousness and reality. If human beings are considered as a whole, without disregarding the spiritual dimension of their existence and their spiritual needs, and without forgetting that human life is not limited to this mortal life and that all people have a great craving for eternity, democracy could reach the peak of perfection and bring even more happiness to humanity. Islamic principles of equality, tolerance, and justice can help it do just this.

AT THE THRESHOLD OF A NEW MILLENNIUM

Just as every dawn, every sunrise, and every coming spring signifies a new beginning and hope, so does every new century and every new millennium. In this respect, within the wheels of time, over which we have no control, humanity has always sought a new spark of life, a breath as fresh as the wind of dawn, and has hoped and desired to step into the light, leaving behind the darkness, as if one were crossing a threshold.

We can only speculate as to when the first man and woman appeared on Earth. The Earth is equated with the Heavens as it exhibits the divine creations and because of the ontological meaning it contains; the value of the Earth stems largely from its chief inhabitant: humanity. According to the calendar we use today, we are at the threshold of the third millennium after the birth of Jesus, peace be upon him. However, since time revolves and advances in a helicoidal relativity, there are different measures of time in the world. For example, according to the measure of time that currently enjoys global acceptance, the world is about to cross the threshold of a new thousand-year period. According to the Jewish calendar, we are already in the second half of the eighth millennium. Within the Hindu timeframe, we are living in the Kali Yuga era. If we follow the Muslim calendar, we are approaching the end of the first half of the second millennium.

We should remember, however, the fact that each measure of time is nothing more than a relative measurement. While a 100-year period is assumed to be the measure for a century, the idea of a 60-year century, based on the life span of an average person, is also worth mentioning. From this point of view, we are already in the fourth millennium after the birth of Jesus, peace be upon him, and the third millennium after the *hijrah* (the Emigration of the Prophet from Makka to Madina), the starting point of the Muslim calendar. I bring up this issue because there are people suffering spiritual discomfort engendered by the terrifying auguries believed to be associated with the upcoming millennium, especially in

---

This article originally appeared in *The Fountain,* Issue No: 29 (January-March 2000): pp. 4-9

the West.

People live in perpetual hope, and thus are the children of hope. At the instant they lose their hope, they also lose their "fire" for life, no matter if their physical existence continues. Having hope is directly proportional to having faith. Just as winter constitutes one-fourth of a year, the periods in the life of a person or a society that correspond to winter are relatively small. The gears of Divine acts revolve around such comprehensive wisdom and merciful purposes; these inform us, just as the circulation of night and day builds one's hope and revivifies one's spirit and every new year comes with the expectation of spring and summer, that both in the life of an individual and in the history of a nation the disastrous periods are short and they are followed by happy times.

This cycle of the "Days of God," which is centered in Divine Wisdom, is neither fearful nor overly pessimistic for those who have faith, insight, and real perception. Rather, it is a source of continuous reflection, remembrance, and thanksgiving for those having an apprehensive heart, inner perception, and the ability to hear. Just as a day develops in the heart of the night, and as the winter furnishes the womb in which the spring grows, so one's life is purified, matures, and bears its expected fruits within this cycle. Also within this cycle, God-given human abilities become aptitudes and talents, sciences blossom like roses and weave technology at the workbench of time, and humanity gradually approaches its predestined end.

Having stated this general view, which is neither personal nor subjective, but rather an objective fact of human history, it should not be thought that we welcome either winter or the winter-like events corresponding to sorrow, disease, and disaster. Despite the general fact that disease eventually increases the resistance of the body, strengthens the immune system, and drives medical progress, it is pathological and harmful. It is the same with terrestrial and celestial disasters. From a theological and moral point of view, they result from our sins and oppression which are great enough to shake the Earth and the Heavens, and from engaging in deeds that have been declared forbidden and despised by law and ethics (whether religious or secular). Even though these diseases awaken people to their mistakes and negligence and provoke developments in geology, architecture, engineering, and related safety measures, even though they elevate the demolished belongings of believers to the level of charity, and the believers themselves to the level of martyrdom, these disasters cause much destruction and harm humanity.

In the same way, we read in the Qur'an:

> If God had not hampered some (of you) with some other (of you), the mosques, monasteries, and synagogues in which God is worshiped would have fallen into ruins. (Al-Hajj 22:40)

In other words, God would be so little known that men and women, who are inclined not to recognize anything as superior to themselves nor to believe that their deeds will be questioned in the Hereafter, would have gone completely astray, thereby making Earth unsuitable for human life. There is also the divine decree:

> You consider something as evil although it is good for you; you also consider something else as good although it is bad for you. (Al-Baqara 2:126)

For example, war is permissible. Although wars based on specific principles and with the intention of improving the existing situation may have benefits, they should not be mandate as they bring harm; they leave behind ruined houses, destroyed families, and weeping orphans and widows.

Moreover, the realities of life cannot be neglected, nor should they be ignored. Human beings are mirrors of the Names and Attributes of God, and therefore have been distinguished from the rest of creation by being honored with the responsibility for making Earth prosperous in His name. If they cannot grasp the wisdom and purposes behind any good or evil that has been sent their way by their Creator, then they cannot escape despair or pessimism. For such people, as can be seen in Existentialist literature, life turns into a meaningless process, existence into a purposeless vacuity, nonsense into the only criteria, suicide into a meritorious act, and death becomes the only inevitable reality.

The Basic Nature of Humanity

After presenting the issues that constitute the basis of this subject as an introduction, we can switch to our considerations regarding the third millennium.

Human history began with two people who constituted the essence of humanity and complemented one another. People lived a tranquil life during this time of the original mother and father and the families that descended from them. They were a united society that had the same views and shared the same environment and lives.

From that day on, the essence of humanity has remained unchanged, and it will remain so. The realities surrounding their lives, their physical structure, main characteristics, basic needs, place and time of birth and death, the selection of the parents and their physique, their innate characteristics, as well as the surrounding natural environment, have not changed. All of these require some essential, vital invariable realities and values. Thus, the development and alteration of the secondary realities of life should be based on the axis of these primary realities and values, so that life will continue as a worldly paradise under the shadow of Heaven.

We mentioned above some issues that seem to be harmful or unpleasant. Similarly, there are human traits that seem to be evil at first glance, such as hatred, jealousy, enmity, the desire to dominate others, greed, anger, and egoism. A human being also has other innate drives and needs that allow the continuation of his or her worldly life, such as the need to eat and drink and the drives of lust and anger. All human drives, needs, and desires should be guided and trained in the direction of the eternal, universal, and invariable values that address the fundamental aspects of humanity. In this respect, the need to eat and drink, and the desires associated with lust and anger can be tamed and transformed into means of absolute or relative good.

Likewise, egoism and hatred can become sources of fine attributes and goodness. Jealousy and rivalry can be transformed into competition in charitable and good deeds. The feeling of enmity can be transformed into enmity against Satan, the greatest enemy of humanity, and against the feeling of enmity itself and hatred. Greed and rage can force one to perform good deeds without tiring. Egoism can point out the evil aspects of the carnal soul (*nafs*), thereby seeking to train and purify the soul into not excusing its evil actions.

All negative feelings can be transformed into sources of good through training and making an effort. This is how one reaches the level of "the best of Creation" by traveling on the way of transformation from a potential human being to a real and perfected human being, to the best symbol, model, and personal representative of creation and existence.

Despite this fact, the realities of human life do not always follow these guidelines. Negative feelings and attributes often defeat people, dominating to such an extent that even the religions that guide people to goodness and kindness are abused, not to mention the feelings and attributes that are sources of absolute good. Human life, at the level of the individual and of humanity as a whole, is merely the summation of internal, personal struggles and their external manifestations. These tides make society, history, and the personal world of the individual an arena of battle, struggle, war, oppression, and tyranny. As a result, it is usually human beings who suffer the consequences.

We always reap the harvest of our deeds. In the first period of its history, humanity lived a happy life as a united society, the members of which shared their joys and sorrows. But later on they bound their necks and feet to a rusty yoke composed of the chains of oppression; this was the result of jealousy, greed, and the coveting of the rights and property of others. The consequence was the murder of Abel by Cain. As a result, humanity stepped onto the path of disunity. Despite millennia flowing one after the other, like days, seasons, and years, this "cycle" still continues.

The Second Millennium

The second millennium started with the Crusades and then the Mongol invasions of the Muslim world, which at that time was the heart of the world and history. Despite the wars and destruction, and despite the crimes committed, sometimes in the name of religion and sometimes in the name of economic, political, and military supremacy, this millennium saw the apex of the civilizations of the East, civilizations based on spirituality, metaphysical, universal, and eternal values, and of the civilizations of the West, those based on physical sciences. Many significant geographical discoveries and scientific inventions occurred during this millennium.

Yet, the civilizations of the East and the West existed separately from each other. This separation, which should not have occurred, was based on the fact that the former retired from pursuits of intellect and science, while the latter retired from spirituality, metaphysics, and eternal and invariable values. As a result, the last centuries of the second millennium witnessed disasters that we find hard to comprehend. Due to the growing arrogance and egoism of humanity, caused by its accomplishments, people had to experience worldwide colonialism, rampant massacres, revolutions that cost millions of lives, unimaginably bloody and destructive wars, racial discrimination, immense social and economic injustice, and iron curtains built by regimes whose ideology and philosophy sought to deny the essence, freedom, merit, and honor of humanity. It is partly because of this and partly because of some auguries from the Bible that some people in the West fear that the world will again be soaked in floods of blood, pus, and destruction. They are quite pessimistic and worried about how the new millennium will proceed.

Our Expectations

Modern means of communication and transportation have transformed the world into a large global village. So, those who expect that any radical changes in a country will be determined by that country alone and remain limited to it are unaware of current realities. This time is a period of interactive relations. Nations and peoples are more in need of and dependent on each other, a situation that causes closeness in mutual relations.

This network of relations, which has surpassed the period of brute colonialism and exists on the basis of mutual interest, provides some benefits for the weaker side. Moreover, owing to advances in technology, especially digital electronic technology, the acquisition and exchange of information is gradually growing. As a result, the individual comes to the fore, making it inevitable that democratic governments which respect personal rights will replace oppressive regimes.

As every human, unlike animals, represents the whole of humanity, individual rights cannot be sacrificed for society, and social rights should depend on individual rights. This is why the basic human rights and freedoms found in the revealed religions were taken on board by a war-weary West. These rights are given priority in all relations. The primary right is the right to life, which is granted by and can only be taken by God. To accentuate the importance of this right in Islam, a basic Qur'anic principle is that:

> If one person kills another unjustly, it is the same as if he has killed all
> of humanity; if one saves another, it is the same as if he has saved all of
> humanity. (Al-Ma'ida 5:32)

Other rights are the freedom of religion and belief, thought and expression, to own property and the sanctity of one's home, to marry and have children, to communicate and to travel, and the right to an unimpeded education. The principles of Islamic jurisprudence are based on these and other rights, all of which have now been accepted by modern legal systems, such as the protection of life, religion, property, reproduction, and intellect, as well as the basic understanding of the equality of people, which is based on the fact that all people are human beings, and subsequently, the rejection of all racial, color, and linguistic discriminations. All of these will be—and should be—indispensable essentials in the new millennium.

I believe and hope that the world of the new millennium will be a happier, more just, and more compassionate place, contrary to the fears of some people. Islam, Christianity, and Judaism all stem from the same root; all have essentially the same basic beliefs, and are nourished from the same source. Although they have lived as rival religions for centuries, the common points between them and their shared responsibility to build a happy world for all of the creatures of God make interfaith dialogue among them necessary. This dialogue has now expanded to include the religions of Asia and other areas. The results have been positive.

As mentioned above, this dialogue will develop as a necessary process, and the followers of all religions will find ways to become closer and assist each other.

Previous generations witnessed a bitter struggle that should never have taken place: science versus religion. This conflict gave rise to atheism and materialism, which influenced Christianity more than other religions. Science cannot contradict religion, for its purpose is to understand nature and humanity, which are each a composition of the manifestations of God's Attributes of Will and Power. Religion has its source in the Divine Attribute of Speech, which was manifested in the course of human history as Divine Scriptures, such as the Qur'an, the Gospels, the Torah, and others that had been revealed to just prophets since Adam. Thanks to the efforts of both Christian and Muslim theologians and scientists, it seems that the religion-science conflict that has lasted for a few centuries will come to an end, or at least its absurdity will finally be acknowledged.

The end of this conflict and a new style of education that fuses religious and scientific knowledge with morality and spirituality will produce genuinely enlightened people with hearts illuminated by religious sciences and spirituality, minds illuminated by positive sciences, characterized by all kinds of humane merits and moral values, and cognizant of the socio-economic and political conditions of their time. Our old world will experience an amazing "springtime" before its demise. This springtime will see the gap between rich and poor narrow; the world's riches will be distributed more justly, according to work, capital, and needs; there will be no discrimination based on race, color, language, or worldview; and basic human rights and freedoms will be protected. Individuals will come to the fore and, learning how to realize their potential, will ascend on the way to becoming "the most elevated human" on the wings of love, knowledge, and belief.

In this new springtime, when scientific and technological progress has been taken into consideration, people will understand that the current level of science and technology resembles the stage of life when an infant is learning how to crawl. Humanity will organize trips into space as if they were merely traveling to another country. Travelers on the way to God, those devotees of love who have no time for hostility, will carry the inspirations within their spirits to other worlds.

Yes, this springtime will rise on the foundations of love, compassion, mercy, dialogue, acceptance of others, mutual respect, justice, and rights. It will be a time in which humanity will discover its real essence. Goodness and kindness, righteousness and virtue will form the basic essence of the world. No matter what happens, the world will come to this path sooner or later. Nobody can prevent this.

We pray and beg that the Infinitely Compassionate One will not let our hopes and expectations come to nothing.

AS A NEW WORLD IS BEING BUILT

Life and the Spirit of Hope

If life is viewed through the window of He Who Has Given Life, then hope is the dynamic of action that does not fade. It is nourishment for those who do not think continuously of themselves, but rather of others, for those who find true happiness in the happiness of others and for those who find a life in bettering the lives of others; it is also a source of energy which never diminishes for those who have devoted themselves to a blessed ideal of leading life at the level of the heart and soul, having freed themselves of the prisons of time, space, matter, physicality and self-interest. In that respect, at a time when all others are of the belief that "everything is over," a time when the great figure of a nation has been bent to breaking point, a time when resolve and will, adrift with tremors, storms and floods, die away, a time when those who have grown to depend on office, degree, wealth and prosperity and powers that are not derived from the true possessor of strength and power, and those who, due to not being able to find the truth, have bound their hearts to the stars, the Moon and the Sun, objects that fade from the sky, begin to face despair, the hope of the people of ideals, these people whom we have described in the beginning lines of this paragraph, takes on such an epic quality that in all circumstances they can challenge the universe. They continue on their way unshaken, even if their calculations and their plans should fail fifty thousand times, taking on an attitude of prosperity even in the face of poverty. They become life for dead souls and strength for those bent at the knees.

A certain person from the West said, "When all give up hope, even hope of defense, this is when the attack of the Turkish nation begins." The new, fresh shoots that emerged after the Mongol invasion and the division of Anatolia, the re-gathering of power and the increasing vitality after the defeat at Çubuklu Valley, Gallipoli and subsequently, the War of Independence, all of which were fought to the point of annihilation and which are epics without equal set down in history, all these give the im-

This section is taken from the supplement to the book prepared by Nevval Sevindi entitled *New York Conversation with Fethullah Gülen and Global Tolerance*, Timaş Yayınları, April, 2002.

pression that our nation's essential function in history is to write and re-write epics of regeneration, built upon the foundations of hope and faith.

Today in gratitude, I am trying to be patient in the face of serious medical problems; I am experiencing the homesickness caused by being far away from my homeland, a place that I love more than life itself; away from the water, the air, the rocks, the soil, the sky and the rosy-faced people—I miss them all terribly. This homesickness is reflected in my soul as if it were a bottomless well. I watch, anxiously, but at the same time hopefully, what is happening in my land—even though I may only see glimpses or only be able to see what is on the surface—a land that many now consider a place impossible to live in. I am trying to see what direction the latest attempts of America will take, and still, I am keeping my hope alive for the world and humanity, fresh as evergreen leaves and I keep on looking upon tomorrow with a smile.

Humanity Is the Source of Everything

Humanity, with all of its attributes, is a creation that is difficult to understand. As with all the realms, the essence of all created things is present in humans, and in a way, with their characteristics, in one respect it is possible to understand existence by knowing humanity, while, in another respect, knowing humanity is possible by understanding existence. In truth, understanding humanity is the principle mission of humanity, since humanity is also the window that opens on understanding the Creator. For this reason, the first and foremost duty of human beings is to discover and know themselves and then to turn their gaze toward their Lord with the lens of their enlightened nature. It is an unfortunate fact that this is what most of us neglect to do. Indeed, how many people can we name who exercise self-criticism often enough? How many people can we name who every day rediscover themselves anew, a rediscovery of their weak-nesses, their abilities, their absences, their sources of strength, along with the things that they have gained or lost; how many people can stroll through their own inner selves? How many people can we name who try to examine their own beings—not with a passing awe or a casual curios-ity, and not by looking deep into faults and degrading themselves—but like a fair, professional and rational doctor, sitting themselves on a stool to be examined, desiring to investigate and to become acquainted with their true selves, trying to study themselves realistically in order to diagnose the disease? It is simply because this deed has not been performed that humanity cannot find the happiness it desperately seeks in this "lost paradise"; more precisely, humanity cannot find the lost paradise.

The Patent Right of a Small Minority

It is impossible not to appreciate the results of scientific research, the wonders of civilization, the products of technology. But have we succeeded in employing this science and technology—the product of all this effort and intellectual labor—and the speed and globalization that they bring, in the service of more exalted purposes? Do space, which is being compressed more and more each day, until it is no larger than a village, and time, which people are attempting to shrink to zero, serve a goal beyond themselves? Or do they, despite the greater majority, serve the worldly prosperity of a small minority who hold the "patent" of all these? Reaching the furthest corners of the universe, investigating every existing thing, becoming as familiar with the world as we are with our village or district, discovering information about even the most hidden aspects of things—if all this is placed above human needs and desires, if respect for human privacy and values is uprooted and let adrift, then the time has come to consider whether it is preferable to live in a world with all these modern products, or whether it is better to live without them, in a world of bygone ages when human beings were happier and when personal and social life and relationships were founded on human values.

Up until now, science, technology, and speed have never been the principle needs of humanity. But it would be incorrect to oppose science and technology with "idealistic" thoughts; such an opposition is only a form of utopia. No good for humanity can come from ranting at machinery or cursing the factories. The machines will continue to operate; the factory will continue to exude its fumes, even if we heap curses upon it. For this reason, it may be said that what is important here is not this or that technology, but rather who controls science and technology and what purpose they serve. Science and technology can turn the world into a hell in the hands of an irresponsible minority; if the same tools are in the hands of angels no one will suffer. Humanity has suffered most from those who see right as belonging to those who have power and insatiable ambition. Science and technology and the speed with which they allow us to perform are sacred and worthy of respect only in proportion with how much they direct humans toward humane goals, facilitate the accomplishment of these goals, bring about peace and happiness, extinguish longing and the pain of separation, deal with a multitude of ills before time runs out, serve the general harmony of the world, provide balance between states, participate in the resolution of worldly and spiritual problems and give momentum to research and establishing facts that will enhance our understanding. But when science and technology are distanced from the goals mentioned and when they become values in and of themselves, when it is expected that they will only serve themselves, or only the interests of a small minority, it is then that their absence is much better than their presence.

Technology and Science in the Service of Humanity

I believe that both science and technology should be viewed from this very perspective. We have to ask in whose service science and technology are today. Do they serve the relationship between individuals, between the individual and society, between society and the state; do they serve mutual love, respect and support for one another in all good things, tolerance, the acceptance of everyone in their own context, truth, loyalty, a respect of rights, or do they serve mendacity, deceit, malicious conjecture, slander and an unnatural interest in other people's sins and faults, a violation of privacy and intrusion into the lives of others? Do they serve respect, from the heart, of the rights of all, something that should be protected, for example, the right to belief, life, personal possessions, reproduction, and mental and physical health? Do they serve good intentions, mutual understanding; do they serve in the relationships between states and nations, do they serve what is right, what is just? Do they encourage sharing, abstinence from exploitation, respect for basic human rights and freedoms or do they serve the sovereignty of capital and crude force? If science and technology emphasize the negative elements stated above, this then is a nightmare scenario for the future. Indeed, if the values which are universally valid today and upon which globalization is founded are the negative ones enumerated above, then the fact that at the present time half the world is living on two dollars a day, with a billion people surviving on even less, the fact that a quarter of the world does not have access to healthy drinking water, that the most terrible of diseases, like AIDS, have a tendency to spread rapidly and thus threaten humanity, the fact that health, which is the most vital need of humanity, has become an industry with very expensive services, the fact that global warming and pollution is rife, the fact that a major proportion of the world's population is living without any democratic rights, the fact that human rights violations have become the norm, that living conditions in many places of the world are abysmal, and that unpreventable acts of local and international terrorism reign will be the fearful reality for the whole of humanity.

A Muslim Cannot Be a Terrorist

I should point out first that the religion that God has sent, whether it be called Judaism, Christianity or Islam, cannot be thought of as allowing terrorism, let alone prescribing it. First of all, in God's regard, life is of paramount importance. All existence has been programmed to give way to life. Life is the name of a divine mystery, which lets one thing retain all things. A thing with no life is an orphan, even though it may be as large as a mountain, and its relationship with what surrounds it is only limited to the place that it inhabits. On the other hand, something that has life, even though it may be as simple as a honeybee, can call the whole universe "my garden" and can look upon all flowers as friends. That bee has many connections and dealings with all different kinds of existence, from the Sun to the air, from the air to humans. Thus, life is the point of concentration for the names of the Excellent Just One, a focal point for the simultaneous manifestation of all these attributes. God, having given such importance to life, has deemed it to be one of the five essential values to be protected with the religion that He has sent. Islam has deemed the killing of any single individual to be equal to the killing of the whole of humanity, as one life represents the life of all; therefore, saving the life of a single individual is the same as saving the life of all. Moreover, as far as rights are concerned, it is said, "there are no minor or major rights"; i.e. it is seen that the right of the individual and the right of society are equal. One cannot be sacrificed for the other, to the extent that it has been decreed "if a ship is carrying nine murderers and one innocent soul, that ship cannot be sunk to punish the nine murderers."

Terror Cannot Be a Means for an Islamic Goal

Secondly, just as Islam prescribes that the goal has to be lawful in all acts of Muslim individuals, so too has it particularly emphasized that the means employed to attain that goal must also be lawful, reminding those who try to reach a lawful goal through unlawful means that they will in the end come face to face with the diametric opposite of that which they were aiming for. In this respect, we can say that terror cannot be a means to realize any Islamic goal. Moreover, Islam has never looked favorably upon war, although it is a reality and one of the most prominent elements in the history of humankind; Islam has bound war first and foremost to the condition of defense, and then, within the framework of the principle "inciting dissent is worse than murder," found in the Qur'an, it has deemed war lawful only to prevent war and disputes which lead to war, to prevent disorder, oppression and subjection. These are the conditions that Islam deems necessary for engaging in war; for the first time in human history Islam introduced serious limitations and principles concerning the matter. Orders like the following have gone down in history:

> Do not let the fear of God go from your hearts. Do not forget that you can do nothing without the help of God, always remember that Islam is the religion of peace and love. The courage, the bravery of the God's Messenger and his keeping to the path that God has ordained should always be a model for you. Do not trespass cultivated land and orchards. Respect the priests and monks who live in temples and those who have given themselves to God; do not hurt them. Do not kill civilians, do not act in an untoward manner toward women, and do not injure the feelings of the defeated. Do not accept gifts from the local population. Do not attempt to house your soldiers in the houses of the locals. Do not neglect to perform your prayer five times a day. Fear God and do not forget that death can find you at any time, even thousands of miles away from the field of battle. So, be ready for death at all times.

These orders are the principles that heads of state have reminded their commanders of throughout Islamic history, and they have been followed to the letter. War, which can only be applied by a state and only perforce within the framework of certain principles, cannot be declared by individuals and organizations; moreover, it is clear that acts of terror which are without restraint, which target human values that must be protected and which destroy safety have no place in Islam. In that respect, just as a terrorist cannot be a genuine Muslim, a Muslim cannot be a terrorist. A Muslim cannot be a terrorist because Islam decrees the severest of worldly punishments on those who target people's lives and security; in the Hereafter those who deny God and who assign Him partners, along with those who kill people and deliberately take lives, are faced with eternal Hell. A person cannot possibly commit an act that is understood to have such a punishment whilst being a Muslim and displaying the characteristics of faith and Islam. Thus, it is not possible for a terrorist to be a true Muslim, just as it is impossible for a Muslim to be a terrorist.

The Problems of Islamic Societies

Moreover, if acts of terror continue to take place in this way, be it in Islamic societies or elsewhere, there must first be a sound diagnosis of the situation, and then whatever treatment the diagnosis calls for must be given. As far as this is concerned, the following can be listed as the principle reasons why certain individuals in the Islamic world become entangled or are made to become entangled in this web of terrorism and the reasons why terror is a serious problem in the world:

a) Islamic societies entered the twentieth century as a world of the oppressed, the wronged, and the colonized; the first half of the century was occupied with wars of liberation and independence, wars that were carried over from the nineteenth century. In all these wars, Islam assumed the role of an important factor uniting people and spurring them to action. As these wars were waged against what were seen as invaders, Islam, national independence, and liberation came to mean the same thing. Afterwards, when national states were established in these parts of the world, the states were not compatible with their public; whereas the states should have instructed the public in Islam with its true identity and nature, they acted in a way which disregarded the public, a way contrary to the values and traditions of the public. This made Islam a pillar, a refuge against the administration in the eyes of the public. Consequently, it is regrettable to say, Islam has come to be regarded as a traditional political ideology by many.

b) In many regions of Islamic geography, administrations that disregard and denigrate the public and which are oligarchic in nature, have worked for the well-being of the dynasties, the families of which they are members, rather than working for the prosperity of their country and trying to establish the unity of public and the state, and thus these administrations have been degraded to the position of mere oppressors and are deserving of loathing in the eyes of the public. The poor and uneducated masses in the public have become the enemies of their own administrations.

c) Both in Islamic societies and other nations, the roots of terror have always grown in poverty, ignorance and lack of education. In many places, feudal and tribal systems still continue and in these places, a great majority of the population regard the developed countries of the West, countries which at one time had invaded and occupied their country, as the protectors and supporters of the administrators ruling over them, and thus they hold these Western countries fully responsible for the wrongs and oppression that they suffer in their own country.

d) Values like democracy, basic human rights, the spread of knowledge and education across society, economic prosperity, equality in production, the institutionalization of consumption and income in a way that prevents class formation, the supremacy of law and justice, values which today are general accepted throughout the world, have never been fully realized in Islamic societies, nor in other regions designated as Third World countries. Doubtless, those who are primarily responsible for this situation are the administrators of these countries and their supporters—the developed Western countries that have helped them stay in power. Thus, even though these countries may assume the championship of the said values, as far as the people of the Third World are concerned, they have not been seen as being sincere and are seen as those who are exploiting these values.

e) Today's world has, as we have briefly touched on, shrunk to the size of a large village as a result of great developments in information transfer and travel. All people and countries are now neighbors. A few neighbors, a minority, are luxuriating in an ocean of abundance, whereas the greater majority is poor, extremely poor. Colonialism or exploitation, which is exercised very subtly and covertly, is considered to be one of the most significant reasons for this poverty, and moreover, the greater majority is destitute to such a degree that it is unable to meet its most basic needs. All of these factors have led to feelings of rancor, re-

sentment, and enmity. Moreover, it is an unfortunate reality today that unlawful acts have become as much a norm as lawful
acts. Corruption, deceit, the desire for easy money, selfishness,
individualism, international gambling, and international smug-
gling (principally of drugs and arms) can be found in nearly every
country in the world today. The mafia organizations that make
such activities possible, and other similar organizations, like large
holdings, trusts and cartels, are all in deadly competition, employing bloody murderers and thugs who represent crude physical
force. The fact that these organizations feed and support such activities no doubt is another important and undeniable factor in
terrorism taking on an international aspect.

f) Maybe more importantly than all of the above, the fact that relig-
    ion, and the religious values, spirituality and ethics that are con-
    nected to religion have been eroded away throughout the world
    constitutes the most important source of both terrorism and
    other major social problems that threaten humanity today. The
    world is going through a spiritual crisis; all the essential support-
    ing pillars of humanity have collapsed and have been destroyed.
    Philosophies of depression, Satanism, currents that are fundamen-
    tally materialist and naturalist, but which appear spiritual (a new
    one crops up every day), and so called cults all prepare the
    ground for violence and suicide. Indeed, these phenomena are
    like an epileptic attack, shaking our world, or the shivering of one
    with a high fever. To ask why people commit suicide, kill and use
    drugs when these people have lost their hope, when they see the
    past as a vast tomb and the future as a bottomless chasm, finding
    life meaningless can only be put down to blind ignorance, if not
    an artful pretension of ignorance.

g) The final word that needs to be said upon the matter is the fol-
    lowing: the fact that there has been no definition or categoriza-
    tion of terrorism recognized by all nations, or at least set down by
    the United Nations to date is a serious problem. What acts
    should be considered within the term "terror acts" and what acts
    should not, who is a terrorist and who is not? Everybody seems
    to arrive at their own answers to these questions. One person's
    terrorist is another's freedom fighter; one person's warrior for

ideals can be considered as a terrorist by someone else. If there is to be a war against terror in the international arena—and there most definitely should be a serious campaign—it appears that there first has to be a definition of terrorism that is accepted at least by the United Nations. If this can be achieved, an international campaign against terror can gain a lawful status, a status that everyone will accept, a state of affairs where no one will be able to lay blame on anyone else, and maybe this will constitute a first step in the prevention of terrorism. It is hardly necessary to speak of the resolutions, after we have spoken of the essential problems and the issues that are mentioned as their causes: the diagnosis of the problem contains the resolution within itself.

The Principle Fabric of Social Life

The principle fabric of social life is founded upon religion, law, wisdom, and power. A person or society without religion will not be able to continue for long, just as they will not be of benefit to others. In truth, religion is an essential element that has been determined beyond ourselves and that has entered our lives, whether we accept it or not. Even though we may be the most perfect creatures, exalted with our free-will, there are still many indispensable elements that surround our lives and to which we are bound. For instance, where we are born, when we are born, and when and where we will leave this world are all planned and determined extraneous to us. Similarly, we have no say in the determination of our family—of our mother and father—of our race, color, or physical characteristics. Moreover, even our body works totally independent of our will; we cannot help getting hungry, thirsty, or sleepy. Also, the ways and means through which we fulfill these needs are independent of ourselves as well. In our simplest daily activities, such as eating and drinking, our only role is procuring the food and drink and making the decision to do so: in a way, we can say that our role in the act of fulfilling our needs amounts to no more than one percent. This means that whether we like it or not, our actions are limited by certain dominant conditions. Religion, too, is one of these forceful conditions. Whether or not we accept it, religion is one of the most essential elements in our lives, an element that cannot be replaced by any other thing. This is because it plays a vital role in the organization and regulation of our spiritual needs, needs which have a greater meaning and importance to us than material needs. Religion has an importance not only in and of itself, but also in the organization of our individual, domestic, and social life, as well as in our material life. Religion plays a crucial role in determining and enacting the laws that are the regulating principles in certain aspects of our lives. The final goal is not laws or their application; these gain value only to the degree in which they serve humanity and society. Thus, when setting down laws, one has to be well acquainted with humanity and with all its characteristics, taking its essential nature into consideration; one also has to know society, which is made up of people with awareness and will, the needs and means through which society satisfy these needs, and one also must know the sorts of relationships that exist between the individuals within society. Individuals are like the atoms of a whole, and therefore one must also be aware of the connections and bonds individuals have with the collective spirit of society. Thus, in being familiar with society and with the people of which it is composed, religion performs a special function, since both the Creator of Humanity and the One Who Preaches Religion is God. In that respect, the role of religion in understanding humans and society is so critical that it is impossible to estimate its importance.

The Indispensability of Religion in the Order of Society

Secondly, just as force has an undeniable role in law-enforcement, the importance of religion in this arena is also undeniably great. Religion is based upon a foundation of putting faith in the existence of a Being that sees humans, controls them, and knows not only all that they do, but also all that they think and all of their intentions and aims. And this faith is natural to humanity, and always lies dormant in the conscience of humanity, making itself felt at all times. Also, religion, because it may be possible to escape the law, government and enforcement on this Earth, yet it is impossible to be exempt from the boundaries of the divine scrutiny of God, teaches humans that they are responsible for all that they do in this world, and that they will be judged in another world concerning their deeds, and that according to the outcome of that judgment they will either be bestowed eternal happiness or punished. In truth, in educating humans to become poems of virtues rather than of evil, it is inconceivable that any otherworldly system could replace this belief system.

Thirdly, the ethical principles of religion in particular have a priority that is irreplaceable by any otherworldly thing in the cultivation of humanity. In fact, these ethical canons are the criteria that all people have accepted throughout time; this is an undeniable fact. These criteria defy both existence and time. Whether these evoke the necessary impact on people depends again on the state of religious belief and its application in society.

Religion in the Western World Today

Some people might be tempted to say that religion has no place in the life of society in developed countries such as America and those of Western Europe. We must immediately point out that such a statement is in no way correct and that these countries have and are attached to their religions. Just as we have expressed earlier, although religious values may have been weakened over the last two centuries throughout the world, humanity today is again searching for religion, and is once again inclining toward it. Even though the population may be indifferent to religion to a certain extent in Western Europe, those in the administration seem to be, on the whole, rather religious. Among these, there have always been religious people at the highest levels of administration, and there still are today. Moreover, though secularism is the rule in all these countries, there has never been a mentality dictating that the guidance of religion should be abandoned in social or even in the political life of a country. Western historians state that Christianity is the most important element in the formation of the modern social structure of Europe. According to these historians, Christianity has played a role that extends into the political and social arena and it has always played a decisive role in particular areas, with significant laws made concerning blasphemy, religious holidays and collective worship.

Also in countries like the USA and Canada, the majority of the population is attached to their religion, despite what might be said to the contrary, and religiosity is received with serious esteem both within the public and at various levels of the government. When we look at the current body of law in these countries, it is possible to see the influence of religion. For instance, in the USA, the penalties for crimes such as causing the death of a human being can at times exceed the amount of indemnity prescribed by Islam. Secondly, all nations have characteristics unto themselves, stemming from their own nature, history, and culture. Turks have been Muslim for centuries and it is impossible to severe them from Islam. At times when they have distanced themselves from Islam they have never found peace or progress; rather, on the contrary, this way has led to degeneration. This is due to the fact that Islam is unlike any other religion. A Jew does not have to believe in Jesus nor in the Bible, nor in Muhammad and the Qur'an. A Jew is considered faithful if they do not believe in those things. A Christian, similarly, is considered to be religious even though they do not believe in Muhammad, peace and blessings be upon him, or the Qur'an. This is because these religions do not accept the divine systems and books that have followed into their framework. Thus, religion can find a place within the vast spectrum of divine religions that stems from Judaism and Christianity. In this spectrum there is a book, a prophet with which it is connected and thus the system can never become completely corrupted; when someone has put it down, it may sour, like milk, but in the same way, this soured product can still serve a purpose. If we use another metaphor, religion can take refuge in one of the many rooms of a palace and be illuminated with the light found in that room. Islam, on the other hand, encompasses all religions. Believing in Muhammad and the Qur'an as the last and the essential, and thus believing in all the prophets and holy books is one of the pillars of Islam. In other words, Islam is inclusive, uniting everything. If we take up the palace metaphor again, Islam is the electrical system, the main generator for the whole building. If you abandon that system, the whole palace, the whole world will be plunged into darkness; there is no more light that illuminates. Those who abandon this light are the anarchists who deny all order.

In these last three centuries, centuries which have been years of subjection for Muslims, and even at the present time, when the face of Islam has been darkened by those who claim to be the most genuine members—at a time when Islam is presented as being dark by its enemies—the number of people turning to Islam continues to grow at a remarkable pace, while the number of people who estrange themselves from Islam is still very low. This may give some idea about what we have been discussing. Thus, those who want order in Turkey and in the world should conform to Islam and embrace it, not abandoning it to the mercy of those who misinterpret and misapply it. In the fabric of a healthy society, the law should give itself up to wisdom; that is to say, it should not go against the essential nature of humanity and the structure of nature, in short, the laws of creation. Law should take into account the character of the nation, and national-religious values; it should heed the warnings of logic and commonsense and it should be readily acceptable by the majority. Along with religion, history, traditions, and national values, the main principles of sociology, anthropology and even physics and chemistry are vitally important in the determination and institutionalization of laws. Law is not an independent science; it is a science that encompasses religion, history, philosophy, sociology, the sociology of history, psychology, anthropology, physics, chemistry, etc., and it has to be viewed in this light. Otherwise, the regulations made will be like a dress that does not fit; it will need frequent alterations. The material is of poor quality, the pattern is unflattering, it is of the wrong size. This outfit must be cut up and sewn again, taken in here, let out there—such a garment will bring about more harm than good to the composition of society.

Force Cannot Be an End in Itself

Another great element in the fabric of society is force. Undoubtedly, there is a divine reason for the existence of force as well; just as without force it would be impossible to enforce the law, it would also be impossible to protect the safety of the country, especially vis-à-vis foreign powers. Also, force has its particular place in ensuring law and order domestically, and thus it must be respected. But force is not a value or an end in itself; it can and should not be the final objective. Force is worthy of respect only as long as it serves people's rights and justice; force that has gone out of control in the hands of a minority defeated by their own ambitions and selfishness will not revere rights or justice; it will authorize no law, no wisdom. The fact that rights should be sacrificed to force, that considerations of self-interest should rise to the surface above all other values, that bitter racism should replace universal values, that attempts to solve national and international problems should be made with crude force has always been a problem for humanity. In a situation where problems are attempted to be solved through crude force, it is impossible to speak of intellect, judgment, rights, justice, or law. On the contrary, in their stead are unlawfulness, injustice, and oppression. Even though force may be considered a potential power for the removal of problems—in the hands of the just and through the guidance of logic and judgment—it has always been an instrument of destruction in the hands of the cruelty that springs up in the axis of emotions. It is the wildness of force that acts with the supposition of an unlimited freedom that does not secure rights, justice, law, intellect, or judgment their due value. It is this fatal error that made Alexander dizzy and clouded his gaze; it is this that damaged the genius of Napoleon; it is this that transformed Hitler into the crazy man of the century. So, it would not be an exaggeration to say that unbridled force is behind the chain of chaos and the counter-currents that we are experiencing today. It appears that this chaos will continue until the day that those who represent force in the world submit themselves to justice, and the masses following these people be rid of the popular currents of everyday life and look at the world through the prism of justice.

The War Policy of USA

The questions that we have tried to address up until this time in the framework of basic principles and general rules have been expressed clearly enough not to require individual explanations or deeper analysis. Still, if we have to say specific things about recent events, the following can be said: To reiterate a sociological truth—a truth which has been misconstrued by some—that I have expressed many times before: there has always been a power that kept the balance in the world and there always will be. This power was once Rome; then for a time it was Islam, first with the Arabs and then through the Muslim Turks, that assumed this function. Starting with the nineteenth century, the Anglo-Saxon world has taken hold of the position of balancing the world; first it was the British Empire that did this, followed by, after World War II, America. God states in the Holy Qur'an that He gives property to whomever He wishes, and also that He takes it away from whomever He wishes; He makes whomever He wishes respected or degraded; and similarly, He states that He circulates victories, defeats, sovereignty and subjection among the nations.

That is to say, time does not follow a straight course, but rather a circular orbit. Just as the Earth orbits around the Sun or the solar system gyrates toward a destination, so does time and history approach a relative end. All this is determined by God, true, but still the will of humanity, the performance that it makes with its will and its behavior can also have an effect, to a certain degree. Looking at what is happening in the universe we discover the executive acts of the One that has created and the One that administers existence, and we call these "laws." Just as some laws of God are manifested as religion, He also has laws that pertain to His executive acts in the life of humanity and the universe. Just as the fact of whether or not obeying religion or its decrees, which we may call the laws of religion, has results, rewards, and punishments which will be manifested partly in this world, but principally in the Hereafter, so too obeying or ignoring the laws of sciences like physics, chemistry, biology and astronomy have results, rewards, and punishment, most of which come forth in this world, and some in the Hereafter. For instance, among the laws concerning life on Earth are attaining a goal, in most cases, as a result of patient perseverance, or getting mired down in the road due to impatience. Wealth is the result of hard work, poverty the result of laziness; success is the result of systematic and methodical study and failure the result of non-systematic and unmethodical study. God treats people, societies, nations, and states in relation to whether they obey laws of this kind; and accordingly states and nations take their place vis-à-vis the balance of the world.

Today, the USA engages the dominant position in the political balance of the world. However, its dominance depends on whether it continues to act on the basis of human rights and justice. It appears that at the moment the machinery of the system works well in America. But just as each day embraces its night, and each spring and summer reaches winter, if this system leads to a *blindness of system*, if America starts to present disloyalty to values such as democracy, human rights, and the fundamental freedoms which it claims to champion, if it does not wield the domination that fate has placed in its hands on the principles of justice and the protection of human rights, then its day too will turn to night, its summer will turn into winter. Just as has been stated above, no system can live long if it is supported solely by force. Force that does not depend on rights and justice will inescapably diverge toward oppression and thus prepare its own end. Today, the world is being shaken by great problems which have been partly looked at above. In addition to this, countries, like China and India, which are in possession of ancient civilizations and large populations are today in a state of awakening. In Eastern Europe, Russia is another great power. Europe is on the path to becoming a unified state—though it is still uncertain how successful and long-lived this effort will be. Moreover, the countries of Asia and Africa, which see themselves as having been oppressed for centuries, possess a potential that must be taken into consideration. To install a system dependent on force in such a world and to procure such a system's longevity is not a simple task. I sincerely hope that America will not make a regrettable mistake that will undo the existing balance, unleashing events that would turn the world into rivers of blood.

Regimes of Oppression: Not Any Longer

The fact that the world has, in some aspects, shrunk to the size of a village, due to rapidly growing communication technologies, presents a situation where regimes of oppression, like sovereignty thorough force, do not have much chance to continue unchecked. The human being is a noble creature; it cannot bear to be slave or servant for long. For their own good, it is vital for all states and for the people who operate the administrations to establish a governmental system that serves people and acts according to the principle of "the master is the one who is being served." Each individual person has innate honor, self-esteem, and character befitting to a human being. As long as the honor, self-esteem, and character that the Creator bestowed upon a person are not taken into consideration, it is impossible to instate peace and safety in any country or in the world. Believing, living in the way one believes, thinking in liberal ways, expressing what one thinks, and the freedom of communication and travel are all the basic rights of human beings. In a society that cannot procure and guarantee the most basic rights, like the right to life, security, health, employment and earning, and the establishment of a family, in a society where the sharing and consumption of production, and basic values that keep the society alive, like rights, justice, and balance, are not protected, in such a society virtues like love, mutual respect, and co-operation cannot be cultivated. It is impossible for any sovereignty to be long-lived in a world that is poor in these aspects. In fact, any administration or sovereignty that lacks these vital characteristics will always feel insecure and suffer profound uneasiness.

Even though the consideration of the world as a village becomes firmer and more prevalent over the course of time, different beliefs, races, customs, and traditions will continue to cohabit in this village. Each individual is like a unique realm unto themselves; therefore the desire for all humanity to be similar to one another is nothing more than wishing for the impossible. For this reason, the peace of this (global) village lies in respecting all these differences, considering these differences to be part of our nature and in ensuring that people appreciate these differences. Otherwise, it is unavoidable that the world will devour itself in a web of conflicts, disputes, fights, and the bloodiest of wars, thus preparing the way for its own end.

NEW WORLD ORDER

Everyone takes up the matter of a new world order and evaluates it from a different point of view, according to their own thoughts. This is quite natural. For example, people who have suffered from an internationalism disagreeable for many might accept chauvinism as a form of salvation and be inclined toward it. As a matter of fact, in Asia today almost every nation, under the ideal of turning back toward its ancient history, is turning toward its own particular values to such a degree that these nations now see themselves as being nationalistic. In view of the present situation, it is possible to evaluate the changes in the Russians, the Uzbeks, the Kazakhs, and others in this way. Today there are a number of changes with similar significance taking place in other countries in the world. As long as these "changes" and "developments" do not harm anyone else they can be seen as being normal. However, if we can find a way and a method that would make these changes more beneficial it would then be possible to prevent further tragedies.

Some of these developments follow a course based on religion. In relation to these, it is possible to mention both organized and unorganized activities throughout various parts of the world. Unlike others, they approach every matter from the principle that "religion is basic." And naturally they want to evaluate today's unsettled situation in line with their own way of thinking and manipulate and lead people to the position required by religion.

In addition to this is the fact that the attempt by the powers which have exploited the world many times to take advantage of this period of restructuring seems normal from their own perspectives. Is there full agreement among these powers? Of course not. However, it is widely believed that they are trying to come together and to reach an agreement as soon as possible. As is known, Britain does not think very differently on this matter from America. Although they had a small difference of opinion regarding the Sarajevo issue, the British are now also following America's line. Sometimes France appears to have different views, but

---

This very important speech was made in answer to a question about the New World Order in 1995. It is highly interesting that what was discussed then is proving to be true as time passes.

that derives more from their effort to get a share in the new structure and formation rather than a genuine difference in view.

In addition, there are some countries in which it is difficult to tell whether they are comfortable with the new order or not. It is quite difficult to understand the situation of these countries, just as there are some diseases that are hard to diagnose. As a matter of fact, they do not expect a share in the general advantages. In fact, it is not obvious what they really want at the present time.

It is also necessary to take note of the internal change that every country expects from itself. Of course, the manifestation of this expectation will vary according to the country, and it is impossible to consider and analyze all of them separately. If you like, let us make a few points about expectations in our own country and then move on. Our society is prudent and vigilant; one day it will assuredly listen to its intuition and conscience and, adopting the change most suitable to its nature, it will realize this change. This situation being surmised, many differences in thought have emerged in our country. Hopefully those who possess all these different views and thoughts are sincere in what they say and want to do. In this broad spectrum some differences in line and motif are quite normal and, in fact, in one respect they should be accepted as being beneficial.

After these general remarks we can briefly consider the matter within a technical perspective. The idealized peaceful world cannot be established by war and spilling blood. Nor will camouflaging activities of aggression and occupation yield positive results. For this reason, it is beneficial to repeat clearly and precisely once again that any balance of power that is made by using force will collapse in the shortest period of time, and those who were responsible for it will be the first to be buried under the debris.

I think we have witnessed that, in this sense, Korea, Vietnam, the Gulf, and Somalia are some of the most striking examples. Examples of reaction are likely to be even more violent in the future. The sympathy among Muslim peoples in the Muslim world, a sympathy which was once felt for the leaders of the free world, will slowly melt and antipathy will take its place. It appears that if the new world order is founded upon explicit or implicit exploitation by force, instead of democracy and full enjoyment of basic human rights and freedoms, then this antipathy will continue in expanding dimensions.

Our ancestors said, "the water jug breaks on the way to the well." Those who have gained a position by destroying something will themselves collapse and lose that position later on, in the same way. If we look all around us today and take into consideration the recurrence of history, we will be able to see more clearly what is awaiting us tomorrow.

Even if the world is not in a process of renewal, and it is clear today that it is not, it definitely is in a process of reconstruction. When the correct time arrives, this reconstruction will certainly be realized. When this happens, instead of having a world that has been shaped with malice and hatred, a surprising world that has taken its form in a climate of love, tolerance, and forbearance will appear before us. The collective conscience will gladly welcome and place it in its heart, not neglecting those who have a share in this reformation. These people will leave permanent tracks and, even if they have physically left this world, their tracks will remain for centuries. I believe with my whole heart that the only thing to do today in order to realize these spring-fragranced dreams is to perform this kind of service for humanity. For this reason, instead of temporary, fleeting, and un-promising efforts, I would advise a type of movement that is lasting and fully beneficial in every way. I think that as long as I am alive I will not hesitate to repeat these recommendations.

REGARDING THE INFORMATION AGE AND
THE CLASH OF CIVILIZATIONS

As in the past, there are some conjectures being made about the future today as well. One of these is the claim regarding the future as an age of information. Those people who are discussing the future in this way are basically futurists. There are many who see the people who are making these kinds of conjectures as oracles of the second millennium. Yet, rather than being objective evaluations, some of the claims that are made related to the future in terms of historical cycles are efforts to develop ideas around some particular desires and therefore they carry no more value than any other predictions. In other words, I think that as a result of these claims, people form expectations in the same way that they expect an answer to a prayer. Thus, while saying that the expectation produced by these types of claims that "the future will be like this" gives birth to certain efforts in that direction, these expectations eventually become goals and purposes. Once the goal has been determined, different strategies and policies will be produced to reach that goal and efforts will be made to fulfill it. I think this is the crux of the matter.

Along with this, there has been an extension of the prophetic mission of God's Messenger up until the modern day through the line of representatives, through people like Muhyiddin ibn al-'Arabi,[1] Imam al-Ghazali, Imam Rabbani, Mawlana Khalid, and Bediüzzaman. We hope that the function of this fortunate line of transmission is to prepare a foundation for the rebirth of the prophetic spirit in the years to come, and, in this respect, we hope that this spirit will live again. Of course, the Prophet will not be there, but Islam, in the pure understanding of the Companions, will be ever-ready to greet life once again.

But apart from all this, as we live in a world where causality and certain other laws are operative, if we act without taking such laws into con-

---

[1] Muhyiddin ibn al-'Arabi (1165-1240): A Sufi of great renown, he wrote *al-Futuhat al-Makkiyah* [Makkan Revelations], a twelve volume encyclopedia of Sufi beliefs and doctrines, which is considered to be a compendium of the esoteric sciences in Islam.

sideration we are in danger of falling into determinism. However, Muslims, by using their will, are able to consider the causes carefully enough so that someone looking from the outside would think that they are acting only according to laws of causality. On the other hand, regarding results obtained from actions, Muslims should be so completely submitted to and trusting in God's will that someone looking from the outside would will think that they have completely rejected causes. Acting in this way shows that, on the one hand, causes are very important and everything humanity does should definitely be planned around them and put into effect accordingly. On the other hand, while so doing, due to their fear of falling into the error of speculating partners to God Almighty, they should also know that they have not personally achieved any success themselves, rather all success is directly from God.

After determining the matter in this way, we can summarize our thoughts regarding the future in the following way. In the future, everything will be within the orbit of knowledge, and the horizons that have been darkened by our neglect for a period will once more be enlightened. To a large extent, we have been particularly neglectful of the scientific knowledge obtained during the fourth and fifth century A.H. (after the Hegira) that is based on the Qur'an and we have turned our backs on the very important dynamics that could keep us on our feet. Personally, I have always been saddened that the *madrassa*s got rid of Sufism, of what can be called Islam's spiritual life. Later their decrease in interest in the experimental sciences and the eventual expulsion of the same contributed to our falling far behind the newly scientifically developing countries. So the neglect we showed in the past should be made up for, and our tomorrows will be built on knowledge, and everything will take its strength and power from knowledge.

Knowledge will occupy a very important place in a world that is rapidly becoming smaller and in an era when time and space are shrinking. The important point here is whether or not we will be ready for such a world.

Today, there are many scientists in the world, in many different countries, but, in my humble opinion, they are not enough to establish a new, happy world, even if they were to work all together. For this reason, there is a need for a new way of thinking today, a new approach to the sciences, a new life philosophy, and new educational institutions. New generations should be mobilized at every period of their lives, from kindergarten to high school and from there onto university. Since everything will obtain power from knowledge in the future, it will only be possible to build knowledge for the future with this kind of effort.

Huntington's Assertions

Regarding Huntington's claim about the clash of civilizations, I think that rather than being realistic evaluations regarding the future, these types of claims seem to me to be determining new goals in an attempt to influence public opinion within the framework of these goals. Until the disintegration of the Soviet Block, there was the idea of a clash between the East and West, or between NATO and the Warsaw Pact countries. This time, by creating new enemy fronts, a clash between civilizations based on religious and cultural differences is being prepared and a new foundation is being laid for the continuation of the rule of the power blocks.

Actually, up until now, conflict is something that is desired by certain power centers. The masses have been put on alarm against a frequently conjectured and feared enemy; this enemy is more imaginary than real. It is in this manner that the masses have been prepared for every kind of war.

In truth, no divine religion has ever been based on conflict, whether it be the religions represented by Moses and Jesus, or the religion represented by Muhammad, upon them be peace. On the contrary, these religions, especially Islam, are strictly against disorder, treachery, conflict, and oppression. Islam means peace, security, and well being. Thus, in a religion based on peace, security, and world harmony, war and conflict are negative aspects. In exceptional cases there is a right to self-defense, just like when the body tries to rid itself of germs that have attacked it, but this can be done only according to certain principles. Islam has always breathed peace and goodness. Islam considers war as an secondary event. Rules have been placed in order to balance and limit it. For example, Islam takes justice and world peace as a basis:

> Let not the hatred of others to you make you swerve to wrong and depart from justice. (Al-Ma'ida 5:8)

Islam developed a line of defense based on certain principles in order to protect the freedom of belief, life, property, the mind and one's descendants, as has the modern legal system. Christianity, as a religion of abstract love, from the very beginning categorically condemned war and did not lay down any rules regarding this human and historical reality. But it was not able to prevent wars like the World Wars or the Hundred Years' Wars or the Nagasaki and Hiroshima incidents from occurring. The views of Huntington and others like him of the future are unfortunately based on conflict, and reflect plans to continue domination through conflicts.

With the blessings and beneficence of God, we are going to do our best to help this breeze of tolerance and dialogue to continue blowing; it is a breeze that has only recently begun to blow and it shows a tendency toward spreading over the entire world. God willing, we will prove the predictions of such scholars to be false. We believe that these breezes are powerful enough to overwhelm lethal weapons, to subdue mechanized military units and much of any other negativity that may arise. The fact that every segment of society is expressing and enacting this brand new message, the roots of which lie in the past, in the message of the prophets, is a divine favor to today's devotees of love. In this respect, we state that tolerance and dialogue should be represented in our country in the best possible way and should be an example to the whole world. Such an example will encourage people to come together, to gather round the same basic human values and, God willing, humankind will live one more spring before seeing the end of the world.

"I TRUST IN THE BEAUTY
FOUND IN THE MAKE-UP OF HUMANITY"

Your Most Respected Holiness,

We bring you the sincerest greetings from the people of the land known to be the birthplace of the three great religions, people who have full knowledge of your sacred mission to make the world a better place in which to live. We also thank you from the bottom of our hearts for granting us an audience, and for taking time from your most hectic schedule.

We are here to be a part of the continuing mission of the Pontifical Council for Interreligious Dialogue (PCID), instituted by His Holiness Pope Paul VI. We would like to see this mission reach fruition. We come to you most humbly, yet with some audacity, to offer our modest assistance in accomplishing this most worthy task.

Islam has been a misunderstood religion, and for this the Muslims are mostly to blame. A timely effort in an appropriate venue can help to greatly reduce this misunderstanding. The Muslim world would welcome the opportunity for a dialogue that would work toward eradicating centuries-old misconceptions about Islam.

Humankind, from time to time, has denied religion in the name of science and denied science in the name of religion, arguing that the two present conflicting views. All knowledge belongs to God and religion is from God. How could the two then be in conflict? To this end, our joint efforts directed toward inter-religious dialogue to improve understanding and tolerance among people can go a long way.

We have, in our country, been in dialogue with the leaders of several Christian denominations for sometime now. We humbly claim that these modest efforts have not been in vain. Our goal is to establish fraternity

The letter which Gülen presented to Pope John Paul II during his historical visit to the Vatican on February, 8, 1998.

among the faithful of the three great religions through tolerance and understanding. We can, by coming together, stand up against those misguided souls and skeptics to act as breakers, barriers if you will, against those who wish to see the so-called clash of civilizations become a reality.

Last year we held a symposium on peace and tolerance between civilizations, attended by international scholars of some renown. Encouraged by the unqualified success of this effort, we would like to try to repeat the event. We are currently in the process of organizing a conference on inter-religious dialogue directed toward strengthening the bond among the adherents of the three great religions; an event at which we hope the Vatican will be present.

We will be pleased and greatly honored if you would be kind enough to accept the invitation extended to you by Mr. Demirel[1] to visit our country so that your Holiness can see the holy places in Turkey. The people of Anatolia await with great eagerness the possibility to demonstrate their hospitality and to warmly welcome you. After discussing the matter with the Palestinian leaders we are able to secure an invitation to jointly visit Jerusalem; a visit that may prove to be a significant step toward efforts to proclaim that sacred city an international zone; a place where Christians, Jews, and Muslims alike would be free to go on pilgrimage with no restrictions, without even needing a visa.

We also would like to propose the establishment of a conference series to be held in different world capitals on a rotational basis, the initial one being held in Washington D.C., with the collaboration of the leaders of the three great faiths. The timing for the second series might be ideal for the occasion of the 2,000th anniversary of the birth of Christ.

A student exchange program would also be most beneficial. Having young people of faith study together will enhance their affinity for each other. Within the framework of a student exchange program, a college of divinity could be established in Harran, in the Urfa Province, known as the birth place of Prophet Abraham, who is professed to be the father of the three great religions. This could be accomplished by expanding the programs at Harran University or in setting up an independent university with a comprehensive curriculum that would satisfy the needs of all three faiths. The latter may prove problematical owing to obstacles due to state policies.

[1] Süleyman Demirel (b. 1924): Eighth president of Turkey.

The suggested programs may sound overambitious, but they are well within reach. There are two types of people in the world: conformist and non-conformist. Conformists try to adopt themselves to whatever takes place in society. Not-conformists, on the other hand, try to adopt the society to perennial values and to favorable new developments. Therefore, all the progress in society is due to non-conformist people. Thank God for non-conformist people.

M. Fethullah Gülen,
God's humble servant

MESSAGE CONCERNING THE SEPTEMBER 11th TERRORIST ATTACKS

I would like to make it very clear that any terrorist activity, no matter by whom it is carried out or for what purpose, is the greatest blow to peace, democracy, and humanity. For this reason, no one—and certainly no Muslim—can approve of any terrorist activity. Terror has no place in a quest to achieve independence or salvation. It takes the lives of innocent people.

Even though at first sight such acts seem to harm the target, all terrorist activities eventually do more harm to the terrorists and their supporters. This latest terrorist activity, which is a most bloody and condemnable one, is far more than an attack on the United States of America—it is an assault against world peace as well as against universal democratic and humanistic values. Those who perpetrated this atrocity can only be considered as being the most brutal people in the world.

Please let me reassure you that Islam does not approve of terrorism in any form. Terrorism cannot be used to achieve any Islamic goal. No terrorist can be a Muslim, and no real Muslim can be a terrorist. Islam demands peace, and the Qur'an demands that every real Muslim be a symbol of peace and work to support the maintenance of basic human rights. If a ship is carrying nine criminals and one innocent person, Islam does not allow for the ship to be sunk in order to punish the nine criminals; doing so would violate the rights of the one innocent person.

Islam respects all individual rights and states clearly that none of these can be violated, even if doing so would be in the interest of the community. The Qur'an declares that one who takes a life unjustly has, in effect, taken all the lives of humanity, and that one who saves a life has, in effect, saved all the lives of humanity. Moreover, Prophet Muhammad stated that a Muslim is a person who does no harm with either the hands or with the tongue.

I strongly condemn this latest terrorist attack on the United States. It only deserves condemnation and contempt, and it must be condemned by

---

M. Fethullah Gülen issued this message just after the September 11th terrorist attacks in order to condemn them and any other terrorist activity.

every person in the world. I appeal to everyone for calmness and restraint. Before America's leaders and people respond to this heinous assault out of their justified anger and pain, please let me express that they must understand why such a terrible event occurred and let us look at how similar tragedies can be avoided in the future. They must also be aware of the fact that injuring innocent masses in order to punish a few guilty people is to no one's benefit; rather such actions will only strengthen the terrorists by feeding any existing resentment and by giving birth to more terrorists and more violence. Please remember that terrorists represent an extremely small minority within any society or religion. Let us try to understand each other better, for only through mutual understanding and respect can such violence be prevented in the future.

I feel the pain of the American people from the bottom of my heart, and I assure them that I pray to God Almighty for the victims and I pray that He give their loved-ones and all other Americans the necessary patience to endure their pain.

I would like to take this opportunity to once again send my regards to everybody.

INDEX